DEMOCRATIZATION IN RUSSIA UNDER GORBACHEV, 1985–91

Also by Anne White

DE-STALINIZATION AND THE HOUSE OF CULTURE
Declining State Control over Leisure in the USSR, Poland and Hungary, 1953–1989

DEMOCRATIZATION IN RUSSIA UNDER GORBACHEV, 1985–91

Also by Anne White

DE-STALINIZATION AND THE HOUSE OF CULTURE
Declining State Control over Leisure in the USSR, Poland
and Hungary, 1953–1989

Democratization in Russia under Gorbachev, 1985–91

The Birth of a Voluntary Sector

Anne White
Lecturer in Russian
University of Bath

First published in Great Britain 1999 by
MACMILLAN PRESS LTD
Houndmills, Basingstoke, Hampshire RG21 6XS and London
Companies and representatives throughout the world

A catalogue record for this book is available from the British Library.

ISBN 0-333-74775-5

 First published in the United States of America 1999 by
ST. MARTIN'S PRESS, INC.,
Scholarly and Reference Division,
175 Fifth Avenue, New York, N.Y. 10010

ISBN 0-312-21993-8

Library of Congress Cataloging-in-Publication Data
White, Anne, 1959–
Democratization in Russia under Gorbachev, 1985–91 : the birth of a voluntary sector / Anne White.
  p. cm.
Includes bibliographical references and index.
ISBN 0-312-21993-8 (cloth)
1. Voluntarism—Soviet Union—History. 2. Associations, institutions, etc.—Soviet Union—History. 3. Charities—Soviet Union—History. 4. Pressure groups—Soviet Union—History. 5. Perestroika. 6. Soviet Union—Social conditions—1970-1991.
I. Title.
HN530.Z9V649   1999
361.3'7'0947—DC21   98–47534
                                                                                                  CIP

© Anne White 1999

All rights reserved. No reproduction, copy or transmission of this publication may be made without written permission.

No paragraph of this publication may be reproduced, copied or transmitted save with written permission or in accordance with the provisions of the Copyright, Designs and Patents Act 1988, or under the terms of any licence permitting limited copying issued by the Copyright Licensing Agency, 90 Tottenham Court Road, London W1P 9HE.

Any person who does any unauthorised act in relation to this publication may be liable to criminal prosecution and civil claims for damages.

The author has asserted her right to be identified as the author of this work in accordance with the Copyright, Designs and Patents Act 1988.

This book is printed on paper suitable for recycling and made from fully managed and sustained forest sources.

10 9 8 7 6 5 4 3 2 1
08 07 06 05 04 03 02 01 00 99

Printed and bound in Great Britain by
Antony Rowe Ltd, Chippenham, Wiltshire

Contents

Acknowledgements		vi
List of Abbreviations		viii
1	*Demokratizatsiya* and the Voluntary Sector	1
2	1985: the State in Crisis	19
3	1985: Society in Crisis	41
4	*Perestroika* and the Immediate Causes of the Voluntary Sector's Emergence	66
5	Charities	86
6	Self-Help Organizations	118
7	The Communist Response	140
8	Building Political and Civil Society	158
9	Conclusions and Epilogue	182
Appendix: the Survey		193
Notes		199
Bibliography		227
Index		244

Acknowledgements

Much of the material for this book comes from postal questionnaires completed by Russian voluntary organizations in 1992–3. I am extremely grateful to all the respondents, who are listed in the Appendix. I should also like to thank all the interviewees mentioned in the endnotes. They gave generously of their time, the average length of interview being two or three hours. The British Academy funded a research visit to Moscow in 1992 and the postal survey in 1993.

Above all, I wish to acknowledge the generosity of Helvi Häkkelä and Yurii Misyurev, who gave me their rich archives of newspaper cuttings, *samizdat* and personal letters. The research would also have been impossible without the help of numerous other people: in Russia, Alla Barskaya, Nina Belyaeva, Olga Burkova, Mikhail Karev, Sergei and Alla Kolmakov, Viktor Lisov, Vadim Lugov, Daniil Neklyudov, Andrei Verbitsky and his colleagues at *Soprichastnost'*, Evgenii Vodichev, Lena Young, Mary Yntemna and Lyudmila Zhukova; in Britain: Megan Bick, Mark Brace, Ed Cairns, Samantha DeBendern, Judith Harwin, Duncan Leitch, Sergei Oumow and Jonathan Sutton. Colleagues at the University of Bath reorganized their teaching to let me take study leave in 1996.

Some of the material in the book was previously published as: 'Unofficial Associations and Social Welfare in Novosibirsk', *Detente*, no. 16 (1989); 'Charity, Self-Help and Politics in Russia, 1985–1991', *Europe-Asia Studies*, vol. 45, no. 5, 1993; '*Invalidy i politika v Rossii. 1985–1991 gody*', *Golos* (Ekaterinburg), nos 2 and 3, 1994; 'The Memorial Society in the Russian Provinces', *Europe-Asia Studies*, vol. 47, no. 8, 1995.

Finally, I am grateful for the support of my family: my husband and colleague, Howard White, our daughters Tama and Lucy and my mother, Naomi Connelly. My husband and mother gave invaluable advice at every stage of the research. Tama also participated, visiting Moscow at the age of eleven months – according to her visa, 'on an academic exchange'.

The British Standard system has been used for the transliteration of Russian words.

List of Abbreviations

CPD	Congress of People's Deputies
CPSU	Communist Party of the Soviet Union
FMZ	*Fond miloserdiya i zdorov'ya* Charity and Health Foundation
FSI	*Fond sotsial'nykh izobretenii* Foundation for Social Innovations
gorkom	*gorodskoi komitet* town/city party committee
Goskomtrud	*Gosudarstvennyi komitet po trudu i sotsial'nym problemam* State Committee for Labour and Social Issues
Minsobes	*Ministerstvo Sotsial'nogo Obespecheniya RSFSR* Russian Ministry of Social Security
NGO	non-governmental organization
raikom	*raionnyi komitet* borough/district party committee
RSFSR	*Rossiiskaya Sotsialisticheskaya Federativnaya Sovetskaya Respublika* Russian Socialist Federative Soviet Republic
VOG	*Vserossiiskoe obshchestvo glukhikh* Russian Society of Deaf People
VOI	*Vsesoyuznoe obshchestvo invalidov* (the pre-1988 aspiration) Soviet Society of Disabled People *Vserossiiskoe obshchestvo invalidov* (the post-1988 reality) Russian Society of Disabled People
VOS	*Vserossiiskoe obshchestvo slepykh* Russian Society of Blind People

List of Abbreviations

VTEK	*Vrachebno-trudovaya ekspertiznaya komissiya* Commission of doctors and employment specialists (responsible for determining category of disability and work recommendation)
VTsSPS	*Vsesoyuznyi Tsentral'nyi Sovet Professional'nykh Soyuzov* Soviet Central Trade Union Committee

1 *Demokratizatsiya* and the Voluntary Sector

PURPOSE AND FOCUS OF THE BOOK

The book examines the evolution of Russian society and its relationship with the party-state during the period 1985–91. During these years, when Mikhail Gorbachev was General Secretary of the Communist Party of the Soviet Union (CPSU) Central Committee, both society and the party changed profoundly. The causes and nature of the transformation are still imperfectly understood and this book attempts to fill in part of the jigsaw. It provides a case study which is intended to aid understanding of the wider process of *demokratizatsiya*: democratization as it occurred in Russia during this period. Gorbachev's democratizationprogramme included the introduction of multi-candidate elections both for the soviets and within the party, but also a much wider process of removing prohibitions on freeassociation and encouraging social initiatives. This book analyses the emergence of social initiatives, initiatives which could be described as 'building civil society'. 'Civil society' is understood to mean the area of public activity, normally non-economic in character, involving the creation and functioning of independent, non-governmental organizations and movements, which by their being and actions contributed to the curbing of the party-state and the evolution of democratic values and procedures.[1]

Other analysts have discussed areas of civil society such as the media, labour movement, women's organizations, or environmental and cultural groups. This book instead discusses the new voluntary sector, consisting of organizations which, usually trying to act independently of communist party control, sought to improve welfare and/or health provision and addressed connected issues of morality, education and civil rights. The organizations were almost all pressure groups, to a greater or lesser extent. They may be roughly subdivided into service-providing organizations, which will be referred to as 'charities', and 'self-help' associations, in which members sought to advance their common interests by a mixture of mutual aid and lobbying. A number of 'hybrid' organizations, with a diverse membership, were seen by some participants as charities, by others as self-help groups.

In the USSR, 'charity' was a concept officially associated only with 'feudal' or 'bourgeois' societies.[2] Symbolically, Charity Street, St Petersburg, was renamed Textiles Street after the 1917 Revolution.[3] Autonomous self-help groups were also officially forbidden, since the communist party was supposed to supervise all organizations. A genuine voluntary sector therefore did not exist in the USSR in 1985. By 1991 it did exist: thousands of organizations had been created, in many locations across the Soviet Union. Charity and self-help had been recognized by officials and ordinary citizens alike as acceptable activities. (In the post-communist period, 'charity' recovered some of its negative connotations among people working in service-providing organizations. However, the term was normally used very positively during the early days of the voluntary sector, hence its adoption in this book.)[4]

The book focuses mostly on Russia, although inevitably in the Soviet period many of the generalizations apply to the entire USSR. Russia is not equated with Moscow and Leningrad: the provincial experience is examined as closely as possible.

The book is intended to be a history of *demokratizatsiya* as it occurred in Russia, written primarily for readers interested in Gorbachev's Russia or in Russia's voluntary sector. It is not a comparative study of democratization or civil society,[5] but this does not imply complete agreement with the nineteenth-century poet Tyutchev that 'Russia cannot be measured with a common yardstick'.[6] While there are many important respects in which Russia is unique, it is hoped that this book will also suggest fruitful comparisons to those interested in voluntary sectors elsewhere and in theories of democratization.

STRUCTURE OF THE BOOK

After a brief discussion of the existing literature and explanation of the research methodology, Chapter 1 is devoted to general issues connected with democratization under Gorbachev. It discusses different interpretations of the period and explains some of the assumptions and hypotheses which inform the book. It also sketches a portrait of the new voluntary sector, considering factors such as size, typology of organizations, geographical location, chronological development and social composition of participants.

Chapter 2 examines the Soviet welfare state before 1985 and suggests that crisis is an appropriate word to describe its condition. The perceived crisis of the welfare state motivated many participants in the new voluntary sector to take action and also contributed to the legitimacy crisis experienced by the regime in the 1980s.

Chapter 3 explores public involvement in welfare provision before 1985. It discusses the increasing ineffectiveness of much party-organized 'voluntary' work; citizen involvement in social policy discussions through letters and appeals to officials and the press; and the growth before 1985 of illegal, independent self-help groups and movements, particularly those working for the creation of a national Society of Disabled People (VOI). In other words, after considering the spurious, official voluntary sector, it looks at early attempts to create a genuine civil society, involving both the founding of independent groups and their attempts to communicate their interests to the state and general public.

Chapters 4 to 8 examine the *perestroika* era, 1985–91. Chapters 4 to 6 analyse the evolution of charities and self-help groups, exploring why the voluntary sector emerged when and in the shape it did. Chapter 7 looks at how voluntary organizations and the authorities interacted and how well the independent organizations were able to resist attempts at control. Gaining autonomy from the party was an essential precondition for the creation of a civil society. Chapter 8 discusses organizational aspects of building civil society: the voluntary groups' success in creating viable organizations and networks. Successful democratization required a substantial change in political culture: Chapter 8 also examines how voluntary organizations tried to change public attitudes and how perceptions of the state, society and voluntary sector did indeed evolve. Chapter 9 presents conclusions about the *perestroika* period and discusses the fate of the voluntary sector after the coup which led to the end of communist power in August 1991.

EXISTING LITERATURE

There is a sizeable literature on informal organizations in general, particularly those with political and national agendas. The evolution of new political parties has also received attention. Environmental, workers' and women's organizations are all the subject of an emerging Western scholarly literature. Charities and self-help groups, however, have hardly been studied by Western scholars, although the Russian voluntary sector, particularly after 1991, has been the subject of much description and some analysis by practitioners within both Russian and foreign voluntary organizations.[7]

METHODOLOGY

Traditionally, analysts of the Soviet Union have used as wide as possible a range of sources and methods to overcome the obstacles imposed by official policies of secrecy and deception. Although Russia has 'normalized' immensely in terms of access to information, too strict an adherence to one academic discipline remains unhelpful. It seems most useful to view politics and society as a whole, given the all-pervasive nature of ideology in the Soviet system and the totalizing aspirations of the party authorities, which persisted in many cases to 1991. Every field of activity had political implications.

This book uses historical research methods: analysis of official publications, newspapers, a personal diary and unpublished correspondence. I was particularly fortunate in being given a large archive of letters written between disabled people from the 1960s to the 1980s.[8] The book is also based on social research methods: observation during a number of personal visits;[9] interviews conducted in 1989, 1990 and 1992; and a postal survey of voluntary organizations in 1992–3. The respondents are listed and the survey questions translated in the Appendix. All questions were of the open-ended variety. The sources of the research were almost all in Russian; the translations are my own.

Assessing the reliability of one's sources is a problem for any researcher. It is especially problematic when researching the Soviet period: bare-faced lying remained commonplace even during *glasnost*. Moreover, volunteers and journalists who described the new sector inevitably had complex and often confused perceptions of what was taking place. Hence the same respondent can claim that 'no one interfered because we were just a women's organization' and point out that 'they did try to supplant us with the official women's council'.[10] Despite the evidence of actual interference, the first statement is still significant, pointing as it does to how a member of a soldiers' mothers' association assessed the low esteem in which her group was held, and why. In the end, one can only make a personal judgement based on one's wider knowledge of the context, pulling out as much truth as possible.

GORBACHEV AND DEMOCRATIZATION IN THE USSR: SOME ISSUES

The Character of the Party-State before 1985

Interpretations of the Gorbachev era are determined to some extent by the analyst's understanding of the nature of the Soviet regime before Gorbachev came to power.

Unfortunately, *mis*understanding of the pre-1985 regime is not unusual. Today one often encounters references to the 'totalitarian' character of the 1985 system, as if Stalin had never died. Conversely, Russian opponents of marketization tend to idealize the Soviet period. The dramatic events of the years since 1985 seem to screen the complexities of the old regime. However, before 1985 sovietologists subjected the system to more careful scrutiny and as a result suggested very different explanatory models, ranging from neo-totalitarian to semi-pluralist.

The great range of viewpoints was possible partly because of insufficient knowledge, deriving from the secrecy which shrouded the political process, the absence of opinion polls and the inacessibility of most of the country to foreign observers. More seriously, however, the old regime presented a series of genuine conundrums. Contradictory trends were at work and the study of different objects – central/local politics, state/society – suggested different conclusions.

This study will assume that many of the interpretations are more compatible than they first appear, since scholarly debates often reflected *where* the scholars looked, rather than indicating that some analysts saw incorrectly. There is no necessary incompatibility between 'revisionist' views stressing signs of pluralism in Soviet society before 1985 and more traditional interpretations which underline the authorities' totalizing aspirations. The ruling elite – with honourable exceptions, like Gorbachev – was certainly reluctant to embrace the implications of de-Stalinization. However, the authorities were less and less able in the years before 1985 to assert total control in the face of greater societal activity and *de facto* autonomy. George Schöpflin writes of 'decay' in the analogous case of East-Central European communist systems. The USSR was not Poland or Hungary, but nevertheless the process of decay, though less advanced, was equally apparent.[11] Paul Hauslohner, for example, suggests that 'during the final decade of Brezhnev's rule, Soviet power began unmistakeably to lose its effectiveness.'[12]

Social Evolution before 1985

Neo-totalitarian interpretations, based on assumptions of continuity before and after Stalin's death in 1953, suggest that 'independent movements and initiatives...did not emerge in the pre-Gorbachev period' and that 'all social initiative was either effectively chanelled through official organs or repressed'.[13] Analysts who deny the existence of a significant level of autonomous social activity before 1985 then have to search to explain the apparent 'sudden explosion' of independent activity under Gorbachev. Inevitably, they tend to focus on reasons particular to the early Gorbachev period – such as the theory of 'rebound', which suggests that passivity naturally engendered its reverse.[14]

If one were to assume that a 'sudden explosion' model held good for the entire informal sector, Gorbachev's project of democratization would seem *prima facie* unrealistic and doomed to no more than partial success – as indeed is the implication of writers like Steven Fish and Kathleen Smith, who emphasize the still-atomized quality of Soviet society in 1991. Moreover, Fish suggests that leadership of the new civil society under Gorbachev was weak partly because specific individuals were not continuing and developing pre-1985 activities. Hence they must have been either novices in the political game or defectors from the *apparat*.[15]

However, social passivity before 1985 can be exaggerated. Inevitably independent political activism was rare, but other types of informal activity were more widespread. Those analysts, especially sociologists, who had the greatest direct familiarity with Soviet society before 1985 tended to see an embryonic civil society already forming. In the words of Moshe Lewin, 'observations that confined themselves to the top of the hierarchy could not yield insights into the regime's trajectory. For the most dynamic events were taking place outside the Kremlin, in the social sphere, well beyond the view of most political scientists.'[16] Similarly, Shlapentokh suggests that 'the decline of the legal public sector is the most prominent process of Soviet society in the post-Stalin period.' Instead, people's most important loyalties were within the personal sphere, second economy and embryonic civil society.[17] Lapidus also asserts the 'emergence of a rich array of informal and unofficial groups pursuing a broad range of cultural as well as sociopolitical activities'.[18]

The clearest evidence of widespread unofficial activity before 1985 was among young people.[19] In other words, this was the social group whose tendency to 'exit' or opt out of the norms and compromises of official Soviet society had the most worrying implications for the future control of that society.[20] Social problems such as drug abuse and alcoholism are discussed in the next chapter. The interesting feature of 'exit' in the present context is the existence of groups and even organizations and movements which were independent or semi-independent of party control.

Some groups and movements existed over several generations. In music, the 'Amateur Song Club',[21] dating from Khrushchev's thaw in the late 1950s, was a movement uniting singer-songwriters such as Galich, Okudzhava and Vysotsky and their many imitators and listeners. The clubs and their festivals veered between approved and illegal status, depending on the politics of the period.[22] They were immensely popular: Vysotsky has been aptly described as a 'veritable icon of authenticity for a mass public'.[23] In the 1960s the popularity of Western pop music led to the emergence of a 'rock community' which 'adopted a strategy of disassociation' from official norms.[24] A large 1981–2 survey found that 'amateur arts' (mostly amateur pop groups) were commonly located outside official cultural institutions: a finding which prompted attempts to organize such 'unorganized independent activity' under the proper auspices.[25] The threat to party control was particularly explicit in the case of the Novosibirsk dance company 'Terpsichore', established in 1970. Its creator, Gennadii Alferenko, who would be one of the leading figures in the Gorbachev-era voluntary sector, confessed: 'I worked with dance. But in actuality I was working on a social, economic and political experiment.' His attempt to run a genuinely independent organization unsurprisingly led to fifteen years of harassment.[26]

Youth groups often lacked campaigning characteristics and in this sense did not challenge the system. However, pressure groups also existed, although naturally they were fewer in number. The dissident human rights movement is the most obvious example. Dissident activities included, *inter alia*, charity – the collection of funds for political prisoners[27] – and the efforts of disabled activists to publicize the injustices experienced by disabled people. Apart from dissidents, the most visible groups and movements – to the Western observer – were also intellectual in composition. Often nationalist in orientation, such intellectuals raised issues connected with ecology – for example, about the pollution of Lake Baikal.[28] Less prominent, but more significant in numerical terms, were the 'nature protection teams' (*druzhinniki po okhrane prirody*) attached to academic institutions from 1958 onwards.

These were student/staff conservation teams which, although officially-sanctioned, nevertheless maintained a strong sense of self-identity and, particularly in the 1960s, a degree of autonomy. Idealistic and determined, they have been compared to members of a monastic order. Although they perforce sought a *modus vivendi* with the regime, they nevertheless maintained qualities which contrasted strongly with official cynicism and wastefulness. They avoided the construction of hierarchical structures and instead cultivated horizontal links between regions of the USSR: an endeavour which the authorities regarded with considerable concern.[29]

Non-dissident pressure groups also existed before 1985 in other areas of society, notably among disabled people and parents. In addition to mutual support, these organizations – which really were organizations, not campaigns – articulated interests. The issues with which they dealt were not the most sensitive policy areas and, as in the case of the environment, relatively free media discussion sometimes prevailed. Opportunities for discussion were limited, however, by the activists' low social status – as compared with the high-profile literary figures who championed the cause of Russian nature. It was only in the 1980s that the intelligenstia elite adopted welfare issues as one of their causes.

Gorbachev: Pushed, Pushing, or Walking Hand-in-Hand with Society?

It is commonplace – particularly among authors writing on nationalist themes or using interview evidence from after 1991 – to downplay Gorbachev's radicalism, and with it, his significance in moving events.[30] More reliable evidence – of the type presented by Chernyaev or Brown – suggests that Gorbachev was a genuine radical who rapidly realized the need for 'system transformation' and implemented it as effectively as he could, given the political constraints.[31]

Gorbachev will not be mentioned often in this book, but this does not imply that his role is considered unimportant. Indeed, both Gorbachev's general programme and his specific interventions in particular cases aided the conception of the voluntary sector. At the Nineteenth Party Conference in June 1988 Gorbachev welcomed the emergence of 'the [grassroots] charity movement' as well as of official charities such as the Children's Fund.[32] The revival of charity fitted in well with his hopes of creating a society in which individuals would have greater input and behave with more social responsibility.

A related issue concerns the extent to which Gorbachev was forced to introduce reform as a result of pressure from below in 1985. This possibility is dismissed by many analysts, but they are in a sense tilting at windmills, since even those observers furthest from the 'totalitarian' school are unwilling to assert too strong a link between social discontent and leadership policy changes. On the other hand, it seems evident that there was *some* link between social change and policy change. Gail Lapidus's delicate formulation, that 'fundamental social changes [were] altering the relationship of state and society', is corroborated by evidence presented in this book.[33]

If one accepts that society did exert some kind of pressure on events, one may also be tempted to deny Gorbachev's role. Leitch, for example, argues that 'the expansion of unofficial activity in the second half of the 1980s was the culmination of long-term social processes rather than a deliberate policy initiative of the Gorbachev administration'.[34] However, there seems no reason not to square this particular circle and suggest that the most convincing interpretation of events in 1985, if one accepts that Gorbachev was committed to radical change, is that he represented the public – and especially the Moscow intelligentsia – much better than did his colleagues. He shared the public sense that 'this is no way to live'.[35] Speaking on British television in 1996, Gorbachev responded to criticism that he had merely gone with the flow by interpreting the accusation as a compliment, pointing out that former Soviet leaders had tried to divert the evolution of society into the opposite direction from that desired by the population and taken in the Western world.[36] There was an important moral dimension to this sense of need for change, a 'troubled conscience' shared alike by Gorbachev and other members of the elite.[37] The moral dimension was to emerge clearly in discussions about the revival of charity.

Conflictual Models of State–Society Relations after 1985

Once radicalized, 'society in motion' during the later years of *perestroika* sometimes moved too fast for Gorbachev's taste. However, his powerlessness was greater *vis-à-vis* the conservative authorities. It was they who did the most to thwart his policies, not society. If one analyses the later years of *perestroika*, it seems clear from the story of the more political organizations that most authorities, local and central, tried to slow the pace of Gorbachev's revolution. Some scholars investigating these political organizations, such as Moses and Fish, argue that this was a zero-sum game: there was little 'middle ground' or room for compromise.[38] Others have disputed this model, at least for the first years of *perestroika*, pointing to the importance of party reformers. 'The continuation of genuine reformism from above... did not allow the emergence of a consistent "we-they," friend-enemy scenario of state-society relations'.[39]

One might expect that there would be parallels between the experiences of the more political organizations and others, like charities and self-help groups. On the other hand, if there *were* compromises and constructive mutual work, it would be likely to be found between the authorities and the less politicized groups. This book concludes that conflict was the more common experience, and discusses why.[40]

Number of Informal Organizations

It has already been suggested that informal organizations which flourished under Gorbachev sprang from fertile soil: other organizations had been growing in Soviet society during the years before. It is also possible to dispute the other component of the sudden explosion model and suggest that the size of the 'new' informal movement has been exaggerated. One has to remember the distinction between pressure groups and others. Both before and after 1985, the non-pressure groups were very numerous. The figure of 30,000 informal groups in February 1988, which is often flagged up to indicate how *pressure* groups multiplied in the first years of *perestroika*, includes many groups which had no agenda other than to entertain themselves.[41] The Russian adjective 'informal' (*neformal'nyi*) was used to denote any kind of activities not directly organized by the party: amateur rock groups were a particularly widespread example. One should also take into account that, like so many Soviet statistics, these were inflated, in this case by managers of state-run leisure services demonstrating loyalty to party policy. A fictional or defunct cactus-lovers' club was just as good for a statistic as an operating political discussion club.[42]

Moscow News in February 1990 suggested a figure of 2,000–3,000 'informal groups' in the USSR.[43] An authoritative guide to genuine Russian informal organizations describes 1,114 which had emerged by autumn 1990. This list is certainly incomplete, and mentions hardly any of the groups discussed in this book, but it does suggest that the order of magnitude outside the voluntary sector (defined as charities and self-help groups) was not tens of thousands but rather a few thousand issue-based groups.[44]

FEATURES OF THE VOLUNTARY SECTOR

Size

By late June 1991, the Russian Ministry of Justice had registered about sixty national organizations connected with self-help, human rights or charity: one-third of registered organizations of all types.[45] Harvey estimates the size of the voluntary sector at roughly 2,000 registered NGOs, including [several hundred] environmental groups, in the USSR, towards the end of *perestroika*.[46] The absence of centrally-held information about local registration of organizations meant that there was no accurate overall picture. In Voronezh, 72 issue-based NGOs (not including political and religious organizations) had been registered by November 1992.[47] To obtain information for the whole of Russia one would have to acquire the lists of registered organizations held in each individual *oblast* – lists which are not easy to obtain.[48] Moreover, many organizations do not appear even in local lists, since they did not possess formal status, either because they could not get it or did not want it. This was true even after the law on associations of October 1990 made registration easier.

The classification of branches of national organizations is a problematic issue, which Harvey does not consider. In some cases, national organizations were intended as umbrellas for autonomous local groups. *Memorial*, the society for honouring and helping victims of Stalin's Terror, was so decentralized that its 120-odd branches must be considered individual organizations. The opposite would at first sight seem true for the more 'official' funds, established according to the centralized, hierarchical principles universal among official Soviet organizations and included within the *nomenklatura* system of party-controlled appointments. These official principles partly determined the nature of the largest organization, the Russian Society of Disabled People (VOI).[49] VOI had 2,276 local branches.[50] However, 1989–91 witnessed the breakaway from the centre of local official institutions of all kinds. Hence it is probably legitimate to count most local branches separately by 1991 and this means that the number of charity and self-help organizations must have been substantially more than the 2,000 Harvey suggests.

Membership of voluntary organizations was in the millions. If one discounts the Red Cross, which had a formalistic membership of half the population, the organization with the largest membership was VOI, which had 1,100,000 members by autumn 1991. This represented about one quarter of registered disabled people.[51] 419,000 'multi-child' families, with three or more children, received benefits in Russia in August 1991 and they clubbed together to form organizations with thousands of members.

There were thus almost certainly more people involved in charity and self-help than in informal politics or environmental groups. However, all sorts of questions present themselves. For example, in membership organizations, should passive members be considered significant? Many members joined only to receive benefits. On the one hand, their presence swelled the importance of the organization to which they belonged. On the other, they did not participate in building civil society and sometimes they even thwarted the efforts of the more democratic and self-help oriented activists.

Typology of Organizations

What was the typical range of organizations in a Russian city by 1991? In 1985 the main city of each *oblast* already had branches of the Red Cross and the Societies of Blind and Deaf People, as well as a war veterans' organization. By 1988 these had been joined by branches of the more general Organization of Veterans of War and Labour; the Temperance Society; the Children's Fund; and the Charity and Health Foundation. All were official organizations, created from Moscow. VOI, the organization for all except blind and deaf disabled people, was established from both above and below in 1988. By 1991 grassroots groups in the city would probably include *Memorial*, a committee of soldiers' mothers, Afghan veterans, Chernobyl victims, large families, parents of disabled children and people with diabetes. There might also have been at least one group of lone mothers and possibly a *Miloserdie* group or other general charity, with or without links to the Baptists, Adventists or Orthodox Church who might themselves be engaged in voluntary work in local hospitals and children's homes. Although new charities were founded throughout the years 1985–91, self-help groups were more numerous, as the above list suggests.[52]

Location

Not surprisingly, Moscow and Leningrad housed more voluntary organizations than did other cities. However, the disproportion should not be exaggerated. The compiler of the 1992 directory *Charitable Organizations of Russia* (*sic*) gave up trying to find out about groups outside the two major cities after he found only five registered charities in Volgograd *oblast*. He reasoned that in view of the political conservatism of the provinces it was unreasonable even to look for a provincial voluntary sector.[53] Evidence presented in this book suggests that such a Moscow-centric assumption is unwarranted.

Chronological Development

It is one of the main arguments of this volume that the voluntary sector had roots in the pre-*perestroika* period.

Moreover, quite a large number of grassroots organizations emerged in the first half of *perestroika*, taking early advantage of the opportunities offered by Gorbachev's liberalization. The big national organizations with their multitude of local branches were created at the same time, as were a number of smaller groups with strong ties to the authorities. The contours of the voluntary sector were well-defined by 1989. Nevertheless, setting up an informal organization was a hazardous procedure in the first half of *perestroika*. 1989–91, the years of greatest liberalization and most acute economic crisis, were naturally the period when the greatest number of independent groups emerged. Autumn 1990 was a particular watershed. The laws on association and freedom of conscience and the influx of Western humanitarian aid offered new opportunities to charities and self-help groups.

Involvement and Participation

Survey questions about involvement in charity produced different results, but tended to imply that people were more willing to give to individual beggars than to charitable organizations. One survey, for example, suggested that while only about 11 per cent of respondents had never participated in charity of any sort, less than a quarter had sent money to a charity. 58 per cent had given to beggars.[54] The people who would not give most commonly blamed their own poverty; suspicion that the money would not reach its intended recipients was another major factor influencing their decision.

Surveys conducted in 1989 (USSR) and 1992 (Russia) both suggested that only 8 per cent of the population had themselves received or knew people who had received charity. However, there appears to have been an increase in the proportion of people who had benefited from charity *within Russia*.[55] Given the mushrooming of voluntary organizations and the influx of 'humanitarian aid' from the West after 1989, it is hardly surprising if the number of beneficiaries of charity increased.

Who worked in the voluntary organizations? One respondent reported that 'there were grandmothers and young things of 18, doctors and cleaners, washers-up and teachers, engineers [and] technicians'.[56] One reason for studying the sector is the insights provided into the lives of ordinary people as they experienced *perestroika*. The following suggestions about social composition are, however, necessarily tentative, given the small size of available samples.

Turning first to the issue of gender, it seems, not surprisingly, that men were well-represented in the leadership of organizations. Two-thirds of the leaders mentioned in the index of the most complete directory of voluntary organizations were men.[57] However, in a 1994 directory of organizations in Perm *oblast*, women are better represented than men. Moreover, Perm branches of all organizations established nationally before or during *perestroika* showed a clear predominance of *either* men or women among their chairpersons. Of the groups which were not clearly gender-specific, pensioners' organizations, *Memorial* and VOI branches were normally led by men; other (especially parents') organizations by women.[58]

If one looks, not at leaders, but more generally at the activists, it seems that here too there was some gender bias. My survey suggested that while charities involved both men and women, women were over-represented in self-help groups. This was probably not because they had more time than men (as sometimes happens in the West) but because so many groups were connected with family issues, traditionally the province of women. Women pensioners were also an active group. Men, on the other hand, were more prominent in disabled people's organizations, particularly sports organizations.[59]

It has been suggested that 'the first and most obvious characteristic of the informals [in general] would be their youthful profile'.[60] However, the voluntary sector involved people of all ages, although the under-25s seem to have been less active in self-help than in charity. This seems to have held true of parents' organizations, despite the fact that Russian women tended to have children early. One mothers' group explicitly referred to itself as a group of 'mature mums' who, at 30+, had had time to acquire an acute sense of the real problems facing large families.[61]

Activists in political independent organizations tended to be members of the intelligentsia. This was also true for *Memorial*, which was half-political, half-welfare in focus.[62]

There is evidence of both working class and intelligentsia involvement in other urban voluntary organizations. It may have been the case that the intelligentsia was better represented among volunteers in charities. Self-help groups could also have a definite middle-class character, but there were examples of very mixed composition. The problems of conscripts and people with diabetes, for example, were so urgent that people of every social category seem to have become involved in groups trying to address their needs. However, the most striking point about the social composition of the voluntary sector is that so many of the activists were neither *intelligenty* nor workers: they were non-workers, the people who had been invisible in public life before 1985. One questionnaire respondent replied with the rhetorical question, 'What social status does a disabled person have?'[63] It was the exclusion of these people from many of the benefits of the welfare state before 1985 which prompted their activism after 1985. Their emergence from homes – private and residential – into the public sphere was a significant social development. Given the importance of the disabled people's movement within the Russian voluntary sector, they deserve particular attention.

CONCLUSIONS

This book will argue that, despite the totalizing aspirations of many party officials and leaders before 1985, Soviet citizens were increasingly forming informal groups and even organizations in an attempt to address some of the unresolved social issues neglected by the official welfare state. This activity formed a basis for the open voluntary activity of the Gorbachev period. Even after 1985, officials were often still obstructive, and this created an expectation of conflict which dominated relations between the new groups and the authorities. Gorbachev himself responded to calls for the revival of charity and welcomed its reemergence: demonstrating once again that he was in tune with the thinking of the radical Moscow intelligentsia. However, charity and self-help had advocates throughout urban Russia and participants came from various social groups, including those non-workers who had been almost entirely excluded from public life before 1985. Many of the participants were women, although not necessarily for the same reasons which determine their participation in the British voluntary sector. Although some writers have exaggerated the number of informal pressure groups of all kinds, within the entire informal sector, including political, environmental and other associations, the self-help groups were probably the most common type of pressure group.

2 1985: the State in Crisis

'The creation of a universal, guaranteed system of social security for working people in the USSR is an enormous achievement of the Soviet regime. Over the sixty years of Soviet power the social security system has consistently improved.'[1]

'The achievements seem to fade when we view them set against their true background of social, economic and legal problems.'[2]

INTRODUCTION

This chapter discusses how far the welfare state was in 'crisis' by 1985 and examines political factors which contributed to the situation. Both the extent of crisis and its political causes help explain the emergence and evolution of the voluntary sector after 1985. The creation of a voluntary sector would be connected with attacks on elite privileges and with bids to redistribute resources, including bids by organizations of non-employed people previously at the bottom of the welfare pecking order. The ruling elite had much to lose and its sensitivities and self-interest help explain the story of how it interacted with voluntary organizations.

The chapter discusses the extent and causes of failure of the welfare state associated with (a) trends found throughout the developed world; (b) shortage of resources, caused by specifically Soviet factors; and (c) neglect of problems, a neglect encouraged by the official ideology. Two case studies illustrate how, for all three reasons, problems were accumulating in the areas of residential care and employment provision for disabled people.

The word 'state' is used as shorthand for 'party-state': state policy was party policy.[3] The focus is mostly on the whole USSR, but where it is specifically on Russia, Russia should not be considered typical of all Soviet republics. In some respects the Baltic republics enjoyed better welfare provision and higher living standards, while according less legitimacy to the

Soviet state. At the other end of the spectrum, in Central Asia the failings of the state were at their most extreme, resulting in widespread poverty, high infant mortality and serious pollution.

DEFINITION AND CHRONOLOGY OF THE 'CRISIS'

Was there a 'pre-crisis situation' – to use Gorbachev's phrase – or even a fully-fledged 'crisis'? 'Crisis' is a subjective and imprecise concept. Moreover, it was not as if a single crisis occurred at a particular moment: it is possible to see many strands of failure occurring at different periods. In some cases there were also small improvements in the years around 1985.

Some indicators suggest long-standing problems spanning the whole post-Stalin period: economic growth rates were falling from the 1950s and life expectancy, for example, began to drop in the mid 1960s. On the other hand, despite such warning signals, crisis – if such it was – came later. For most Soviet citizens life did improve overall under Khrushchev and Brezhnev, and the expansion of the welfare state was one aspect of that improvement. Stagnation and, in some respects, declining living standards came for many citizens only in the late 1970s or early 1980s. Detente finally collapsed and the war in Afghanistan began in 1979; the economy ceased to grow around the same time. In response to economic stringency, health spending decreased absolutely – on a *per capita* basis – for the first time in 1981.[4] The same was true of some 'critical' social services.[5] The number of children in state care began to rise in the 1980s.[6] Alcohol sales soared, with related implications for public health. (Deaths from drowning, for example, reached a peak in 1981.)[7]

One should distinguish between the situation in 1985 and the following period. Many of the problems of the early 1980s were described from the vantage point of a few years later, when *glasnost* had widened. It was not always easy to tell how bad the situation had actually been before Gorbachev came to power. There were in fact contradictory trends. Some indicators, such as life expectancy, seem to have improved initially under Gorbachev. Other problems worsened. Drug and substance abuse, for instance, seem to have increased sharply after 1985, after a more gradual growth from 1979.[8] In some areas it is therefore probable that 'crisis' is a term used more appropriately *after* 1985.

However, the perception of crisis in the minds of Soviet citizens is more important than 'objective' statistics, in the current context. One of the causes of tension between state and voluntary sector after 1985 was linked with *differing* assessments of the adequacy or otherwise of the Soviet welfare state. The overall situation seemed less acute to social security officials who confined their analysis to how well they coped, according to their own standards. As this chapter will show, even by these standards there was much to criticize. However, if one believed that standards were already too low, it was more natural to think in terms of 'crisis'.

Citizens' expectations had a tendency to rise over time and assertions that all was well because life had improved since Stalin were often cold comfort. They had a still less convincing quality if Russian conditions were compared with those obtaining in Eastern Europe or even the Baltic republics. Soviet citizens were carefully informed about poverty, unemployment, homelessness and other social problems in the 'capitalist' world, while shielded from information about comparative standards of social welfare in East and West. However, as access to the West increased and rumours about Western prosperity gained momentum this type of propaganda about the Soviet welfare state lost credibility.

In addition, there were large groups of citizens who had long felt a sense of crisis in their lives, connected with inadequacies of the welfare state. They had not benefited from the general increase in prosperity and for them Stalinism never truly disappeared. Soviet official definitions of what were in effect poverty thresholds were considerably lower than those accepted in Western countries. Many Soviet citizens lived in very straitened circumstances, but only they, not the official agencies, perceived such shortcomings as a 'problem'. Moreover, although pensions increased over the period, many pensions did not increase proportionately to wages, and by 1971 the minimum pension was significantly below the minimum wage.[9] Standards in residential care were also open to question. Social security officials – expressing their views in print – might seem satisfied that residential care was not in crisis; letters written by residents suggest quite another view. Many people with disabilities found their lives *more* restricted and uncertain than they had been under Stalin, as a result of decisions taken under Khrushchev and Brezhnev. For people like this, crisis was a constant throughout the period. The analysis which follows will pay particular attention to people trying to exist on pensions and benefits at home or in state residential care: their plight is essential background to the emergence of a voluntary sector. Other individuals, also dependent on the state, experienced a specific moment of crisis. When parents of children with diabetes realised that they were being supplied with insulin past its use-by date, a crisis-point had arrived in their lives. Each individual experience of crisis which led to the formation of a voluntary organization was significant as a contributor to the overall evolution of the sector. There were many such experiences.

WIDER TRENDS: THE AGEING POPULATION, 'NUCLEARIZATION' OF THE FAMILY AND ENVIRONMENTAL DEGRADATION

The editors of *Soviet Social Problems* suggest that the findings of their volume of essays, published in 1991, lend weight to convergence theory. 'It was precisely what we had in common, namely, the industrialization and urbanization of the society, that has led to the current state of affairs... This is not to deny... that the Soviet regime has put its own stamp on the form that these problems have taken.'[10] It is hard to subscribe to this viewpoint, expressed in such extreme terms. In politics, the USSR seemed to be following a trajectory very different from the West's. The main focus of this chapter is on specifically Soviet issues. Nevertheless, it is useful to remember that to some extent the USSR was facing parallel problems, caused by similar trends.

As in most European countries, for example, the population was ageing. By 1986 there were 56.8 million Soviet pensioners of all categories, including disabled people: one in five of the population. The number of people aged over 75 doubled between 1939 and 1987 – with obvious implications for health care.¹¹ (The labour shortage prompted official attempts to draw pensioners into economic production.) However, since opportunities for part-time work were barely increased, there was a limit to how many pensioners would be able or keen to continue in work.¹² This was not a complete solution to the pension problem and could have only a limited impact on the healthcare problem.

The need for the state and/or a voluntary sector to make further provision – in the form of services – to older people was becoming urgent. This was the result of a parallel social trend: the 'nuclearization' of the family. As grandparents increasingly lived on their own, so too grew the number of single elderly people in need of some help to survive within the community. Since the number of elderly people living alone increased from 2.9 million in 1959 to 6.9 million in 1979 their care represented a considerable unaddressed need.¹³

The environment was another area in which problems were building up. Essentially this was an issue connected with modern industrial development, although specifically Soviet technological inadequacies and the callousness and complacency endemic in the system had a special role to play in promoting what has been labelled 'ecocide'.¹⁴ The Chernobyl nuclear disaster of 1986, with its immense implications for the welfare state, was only the most large-scale of innumerable industrial accidents.

POWER AND INVESTMENT

If one considers the more specifically Soviet causes of problems in the welfare state, it is clear that the responsible agencies suffered from lack of power and a confused division of responsibilities.

The Russian Ministry of Social Security (*Minsobes*) belonged to the third and lowest, republican-level only rank of ministry. There was no Soviet Ministry of Social Security and on the national level there was no body to coordinate the fifteen republican ministries until 1976. After this, social security was dealt with by the USSR State Committee for

Labour and Social Issues (usually abbreviated to *Goskomtrud*). Before 1988, the Russian Minister of Social Security was always a women – another good indication of low status.

Moreover, *Minsobes* controlled only part of the social security system – the administration of pensions and some benefits, such as grants paid to people disabled from childhood. Its clientele was the non-working population. Trade unions were responsible for important social insurance benefits, such as sickness and maternity leave payments. Their clientele was the much more significant working population.

The Ministries of Health and Education also administered aspects of the system, such as children's homes. Both ministries were somewhat more powerful and authoritative than *Minsobes*, but inevitably suffered too from the emphasis on military spending and investment in heavy industrial production which was an integral feature of the regime. Spending on health, for example, represented a lower proportion of GNP than in Western Europe. According to Chazov, the Health Minister, it declined from 6.6 per cent in 1965 to 4 per cent in 1987.[15] Health officials were acutely conscious of the USSR's inability to purchase or produce modern medical equipment.[16] However, shortage of resources was not the only problem. How those short resources were distributed and (mis)managed were also significant issues. It was here that the most specifically Soviet forces came into play.

CONCEALING PROBLEMS AND JUSTIFYING PRIVILEGE: LOSERS AND WINNERS IN THE SOVIET SYSTEM

Ignoring and Concealing Social Problems

One of the most revolutionary features of Gorbachev's approach was to acknowledge that problems which were not publicly investigated could not be solved, and were likely to grow worse. The Brezhnev regime was attacked for its 'propaganda of success'. Alcohol abuse was a clear example of a problem which had increased to disastrous proportions, while being almost entirely neglected by the ruling regime. The issue was brought into the limelight by Gorbachev two months after he assumed office and became the focus of the notorious anti-alcohol campaign. However, this was just one of the many social problems which were given wide publicity during the era of *glasnost*.

Historical determinism and the quest for legitimacy had led official ideologists to deny that social problems could emerge within Soviet society after the stage of 'socialism' had been reached in 1935. Progress was often presented in terms of increasing gross output. Propagandists referred, for example, to an ever growing 'army of doctors'.[17] The 1970s slogan 'the Soviet way of life' exemplified this complacency.[18] Anything Soviet was by definition excellent: every aspect of Soviet society was praiseworthy. The New Soviet Person was moral and caring, with healthy habits. He or she worked hard, since 'work has become an organic necessity for Soviet people'.[19] The New Soviet Person did not desire charity, believing that 'pity humiliates' (*zhalkost' unizhaet*). Health was an important attribute of the New Soviet Person. Propagandists portrayed a muscular Soviet Man and Woman, striding forward on healthy legs towards a radiant future. Under communism, there would be no disability, and disability in the USSR was supposedly diminishing. 'The implementation of the decisions of the 25th CPSU Congress... facilitates a continual decline in the number of Soviet disabled people.'[20] As one writer on disability issues complained in 1989, 'How can disabled people even be mentioned, in the society of socialist optimism?'[21] (Although there were no reliable disability statistics, a believable estimate of 23.5 million people with disabilities of all kinds was made for Russia in late 1991.)[22]

Censors were supplied with lists of social issues and terms – such as 'poor' – which must not be mentioned with reference to the USSR.[23] The assumption that conflicts of interest could not exist in socialist society ruled out serious discussion of gender or ethnic relations, or disability issues. In addition to conflicts of interest between social groups, there of course existed citizens whose individual behaviour patterns did not resemble those of the New Soviet Person. The extent of some types of 'deviant' behaviour – such as drug abuse and prostitution – was familiar to the police but could be concealed from the public. On the other hand, problems occurring only within the family home – such as violence towards women or child abuse – were less likely to be officially noticed, partly because there was no professional social work. 'Deviant' behaviour which occurred in public was impossible to ignore. Begging, church attendance or drunkenness on the street were *visible* shortcomings and some kind of explanation had to be found. To some extent, they could be dismissed as 'vestiges' of the tsarist regime or as purely local phenomena – sometimes attributable to the carelessness of local officials. Another favourite cause was the evil influence of the West, which was deliberatedly bombarding Soviet citizens with false values. ('It is youth music which is most often used by bourgeois propaganda for ideological sabotage... This is one reason why the disco had to become a field of active ideological struggle, a channel for propaganda and counterpropaganda.')[24] This explanation was at least located within the credible context of legitimacy crisis and 'exit', even if the causes of attraction to Western values and culture were deliberately misconstrued.

Correction of individual rule-breaking was simple, usually involving punishment and/or medical treatment of the individual concerned. The only approach which dealt with social problems in a more general and prophylactic fashion was the use of propaganda. However, this was frequently a clumsy tool.

Khrushchev's 'state of the whole people' was really a 'state of the whole *working* people', since offical policy, and jargon, was premised on the assumption that real people *worked*. *Trudyashchiesya* – 'working people' or 'toilers' – was an official synonym for 'citizens'. Much of Soviet life centred on the workplace, which provided services such as housing, kindergartens, health care and leisure opportunities.

However, the millions of Soviet workers who became disabled as adults – often as a result of industrial accidents or occupational disease – found that once they had lost their capacity to work their status fell sharply: they were viewed as 'ballast which impedes the pace of the heroic construction of the new society.'[25] Still worse was the fate of people who had been disabled from childhood. They received benefits inadequate to ensure an independent existence. Probably most unfortunate of all were disabled people who lived in the countryside.[26]

1985: the State in Crisis 27

[Official policies ensured that disabled people were invisible to the Soviet and international public. Lack of access to public transport and buildings and inadequate prostheses and wheelchair provision meant that they remained hidden from public view 'The standard approach... is "he gets a pension, so let him sit at home and not cough"'.[27] Many types of disabled people were also officially forbidden to travel abroad[28] and the USSR took no part in world-wide actions such as the 1981 International Year of the Disabled. In 1976 a Soviet official, when asked whether a Soviet team might participate in the International Disabled Olympic Games, even denied, to foreigners, that there were disabled people in the USSR.[29] Deaf people, on the other hand, were allowed to travel abroad to participate in disabled sporting events, perhaps indicating that the problem was seen to lie with disabilities which were regarded as disfiguring and hence inappropriate for the image of the New Soviet Person.[30]

Problems of children in care and young people in hostels were also neglected. Children and students were not toilers either. Inadequate resourcing meant that children in children's homes and students in student hostels were often malnourished and lived in squalor and poverty. There was little effort to mould the fate of people who had recently left state care, either children's homes or prison. Ex-prisoners, for example, found that the militia and the local soviets regularly passed off responsibility for finding them employment and housing onto one another.[31] Homeless citizens fell outside the responsibility of the health and social security ministries, both of whom were said to 'ward off the social problem of homeless people as the devil wards off incense'. Only the militia (which had to check whether homeless people should be prosecuted for vagrancy) provided services (such as referral to a doctor, and 'resocialization centres').[32]

Officials with a strong selfish interest in the maintenance of the status quo were unlikely to take active steps to resolve the burgeoning problems. Moreover, officials created a distorting filter of reality for themselves as well as others. They were deceived and deceivers: they both believed and created ideology. In so far as they believed the official doctrine, it provided them with justifications for ignoring social problems. Since they created the operating ideology, they were also able to fashion justifications for the social injustice which lay at the heart of many of those problems.

Social Injustice, its Justification and the Legitimacy Crisis

'Had there been an atheist heaven, even there the ruling elite would have fenced off a privileged corner for itself.'[33]

The privileges of party officials, already a hallmark of the Stalinist system, were somewhat diminished by Khrushchev but became even more marked under Brezhnev.[34] In particular, the *nomenklatura* – those important officials who were included on party lists of reliable personnel – had separate food supply systems, health care, rest homes and personal pensions. Hence they had nothing to gain personally from improvements in the parallel provision accorded to ordinary citizens.[35] Their separate lifestyle, moreover, isolated them from the rest of the population and awareness of its problems. Finally, knowledge among ordinary people of official privilege was discouraged. The secrecy with which *nomenklatura* privilege was shrouded – unmarked shop doors and guarded *dacha* compounds – reduced the potential for public criticism and meant that the *nomenklatura* need not feel threatened into reducing disparities. However, it is probably accurate to say that public resentment was increasing by 1985. Gorbachev – albeit not an impartial observer – stressed that indignation was growing at 'the behaviour of people who, enjoying trust and responsibility, abused power, suppressed criticism, [and] made fortunes.'[36] The ardour with which the privilege issue was taken up under *perestroika* bears out Gorbachev's comments.

Public resentment inevitably fed into scepticism about the ideological justifications for privilege employed by the party leadership. In a parallel process, declining public faith in the ideology in general meant that official explanations were less likely to be believed in the first place.

The existence of privilege was not easy to combine with the egalitarian implications of 'communism'. Throughout the Soviet period, there was an official assumption that the state could and should to some extent respond to *need*. The health and education services apparently operated on this principle, since users paid directly only a tiny percentage of the costs,[37] and the services were open to all.[38] On the other hand, the leadership – always short of resources – had both to provide incentives for ordinary people to work harder and to justify privilege. Hence it also emphasized that until the historical stage of communism was reached, distribution should be according to *labour* (or more generally, merit), not need.[39]

Stalin built a complex system of privileges for the working class elite. The political contribution of party officials was still more highly rewarded. However, presenting the ruling elite as a meritocracy proved to be a dangerous justification for privilege when, under Brezhnev, they were increasingly perceived as incompetent. The military service of Second World War veterans was also rewarded. (Brezhnev's ruling elite was drawn from a generation of war veterans, so the *combination* of military and political service was also important.) Among disabled people, for example, war veterans received special privileges, such as the right to a disabled person's car.[40] Of course they were a relatively small, and therefore affordable, group. When under Brezhnev disabled activists requested the same rights for all disabled people, they were told by an official that 'the state at the present time does not have the means to do this, as everything is spent on the war disabled.'[41]

If labour was a more significant criterion than need, the old revolutionary slogan 'he who does not work, does not eat' retained its salience. Welfare for non-employed people was in danger of being perceived as charity even before the word became officially acceptable. Many social security staff, responsible for distributing disability benefits and pensions, gave the impression that they were distributing a favour.[42] Disabled people complained of being talked to 'in a fashion one should not even use with criminals';[43] in other words, they were perceived as differing only slightly from those able-bodied non-workers prosecuted as 'parasites'. One disabled person visiting *Minsobes* was rebuked: 'Don't dare equate yourself with healthy people!'[44] The metaphors used by disabled people and journalists – such as describing residential homes as 'almshouses' – reinforced the image of official charity. Such perceptions help explain the relative ease with which the authorities accepted the concept of charity, under Gorbachev, as a partial solution to social problems.

The most important *practical* legitimating factor of the Brezhnev regime was the social contract: the unstated agreement between rulers and ruled, especially Slav manual workers, that economic rights – in particular, full employment – would be guaranteed in exchange for the forfeit of political rights. Once again, privileges were protected, since 'politics' was understood to include the secrecy which surrounded every aspect of the *nomenklatura*'s existence, including their privileges. Moreover, by acceding to the status quo, the working population was also implicitly accepting that living standards would not be high, merely adequate. However, there were problems with the social contract as a legitimating factor: it was not applicable to the entire population, especially non-employed people; and the regime broke its side of the bargain, as living standards fell in the 1980s.

Many of the points raised so far are illustrated in the following case studies. These address in turn the issues of residential care and of employment provision for people with disabilities.

THE ADEQUACY OF STATE PROVISION AND CHANGING PUBLIC ATTITUDES: TWO CASE STUDIES

Residential versus Family Homes

Until the early 1930s, Soviet theorists – town planners, architects, feminists and others – had discussed the future of the home. It was common ground that the home, as it existed in bourgeois societies, was a place of oppression. The preferred solution was the provision of state-run facilities such as kindergartens, boarding schools and canteens, which would all, to some degree, supersede the home. In the 1930s, political repression and economic realities overtook the idealists. State residential care remained limited in scope, but communal living of the most unsatisfactory kind was imposed. For millions, home became the 'barracks' of the new industrializing regions. The Terror imposed its own restrictions on home life, with family members unable to talk openly.

In the aftermath of the Second World War, the state expanded residential care. The war created a mass of homeless disabled people and orphans. Moreover, the need to build up the population led to a policy of encouraging single women to have children and place them in homes. The 1944 regulation which entitled them to place their children in homes entirely at the state's expense was enshrined in the marriage code of 1968. Propaganda suggested that state children's homes were even better places for children than ordinary homes. However, the authorities tended to act on the opposite assumption and attempted to place orphans in families whenever possible.[45]

After Stalin's death in 1953 there was a marked change in official attitudes to the home. Khrushchev and Brezhnev initiated massive house-building programmes, moving much of the population out of communal flats into individual rented family flats. Communal living had probably never done much to boost collectivist values; now the state in effect admitted that modern families preferred privacy. Khrushchev's attempt to pursue a policy of opposite logic to the housing programme – his utopian programme for boarding education – failed because of parental opposition: testifying to the strength of domestic as opposed to collectivist values. Propaganda under Brezhnev strengthened the image of the private family home as a source of social stability and good values. Moreover, living standards in individual family homes were often rising faster than those in residential homes.

Despite Soviet boasts about the generosity of state provision, just 0.137 per cent of the USSR population lived in state homes for elderly and disabled people in 1979.[46] They increasingly resembled nursing homes. Whereas previously relatively young retired people on inadequate pensions had *chosen* to enter residential care, by the 1970s this was no longer true.[47] It was harder to believe in the adequacy of state provision than it had been under Stalin. Survey respondents expressed almost universal reluctance to enter residential care.[48] Paradoxically, however, there were waiting lists in many areas, because of the increased number of very elderly people living alone and because the *Minsobes* was powerless to force construction agencies to complete low prestige projects to build more homes.[49]

Homes for elderly and disabled people were officially presented as havens of comfort. This was part of the 'propaganda of success'.[50] However, presumably because of constraints on state resources, there was also propaganda directed at adults to dissuade them from placing their parents in residential care. The 1977 constitution stressed the primary responsibility of adult children to care for their parents; they, not the state, were the first resort and residential care was only for those who had no relatives to support them. The media emphasized the 'treachery' of selfish children who consigned their parents to state care.[51] Although the public had to wait for *glasnost* to discover the full horrors of residential care, in fact there had already been sharp criticism of practice in a number of homes in the 1970s and 1980s, so their image was already dented.[52]

Entry into Soviet residential care was traumatic for reasons common in any society. However, the Soviet residential home was also a *Soviet* institution and as such its prison-like qualities were often much to the fore. At least one home was sited in a former labour camp.[53] Homes were regarded by many administrators as closed institutions, with frequent searches and confiscations of property, and residents' letters to one another compared the regime to that of a prison. Residents were forbidden to undertake employment outside the home. For young people, entering a home which often housed mostly very elderly people seemed like the equivalent of a life sentence. 'Any young person who enters one cannot avoid feeling that this is the end of all their hopes and aspirations.'[54]

Towards the end of the period there is evidence of a more sophisticated approach on the part of social security experts, bridging gaps between residential and home care. In the late 1970s, for example, residential homes for older people in areas where there was no waiting list were encouraged to take short-term residents. Scholars advocated the creation of day centres and sheltered housing.[55] However, such ideas remained largely on paper only.

The image of children's homes also evolved during the post-war Soviet period. Originally they had been intended for genuine orphans, children who had lost their parents in the war. By 1978, however, the proportion of orphans had dropped to 13.5 per cent. The other children had either been abandoned by their parents or the parents had been deprived of parental rights because of their behaviour. A social stigma now attached to being in care. Deprivation of parental rights – usually leading to the appointment of a guardian for the children concerned – became increasingly common in the 1970s, although it was only in the 1980s that the number of children in state institutions began to rise. The increase in deprivations of parental rights was often regarded as an indicator of social decay.

By the 1980s conditions in children's homes were beginning to raise public concern. Their most prominent critic was the editor Al'bert Likhanov, who would become head of the new Children's Fund in 1987. Likhanov criticized the lack of priority accorded to children's homes as opposed to housing for the employed adult population. By the 1980s, 'in the majority of cases the decisions [about whether or not] to build new children's homes were taken not in favour of the orphans, but in favour of those whose labour benefited society. Such an unwise policy has left many of these children in old buildings, some of them dilapidated, having been put up before the revolution of 1917.'[56] A survey of children's homes in the early Gorbachev period found that four-fifths were unsatisfactory, 'rife with abuse of office and even downright thievery.'[57]

As in the case of residential care for disabled and elderly people, there were similarities with a prison regime. Life in children's homes was said to be dominated by 'strict regulation' and 'a hospital-like environment; closed doors; and little contact with society outside'.[58] Children's homes were large – usually containing between 70 and 300 children – and this contributed to their inability to imitate normal home life.[59] Moreover, because of the abolition of fostering and restrictions on adoption, children who entered the system of residential care had little chance of escape.

Residential care was the norm for children with learning difficulties. Parents who tried to bring up their children in the family home could find officials unsympathetic.⁶⁰ Moreover, many children found themselves in boarding schools for supposedly unteachable children only because they had been 'misclassified' carelessly or dishonestly, when ordinary schools tried to offload 'difficult' pupils into the auxiliary schools system.⁶¹

Finally, it is worth considering attitudes towards the most frequently encountered type of state childcare: ordinary kindergartens and nurseries. ('State' in this sense includes facilities provided by enterprises.) Childcare facilities expanded under Brezhnev, in an effort to promote female employment. However, although they were used to full capacity and there were often waiting lists for nursery places, this did not always reflect a high public reputation. (A similar paradox was observed in the case of residential homes for elderly people.) Complaints were frequent about the poor quality of staff and high rates of illness.⁶²

To conclude: although official rhetoric denied the existence of social exclusion, residential homes were very different from ordinary family homes and there was little connection between the two worlds. Soviet practice was to consign 'problem' citizens to closed institutions. Increasingly, state homes came to be viewed as outside the norm – they were either for very elderly people or for the children of 'deviant' parents, commonly stereotyped as promiscuous drunkards. Disabled occupants could no longer work outside the residential home and were thereby excluded from ordinary life and imprisoned within the institution. Simultaneously, the family home, located increasingly in an individual flat, came to symbolize the ideal for most Soviet citizens.

Employment Prospects for Disabled People

*'Where the complicated matter of finding work for disabled people is concerned, a great deal is entirely haphazard and depends on chance factors (a "good" factory director, etc.).'*⁶³

The number of disabled people was increasing and this put pressure on available jobs. Disability and employment were linked categories: in most cases, linked as opposites. This was particularly true after the demise of the disabled people's cooperatives in 1956–60 (see Chapter 3).

Until 1989 'disability' was viewed narrowly as inability to work, more specifically, to work in accordance with one's professional qualifications, 'if illness or impairment hinders the fulfilment of a person's professional duties'.[64] In Russia in 1988, about 30 per cent of registered disabled people were employed, and of these the vast majority were in the third and least severe category of disablement.[65] Only about one in thirty-five of disabled people in categories 1 and 2 was employed.[66] A survey in north-west Russia revealed a decline in the number of employed disabled people in the years 1966–76.[67] Rural disabled people's work needs were particularly neglected.[68]

Nevertheless, increasing the number of disabled people in work was official policy, as enunciated at party congresses[69] and in numerous directives. For example, the Council of Ministers attempted ineffectively to increase the number of special workplaces for disabled people.[70]

Enterprises perceived only inconvenience to themselves in moulding the jobs they could offer to suit the needs of disabled people, by creating part-time posts or organizing home working. Home working did increase to some extent in the 1970s.[71] By 1981, however, there were still only 115,000 home workers – not just disabled – in the RSFSR.[72] The type of work available was usually highly unsatisfactory: typical tasks were the production of wire mattresses, string bags, shoe laces and boxes; other disabled home workers stamped hammers and sickles on flags for an average of 32 rubles a month.[73]

Although most employed disabled people worked in ordinary enterprises,[74] enterprise directors, worried about the fulfilment of the plan and the size of the bonus fund, shied away from employing full-time disabled workers on the shop floor:[75] even though employers of people newly disabled because of industrial accidents and occupational disease were supposedly obliged to find them new jobs,[76] and despite the statutory obligation to reserve 2 per cent of workplaces for disabled employees. No legal sanctions could be applied if they broke these regulations. Of course, such provisions, as with equal opportunities policies more generally, are difficult to implement anywhere without the requisite change in public consciousness and level of economic development. The powerlessness of social security agencies *vis-à-vis* industrial ministries and managers added to the problem. *Minsobes* could not compel the latter to supply workplaces for disabled people. In addition, the fact that social security and economic ministries shared responsibility for work placement meant that both had a tendency to evade responsibility.[77]

Further problems were connected with the narrow remit and insufficient resourcing of the social security agencies. The official statute for social security departments was vague about the departments' specific responsibilities for work placement and other services.[78] The departments were hampered by their lack of professional inspectors, who seem to have been abolished in the 1960s. As for so much else, departments used the services of volunteers, often pensioners, who tended simply to count how many disabled people were employed at local enterprises.[79]

Responsibility for determining employability in the first place lay with the VTEK (*Vrachebno-trudovaya ekspertnaya komissiya*, or commission of experts on medical and employment issues). These decided whether applicants for disabled status deserved to be registered and, if so, which category of disability (1, 2 or 3) was appropriate. This was essentially a decision about employment. Disabled people suspected that the VTEK's real aims were to keep as many people as possible in the labour force and to reduce disability statistics – a fusion of practical and ideological requirements. The number of registrations was indeed one indicator on the VTEK's plan.[80]

The VTEK, having decided whether a person was in category 3 (i.e. with some residual employability) also had to recommend what type of work, if any, could now be undertaken by the disabled person.[81] The VTEK was not actually obliged to find employment for specific disabled people.

When *glasnost* arrived, the VTEK system was subjected to a flood of criticism, although, as one VTEK chairperson pointed out, 'We operate in just the same way as the rest of the Soviet system'.[82] The commissions were poorly paid, short-staffed and overburdened with cases. Moreover, they had to make decisions on the basis of paperwork alone; rather than physically examining the disabled person, they would assess whether the paperwork was in order and class a person accordingly. ('He has nice documentation' or 'His forms aren't up to much'.)[83] For disabled people, the VTEK seems to have embodied the most oppressive features of the Soviet state. One man referred to the three doctors who sat on the commission, in an allusion to the purges, as a 'Stalinist *troika*'.[84] It was almost impossible to contest incompetent and unfair decisions or even to discover the grounds on which they had been made. 'The complaints system operates on the principle "the VTEK is always right".'[85] There was no provision for the VTEK to include disabled representatives.

For many residents of homes for disabled people, one of the most onerous features of life in residential care was that they were denied the possiblity of a regular job. Until 1968 they had had this right, but the social security agencies seemingly found it difficult to reconcile the facts that disabled people both worked and received state support. Eventually the simplest solution was adopted: inmates were forbidden to work outside the home for a wage. In other words, this was a decision made completely for administrative convenience, at odds with the ideology about the 'organic need' of Soviet people to find fulfilment through work.[86] The only employment available was temporary manual work organized by the home and classed as 'labour therapy'.[87] Directors seem sometimes to have regarded residents as slave labour, again reminding one of the analogy with the labour camp, and tried 'come what may to squeeze the last drops of their capacity to labour out of disabled people, forcibly setting them to work'.[88] For example, at one home residents were made to pick potatoes despite the protests of their doctor.[89] Writing to a national newspaper in 1974, a group of disabled people requesting the creation of their own society asserted, 'We don't want to be just labourers attached to residential homes, we want to do real work and see the fruits of our labour.'[90] Two issues were involved. One was about a psychological need for real work. In this, Soviet disabled people were no different from their Western counterparts: the financial and status-connected benefits of employment were just as great in the USSR. The other issue was about the 'fruits of labour', particularly pension rights. People disabled from childhood had to acquire some kind of paid employment record if they were to make the shift from benefit to pension. Personal letters suggest that they were prepared to undertake backbreaking and extremely low-paid labour in order to acquire this right.

One is drawn to conclude that the system of (not) providing employment for disabled people was inflexible yet ridden with arbitrariness; laden with absurd regulations and unnecessary paperwork; underfunded and not under the jurisdiction of a single, authoritative agency which could have enforced the statutory provisions; exploitative and at the same time wasteful. In other words, it was like the Soviet system as a whole. Yet in a sense it was worse, since the people affected were among the least able to offer any resistance. As disabled candidate Ilya Zaslavsky was to point out in his election programme for the USSR Congress of People's Deputies in 1989, 'the difficulties experienced by disabled people are the same difficulties as face all Soviet people, but exaggerated to their greatest degree.'[91] All Soviet citizens lacked civil and political rights, but non-working citizens lacked even economic and social ones. Disabled people complained bitterly, displaying a firm adherence to the officially-proclaimed work ethic and strong sense of the discrepancy between propaganda about state provision and the reality.

CONCLUSIONS

The Soviet welfare state was highly inadequate, even in providing what was officially promised. Moreover, problems were accumulating in many areas, to the extent that by the mid-1980s it seems artificial to avoid using the term 'crisis'.

The failings of the Soviet welfare state were not merely the consequence of a faltering economy. The inequities and gaps in the system had political roots, in the priorities of the communist party, which led to the suppression or ignoring of many problems and areas of need and a narrow agenda for both health and social security agencies. It is hard to disagree with Ryan's suggestions that the Soviet health system was 'conceived essentially as a contribution towards national efficiency and economic growth', that the needs of non-workers counted for very little and that they received only 'Cinderella services'.[92] For their part, social security organs confined most of their energies to administering the pensions and benefits systems. Kaznacheev, the new Russian Minister for Social Security, was to point out in 1989 that there was no interest in how – or whether – each individual citizen managed to survive on his or her pension or benefit.[93] A wide range of personal social services which are taken for granted in Britain were either lacking or left to non-professionals, the officially-sanctioned 'volunteers' such as the pensioners who counted how many disabled people were employed in local factories. Reformers within the health and social security apparatus could only accumulate ideas for more comprehensive or subtle approaches to existing problems on their desks or in specialist journals, without any hope of putting them into practice before Gorbachev came to power, except on an experimental and localized basis.

The crisis had ideological causes, but also ideological consequences. By 1985 gaps had appeared between the official doctrine and real policy which promoted questioning and challenges. Official statements seemed increasingly inconsistent – simultaneously advocating the virtues of state provision and attempting to pass on responsibility for children and elderly and disabled people to relatives at home; advocating the virtues of collectivism but providing flats for individual families and presenting life in the family home as the 'norm'; promoting a strong work ethic and in effect penalizing disabled people for being unable to work, while simultaneously creating conditions which made it extraordinarily difficult for them to do so. These discrepancies prompted questions as to whether the state was always the best provider of services and helped undermine fundamental collectivist principles.

Discontent with the welfare state could, of course, simply have been a matter of grumbling about particular shortcomings of the system. It was not necessarily system-threatening. Alternatively, social problems could be generalized in a way which blamed society: the bad behaviour of individuals was perceived as part of a general 'moral crisis'. A typical expression of this point of view was published by the head of a new charity in 1988. 'Over the past few decades the moral climate of our society has changed. Children have begun to abandon their old and helpless parents, packing them off to residential homes, while parents, without a twinge of conscience, deposit their children in children's homes. Morality and the condition of the human soul are inseparably linked to the state of the times.'[94] This type of analysis apparently blamed individuals, not the *state* for social ills. However, in the Soviet context, to also blame 'the times' was to blame the political leadership, although in the early Gorbachev period the state could be identified with Brezhnev, not the one-party system as such.

Unfortunately for the party, however, any more profound analysis of the failings of the welfare state could not avoid blaming the party. Problems stemmed from both the injustice and the incompetence inherent in the Soviet system. Indeed, by setting up the social contract, the post-Stalinist party had made itself vulnerable: when it failed to fulfil its obligations, so its legitimacy waned and, as Gorbachev put it, 'a gradual erosion of the ideological and moral values of our people began'.[95] The connections between party power and social conditions might not be very direct: it would be hard, for example, to substantiate arguments that poverty for the many directly resulted from the privilege of the few. Yet that was the type of argument which began to be heard under Gorbachev. If one examines statements made by people dependent on the welfare state before 1985, only dissident writings make such clearly political points. However, the system was being criticized too in complaints about the overbearing state (which in effect was the same as the party) and the lack of rights of the individual. Such complaints, largely those made by disabled people, will be studied in more detail in the next chapter.

3 1985: Society in Crisis

INTRODUCTION

'All honest people saw with bitterness that people were losing interest in social affairs.'

Mikhail Gorbachev[1]

This chapter considers Soviet society before 1985, examining in turn officially organized 'voluntary work'; public lobbying of official agencies; and independent self-help groups. The chapter continues discussions begun in Chapters 1 and 2. Taking first the issue of whether the system was in crisis by 1985, it is useful to examine the related question of whether there was a crisis located in social behaviour and attitudes (as opposed to social policy and its absence, which was the main focus of Chapter 2). In other words, the focus shifts from the behaviour of the party-state to that of the public. Was the Soviet system failing to work because public participation in making it work was increasingly lacking – as the above quotation from Gorbachev suggests? If Soviet people were failing to behave in system-supportive fashion, this represented a problem for the ruling elite. Both conservative ideologists and radicals like Gorbachev and Zaslavskaya were concerned about social alienation and considered 'the human factor' to constitute a fundamental part of the overall crisis.[2] On the other hand, if 'exit' from the official structures led to the creation of genuinely independent organizations before 1985, these could be considered to lay the way for the mobilization of society which Gorbachev hoped to achieve and of which the creation of an independent voluntary sector would form a part. Referring back to the debates discussed in Chapter 1, Chapter 3 will show how an embryonic civil society existed even before 1985, in the form of independent organizations of various kinds, and a press which helped disabled people in their struggle against *Minsobes*. (The same newspapers would be the main motors of *glasnost* under Gorbachev.)

THE SOVIET VOLUNTARY SECTOR

The Bolsheviks inherited a tradition of voluntary activity, including charitable work, which had blossomed in the Russian Empire from the 1860s onwards despite state attempts to control it.[3] After 1917, independent charities and self-help organizations were closed down or coopted to serve as 'transmission belts' for the party. In 1929 the Church was forbidden by law to engage in charity. However, the highly mobilizational regime enlisted the unpaid labour of citizens on a mass scale. Participation in so-called 'voluntary work' was treated as an indicator of political success and was tightly controlled by the party. 'Public' (*obshchestvennye*)[4] organizations such as the *Komsomol* or trade unions organized a variety of activities. 'Voluntary societies', officially a subset of public organizations, united members who supposedly shared a hobby, such as bee keeping, supporting the armed forces or friendship with various foreign countries. They included 'public aid associations' such as the Red Cross or volunteer fire brigades.

Voluntary organizations could be established according to a law of 1932 and national organizations were set up by Council of Ministers decree. Although they united members who – in theory – shared a common interest, this was not permitted to be a *material* interest.[5] Altruistic service was the assumption. For example, in 1970 at a congress of the Lifeguards' Society[6] 'it was underlined that all the Society's activities are founded on altruistic work for the benefit of the public.'[7] The principle was an important one, deriving from the assumption that there could be no conflict of interests in Soviet society. Since they could not pursue members' interests when these conflicted with the interests of other citizens, it followed that voluntary organizations could not constitute any kind of real civil society.

Moreover, civil society should be separate from the state, and the expression 'voluntary organization' in English implies considerable independence of action, whatever the source of funding.[8] Such independence of action was impossible in the Soviet context, since both state and voluntary organizations in practice shared a common 'nucleus', the CPSU. (Article 6 of the 1977 constitution specified that the communist party formed the 'nucleus' of all organizations, state and 'public'.)

By making people do voluntary work, the party was forcing them to spend their non-working time under party scrutiny. Voluntary work therefore facilitated social control. The Stalinist and all subsequent Soviet regimes, until the accession of Gorbachev, stressed the need to monitor public leisure activities and exploit non-working time for public, i.e. party, benefit.[9]

By the Brezhnev period, however, there is evidence of public cynicism about voluntary work. While one should not exaggerate the situation as being one of total alienation, nevertheless there were signs that people were increasingly failing to behave as model citizens. Shlapentokh, backing his argument with time budget surveys, concludes that people were spending less time on work for the benefit of the community and that the authorities turned a blind eye.[10] Inflated statistics masked disappointing levels of participation in key activities, for example the paramilitary games organized for schoolchildren.[11] Official data recorded 80 per cent adult participation in *subbotniks*, Saturdays of unpaid community service, but the implication that [at least] one-fifth of the population was not behaving as it should was worrying. In addition, such participation as occurred was often far from whole-hearted: while some 'volunteers' laboured busily, others failed to take the occasion seriously.

Survey evidence also betrayed worrying trends. Questionnaires were traditionally worded to prompt, and Soviet citizens conditioned to provide answers which seemed to legitimate the regime. Nevetheless, there was a surprisingly large number of responses indicating that people participated in voluntary work for the 'wrong' reasons, such as a feeling of having been coerced, or some selfish motivation.[12]

Apathy among young people particularly worried the authorities. Kuebart cites a 1986 article describing schoolchildren's attitude to the *subbotnik*. 'The class waits indifferently at the *subbotnik* until the teacher distributes jobs, some senior pupils do not feel ashamed to refuse the social assignment and when they do get down to work they either fail to complete it or find an excuse for not doing it.'[13] Journalists, worried that there was an insufficient culture of voluntary work, pointed to failings in the Pioneer organization. Pioneers were supposed to participate in the *Timurovets* movement, helping disadvantaged members of the community by performing tasks like shopping for housebound people. However, schools often neglected to organize such work. In other cases, schoolchildren pestered or even stole from the elderly people they were supposed to help.[14] The *Komsomol* also neglected its duties. In Leningrad, for instance, it sometimes refused to help out when requested and claimed to operate a 'waiting list' system. One person who suggested that *Komsomol* members might be asked to visit her disabled son was denied with the words, 'We have many objects of patronage. Wait until your son's turn comes up.'[15]

Officials hoped that voluntary work would substitute for inadequate state provision. On paper there was an impressive range of opportunities for citizens to back up official services, for example through their trade union or by attachment to a local authority. Hegelson suggests that 'the absence of an institutionalised system of personal social services hides the existence of a comparable level of services in the Soviet Union'.[16] However, such services were not always efficient. For example, the shortcomings of the system of volunteer inspectors of employment for disabled people were mentioned in Chapter 2. This corroborates Friedgut's picture of a 'vast apparatus laboring mightily to little effect'.[17] As for *subbotniki*, the most useful type was probably when workers worked unpaid at their own factory, and money in lieu of pay was transferred to the health service. Between 1971 and 1975, for example, funds raised by *subbotniks* were used *inter alia* to construct 32 children's hospitals and attached polyclinics, three children's polyclinics and 11 maternity hospitals.[18] Such inefficient, indirect funding created a precedent for much state-sponsored 'charity' in the Gorbachev period.

Although Soviet voluntary organizations were supposed to be altruistic, this proviso was not observed in the case of societies of disabled people, which provided material benefits for their members. These organizations therefore had a special place in Soviet society. They served as sources of inspiration – or sometimes warnings of what to avoid – for the self-help groups which emerged after 1985.

Prerevolutionary equivalents were liquidated after the 1917 Revolution, but during NEP societies of deaf and blind people were recreated as the Russian Society of Blind People (VOS) and the Russian Society of Deaf People (VOG). Analogous societies were established in other union republics. The societies were managed to a large extent by disabled people themselves but naturally subject to CPSU control. They provided employment, housing, educational and other facilities. The societies had a strong work ethic and tried to make members feel that they had a role to play in constructing socialism, although the very facilities provided tended to segregate blind and deaf people from the rest of society.[19]

VOS and VOG were regarded with envy by people with other disabilities, who often agreed that employment was the key to status in society, and who also wished to be able to run their own affairs. They focused on VOS and VOG's apparent self-sufficiency, playing down or ignoring problems,[20] such as inefficient administration and insufficient provision for rural members.[21]

People with other disabilities had in fact also united during NEP. Their Producers' Cooperative Union of Disabled People (*Promkooperatsiya invalidov*) was set up in 1921. *Promkooperatsiya* ran a wide network of small enterprises, producing clothing and other manufactured goods, or operating services such as bath houses and hairdressers' salons. Disabled people also had their own holiday homes and sanatoria and organized job training for their members. However, between 1956 and 1960 *Promkooperatsiya* was closed and its enterprises transferred to various industrial ministries, while social security departments took over responsibility for people with disabilities. It was claimed that the enterprises were economically inefficient and that the state could deal with all disabled people's problems.

Promkooperatsiya's demise was a misfortune, perhaps a disaster for Soviet disabled people. After the workshops had been transferred to state control some were closed[22] and in others the proportion of disabled workers declined.[23] As a result, many qualified craftsmen were left without jobs[24] and opportunities narrowed for disabled people seeking employment for the first time. Disabled beggars appeared on the streets.[25] In 1956 a new official organization was established, the Soviet Council of Veterans of War, but this could only partly replace *Promkooperatsiya*. Non-veteran disabled people began to dream of creating a Soviet Society of Disabled People (VOI). 'One could describe this as our collective aspiration'.[26]

LETTER-WRITING AND PETITIONS

Complaining and lobbying were activities of ambiguous significance; some actions could be classed with the officially encouraged public participation described above, others were associated with the independent movements discussed in the latter part of this chapter.

On the one hand, direct appeals to officials were officially encouraged. They were a crucial part of the system, so rigid in appearance and so flexible in reality. Complaining to official organizations about aspects of the welfare state in particular increased in many regions before 1985, whether because of rising expectations, greater fearlessness or greater cause for complaint. People complained more, even although there was no more chance of redress than in the past.[27]

Face-to-face appeals to officials were increasingly common. In the late 1970s, the Central Committee in Moscow was receiving 20,000 visits annually.[28] Even the least mobile citizens made the effort, appealing both to local officials and to perceived 'good tsars' like the Central Committee or Supreme Soviet. If in Moscow, they would do rounds of official institutions, if necessary by taxi. One activist wrote that [seated on a homemade skateboard] 'I wheeled myself from office to office, beginning with the borough executive committee and ending up with the Supreme Soviet.'[29]

Writing letters to the press was even more widespread. Soviet national newpapers collectively received about sixty to seventy million letters annually in the early 1980s.[30] In addition, citizens were encouraged to write directly to the authorities. The system was institutionalized in official decrees and in 1979 a Letters Department was created in the CPSU Central Committee.[31]

Writing a letter was normally a genuinely voluntary action and the volume of letters sent suggests that Soviet citizens must have considered letter-writing to offer some chance of achieving the desired goal.[32] Letter writing could be an effective way to bypass and pressurize local authorities; newspapers were duty bound to respond to letters and kept staff employed specifically to do so.[33] It was true, however, that sometimes the response was a *pro forma* note on a scrap of paper, saying that the letter would be analysed in due course.[34]

Disabled letter-writers encountered practical obstacles: writing letters was not so easy lying on one's back or using one's toes to hold the pen. For people who lived in residential homes, to complain was often to bring down the wrath of the administration. Yet, given the isolation in which they lived, writing letters was their 'outlet to the world'.[35] Sometimes their behaviour seemed reckless. For example, in the mid-1970s Mikhail Karev, a resident at a home in Orenburg *oblast*, was so furious when he read what disabled people could expect from the tenth five-year plan that he immediately penned, and sent off, a letter to the Central Committee.[36] In 1983, when he sent another letter to the Central Committee, asking them to permit the founding of a VOI, the reply was delivered with abuse and threats from a delegation of party dignitaries, including one who had travelled from the distant *oblast* capital.[37] Nina Sedova, supporting her pensionless parents on a collective farm, with no income except from casual sewing, made it her business to bombard the authorities at all levels with appeals to help her find a better job. She was ready to risk prison to secure her rights.[38]

Disabled people sometimes approached the authorities collectively. For example, many sent their comments and proposals for the 1977 Constitution to the Constitutional Committee in Moscow.[39] Members of *Prometei* (see below) wrote letters to officials requesting help for fellow members in matters such as housing. The most significant coordinated burst of lobbying occurred in 1979–80, before the Olympic Games and after a newspaper article by the Minister of Social Security which roused hopes for the creation of a society of disabled people. In November 1979 66 disabled people, mainly from two residential homes, requested the Supreme Soviet to consider the establishment of a VOI. *Minsobes* replied curtly that such a society would be 'pointless'.[40] At about the same time at least four other appeals were made to official organs: to the Supreme Soviet again (10 signatories); to the Presidium of the Supreme Soviet (with at least 186 signatories from very diverse locations); to Brezhnev (11 signatories); and to the Central Committee.[41] They pointed to the existence of organizations of disabled people in Czechoslovakia as evidence that there would be nothing threatening to socialism in the creation of such a society.[42]

The press also received many letters from disabled people. Occasionally newspapers publicised cases in which only the intervention of the press had forced local officials into action over specific complaints.[43] An outstanding example was that of Veronika Kononenko, a journalist with the women's magazine *Rabotnitsa*, who published a piece in 1974 about the plight of a young disabled woman looking for work in an isolated northern village. The woman had been ignored by the *Komsomol* and social security officials until she wrote to *Rabotnitsa* for help; the journal then persuaded a local newspaper to print her letter, after which she was offered training as a knitting machine operator. Kononenko herself helped transport the machine by boat to the almost inaccessible village.[44] Kononenko received many responses to her article and publicly promised to find work for any disabled people who requested her aid.[45] She successfully placed 154 in one year,[46] after many battles with local social security departments. Disabled people considered this achievement extraordinary compared with the low success rates using normal channels. Kononenko's main aim, however, was to achieve a solution on a national scale. Hence she was not entirely gladdened by her own success: in a private letter she suggested that failure would have justified *Rabotnitsa*'s editor taking up the general issue with the Council of Ministers.[47]

Significantly, disabled people too wrote to the press about nation-wide problems, in effect suggesting changes in social policy. Such actions should not be dismissed as evidence of a naive misunderstanding of the nature of the regime. Often the writers had no illusions, but felt that nonetheless there was virtue in persistence. 'We try not to give in to this feeling of doom, we struggle, try to achieve something, demand, write. Sometimes we find support. But in general our struggle meets with failure, since things always come down to the Ministry of Social Security, which is not at all concerned about our problems.'[48] 'Somehow [at first] I believed in the possibility of a miracle, but while I was writing the letter my enthusiasm waned. Now I'm not at all convinced. Although perhaps miracles do happen! They say a drop of water can wear through a stone – so perhaps we'll be able to wear them down somewhere.'[49]

If they persisted, it was partly because *Minsobes* was not their only interlocutor. They also hoped to arouse public opinion about disability issues: 'to agitate amongst journalists on our behalf, so that they in turn raise public consciousness'.[50] It is interesting that this was seen as important in Soviet context, in so far as public opinion has traditionally been regarded as almost non-existent and/or powerless before 1985.[51] They participated eagerly in debates raised by newspaper articles, with one another – sending clippings or copied articles to friends – and in letters to editors. They wrote to each another asking, 'Did you respond to that article?' and considered it their responsibility to do so. Sometimes they responded collectively. For example, in 1974 a leading activist tried to organize a campaign of letter writing to *Literaturnaya gazeta*.[52] In their letters, disabled people sometimes highlighted political implications which the original article had left vague.[53]

A number of prominent journalists had personal reasons for involvement in disability issues, such as a disabled family member.[54] Journalists and disabled people became friends and allies. Even one journalist on *Pravda* was said to sympathize with the disabled people's cause;[55] the more liberal *Komsomol'skaya pravda* and *Literaturnaya gazeta* contained groups of 'allies'.[56] They corresponded with disabled members of the public, as personal friends, about the progress of the disability movement.[57] A very few journalists were disabled themselves. Nina Vishnyakova, a severely disabled woman who lived in residential homes, mostly in Sverdlovsk, until her death in 1978, was an inspiration to many.[58]

Although articles were produced to a plan, nevertheless debates could also surface as a result of letters from the public. Disabled people tried to start up debates. In particular, they tried to exploit any signs of *glasnost* on the subject of a VOI, and the story of their campaign may be taken as a case study illustrating many of the points already made about interaction between the media and the public. For all the rhetoric about monolithism, in fact censors received contradictory signals and, even more significantly, the press and policy makers were sometimes at cross purposes, i.e. the press could be regarded, very provisionally, as part of an embryonic civil society, mediating between state and public.

There had been some discussion about the putative VOI in the Khrushchev period.[59] In 1969 *Komsomol'skaya pravda* advocated the re-establishment of a VOI, after a journalist met with disabled activists in Voronezh.[60] In 1971, however, the same newspaper carefully crossed out the suggestion for a Soviet VOI when it printed an abridged version of a disabled person's article from a Crimean newspaper.[61] The local press could seemingly be *more* open than the national newspaper, which merely referred to the Czech equivalent disabled people's organization. (A similar event occurred in 1984, when a VOI was mentioned in the Voronezh press.)[62]

In 1973 the Ministry's own journal published a letter from leading Voronezh activist Gus'kov advocating a VOI. The journalists concerned – who had acted against the advice of colleagues – earned a sound rebuke by 'top people in the Ministry'.[63] Disabled people responding to Gus'kov's letter were told to 'forget about it'.[64] However, in 1974 *Minsobes* was outraged by the publication of an article making the same point in *Literaturnaya gazeta*. The article, prepared with the help of the Voronezh group, provoked many letters of agreement, but the newspaper dropped the issue.[65] Disabled people who wrote to the Central Committee and other official bodies, hoping that they had been given a signal to pursue their cause, found their letters sent on to *Minsobes,* which replied in predictably offputting manner.[66] Again, journalists were in effect trying to flout official policy, and this raised disabled people's morale. Mikhail Karev in Orsk, for example, was on the verge of suicide when a disabled acquaintance sent him the 1974 article. Karev decide to befriend the Voronezh activists and work with them to create a VOI.

By contrast, when in 1979 disabled people approached a

journalist from *Pravda* and he tried to take up the issue of a VOI, he was explicitly refused permission to do so.[67] This prohibition cannot have been made explicit to all censors, however, since in the same year Leningrad journal *Zvezda* published the autobiography of a disabled engineer and admirer of the Voronezh group, who advocated the creation of a VOI. Once again, disabled readers inundated the journal with their letters of agreement.[68]

Finally, in February 1985, the *Komsomol* magazine *Smena* published a few of its many letters from disabled people unanimously supporting the creation of a VOI.[69] Perhaps not coincidentally, *Smena* was edited by A. Likhanov, future founder and president of the Children's Fund (1987).

POSTAL NETWORKS AND SELF-HELP GROUPS: THE VOI MOVEMENT

'You spend your whole life like a fish beating against the ice, just slowly killing yourself in the process. What does the ice care? It doesn't melt, it just stays frozen, silent... [However,] it seems the time has arrived when disabled people will try to come to their own rescue... A movement has sprung into being, like a river.'[70]

In a society where telephones were scarce, long distance calls expensive, and internal postage rates cheap, it was not surprising that Soviet people chose to communicate with each other by letter. This is an area which, for obvious reasons, has not been studied. The KGB could not monitor the content of every single letter sent within the USSR and my research – based on letters of disabled people from the 1960s onwards – suggests that letter writers who had not been officially classed as troublemakers often assumed they could write reasonably frankly. It was apparently possible to establish postal networks without experiencing manifestations of surveillance, and perhaps to actually escape surveillance itself, until the writers embarked on some kind of more obvious joint action. (Sheer quantities of post also attracted attention. Tamara Zagvozdina, organizer of the *Prometei* Association, was accused by a local official of 'overloading the postal system'(!)[71])

Writing letters helped disabled people keep in touch with friends and acquaintances made in rare forays into the outside world, to hospitals or sanatoria. Such informal networks had a way of expanding into independent organizations, to be discussed below. It was true that circulating typed journals and conducting an organization's administrative business by the internal post was not always quick. Nevertheless, many disabled people took on huge burdens of letter writing and copying in order to keep the networks alive, and in the penfriend clubs discussed below there was a commitment to democratic consultation and achievement of consensus which often overrode considerations of speed.

The disabled people's movement was a true movement in various senses. First, its adherents made consistent demands. The aim was self-determination and self-realization, the objective was to establish a VOI. The aim was most often couched in terms of the value – to individuals and society – of decent employment opportunities. However, other aspects of the problem, such as living conditions in residential homes, mobility (provision of more acceptable wheelchairs and comfortable prostheses) and education were also frequently raised. Second, there was a clear sense of the enemy to be defeated. This was *Minsobes*. Disabled people had the impression that it was 'almost a matter of honour [for the Ministry] to obstruct disabled people in every way possible'.[72] They correctly saw ministerial opposition as the main impediment to progress. Third, there was a certain cohesiveness of membership within the movement. Most of the activists were people with very limited mobility. Although those who lived at home and in homes had slightly different concerns,[73] overall this was a group with very similar experiences and problems. Their separation from the rest of society was another factor which could enhance their sense of solidarity. Fourth, in a number of cases, these networks were institutionalized. Independent organizations of disabled people, all dreaming of forming a VOI, were created in the 1970s and early 1980s and in some cases existed right up to the Gorbachev period.

Was the VOI movement a daring project in the Soviet context? *Prometei*, one of the key organizations of the 1970s,

1985: Society in Crisis

was described by disabled writer Nina Vishnyakova as 'a kind of utopia'. However, she went on to admit, 'I cannot prove theoretically the essence of its impracticability'.[74] The strange truth was that in fact *Prometei*, like the movement as a whole, was not 'impractical', despite the seeming hostility of the environment. The disabled groups found loopholes in system, hiding places in an emerging 'second society'.[75]

Moreover, the fact that they worked on their own, without official support, meant that the disabled informal organizations were run entirely by disabled people themselves. Had they been incorporated into the system, they would almost certainly have lost this control. There was obviously a strong case, in theory, for integrating more closely into society. Soviet realities, however, meant that Soviet society was not an environment into which disabled people necessarily wanted to be integrated. Their own, informal organizations presented the opportunity not to 'live the lie' – to use Solzhenitsyn's phrase – and they were unwilling to sacrifice this independence.

1956–1980

1) Kiselev (Moscow)
In 1956 a number of disabled people, including future dissident Yurii Kiselev, demonstrated outside the offices of the CPSU Central Committee and Moscow *gorkom*. They met representatives of the *gorkom* and *Minsobes*, but their requests for a national society were rejected, and after the activists had met a few times and conducted a sporadic letter writing campaign the endeavour fizzled out.[76]

2) Golubev and Vinogradova (Ivanovo)
In 1970 Vasilii Golubev and Irina Vinogradova of Ivanovo produced an unofficial questionnaire asking disabled people, *inter alia*, whether they would join a VOI were one created and whether they sought employment. The questionnaires were distributed directly by a committee of disabled people during 1970–1.[77] Golubev hoped to collect thousands of positive responses with which to make his case to *Minsobes*.[78] The plan aroused enthusiasm among disabled people: one woman, for example, desperate for proper employment,

described how she 'wrote and wrote and even filled in all the blank spaces [around the edge of the questionnaire] and wrote down everything I thought about the subject, from the heart.'[79] In 1971 Golubev sent the Ministry 800 completed questionnaires, requesting them merely to set up a fee-paying residential home for at least 100 residents, with employment provided.[80] (There were parallels here with other ideas circulating in the movement.)[81] *Minsobes* ignored Golubev's request and instead sent the completed questionnaires to the local social security departments responsible for the signatories – whereupon victimization ensued.[82]

Golubev's strategy had been bold. First he used the media to introduce himself to the disabled community, publishing an appeal for disabled people to join the labour force in the popular health magazine *Zdorov'e*. His article was a paean of praise for the virtues of work which could only endear him to the authorities and which prompted the journal to append an article about Golubev and his bad luck in losing his job in a photographic disabled people's *artel* when it was closed down under Khrushchev.[83]

Golubev then tried to distribute the questionnaires as quickly as possible, to evade notice. The plan was so unusual that not all the participants were aware that it should be kept secret; for example, one respondent arranged for her nurse to type extra copies of the questionnaire.[84] Unfortunately one of Golubev's fellow organizers decided it was 'stupid' to conduct the survey secretly and sent the questionnaire to *Minsobes*. Another survey participant was also suspected of reporting the project. Golubev subsequently found himself hounded by the local authorities and *Minsobes*, who 'rained down curses' on him.[85] Other survey distributors were visited by party officials and the police, who treated the survey as illegal.[86] Accused with Vinogradova of 'anti-state activity', Golubev was dissuaded from further action and apparently psychologically crushed.[87]

3) Prometei (USSR)
However, this was not the end of the story. Parallel to the survey, several of its participants had been developing other approaches to the creation of associations of disabled people.[88] In the Urals, Tamara Zagvozdina had initiated the

Prometei (Prometheus) Mutual Aid Association in 1970. The association continued to exist into the 1980s. Because of Golubev's survey and *Prometei* Zagvozdina received visits from representatives of the local party committee and social security organs. The authorities – whom she described as being 'up in arms against us' – apparently found it difficult to believe the audacity of the projects and seemed out of their depth, desperately finding pretexts for forbidding the unmonitored activity. Zagvozdina reported, 'We argued about it: I pressed my argument on them, they pressed theirs on me'. She was categorically forbidden to continue her activity and warned that *Prometei* was sowing the seeds of discontent among disabled people.[89] The survey was described as a political matter and participants warned that they could be prosecuted for printing the questionnaire forms without authorization. However, unlike Golubev, the furious Zagvozdina 'did not find it necessary to submit. We still have heads on our shoulders, even though we are usually regarded as idiots. Their eyes pop in disbelief when we have the audacity to assert that we are people.'[90]

Disabled people were obviously in some doubt about how much of a secret *Prometei* was supposed to be. For example, one woman requested and gained Zagvozdina's permission to publicize the association in a national newspaper in 1981, but then thought better of it and decided not to do so.[91]

Prometei was run by a council, originally consisting of seven women, all from small towns or villages, and all of whom had to be consulted before decisions to aid members were made.[92] The association produced a bulletin, *Ogonek*, one of whose functions was to keep members informed of developments in the disabled people's movement. *Prometei* had members in Russia and other republics[93]; they totalled two to three hundred in the 1970s. They included some of the most active and influential members of the movement. They had a treasurer, but not an official account, since they were not registered. ('And who would let us be an official organization?' Zagvozdina asked rhetorically in 1971.)[94] Their financial arrangements aroused suspicion from the authorities. Zagvozdina argued that there was nothing wrong or unusual about their activities, since disabled people were friends, providing the type of support that

Russians traditionally extend to friends.[95] Members acquired medicines, food products and other goods for one another. They helped members to travel for treatment[96] and collected money for projects such as repairs to members' cottages or the purchase of a motorized wheelchair. They exchanged books and journal articles. Their letter-writing campaigns had some success in persuading local authorities to help individual members, for example by installing a telephone.[97]

4) Friendship (Lithuania)
Outside Russia, a Lithuanian social club called 'Friendship' (*Draugiste/Druzhba*) was established in about 1971. It published a monthly *samizdat* journal, *Draugo Jodis/Slovo druga*. In 1983 its members were meeting on a river bank. Also in 1983, they unsuccessfully petitioned the Central Committee of the Lithuanian Communist Party to establish a society for disabled people.[98]

5) The Voronezh Group
The best publicized and in some respects most significant of the non-dissident disabled people's efforts was the Voronezh group. In this central Russian city, a prototype of a future VOI had been set up with the blessing of the local authorities. Inventor and engineer Gennadii Gus'kov[99] had a draft Charter of VOI ready in 1969. In the same year, he created a workshop in a residential home and proved that even severely disabled people could perform skilled manual work, if they lived where they worked, to the benefit of state and society.[100] 'It was impossible to overestimate what employment and financial independence had done for the morale of the disabled people involved.'[101]

Gus'kov's conclusion – which he continued to pursue through the 1970s and 1980s, with support from some other disabled activists – was that a national society should not be traditionally, hierarchically structured, based on the normal Soviet principle of democratic centralism. Instead, it should consist of a network of disabled communes or 'residential-production complexes'. He treated his workshop as the first cell of the society and its headed notepaper contained the initials of the putative Society of Disabled People (VOIN).

Initially, Gus'kov's experiment was officially praised, and in 1976 a Council of Ministers' resolution recommended that more workshops be created in residential homes.[102] Gus'kov faced constant antagonism from the management of the residential home and local social security organs.[103] As a result, he tried to remove the workshop from the jurisdiction of *Minsobes*.[104] Gus'kov was taken one night without warning and placed in a succession of residential homes in the Saratov area. His complaints were met with violence and when he returned to Voronezh to argue his case he was put in prison for twenty-four hours and 'deported' to Saratov.[105] Zagvozdina and possibly also other members of *Prometei* campaigned unsuccessfully for his return.[106]

6) Omsk
A more inward-looking local group was formed in Omsk, some time before 1980. Unusually, Omsk possessed a rehabilitation centre, visited frequently by local disabled people, who made friends and often phoned one another. Together with the nurses, they met socially, for example at communal drinking sessions on public holidays.[107]

7) Iskra (Gorky and Moscow)
Iskra (Spark) was a 'mutual aid association of disabled letter-writers' which was founded in Gorky in 1979.[108] Its centre then moved to Moscow, where it was organized chiefly by Ol'ga Kameneva, a young severely disabled woman who lived in a residential home. They published a newsletter, *Vestnik*, purchased medicines for one another, and ran a lending library.[109] By May 1982 the club had fifty members, by March 1985, 250.[110] Most of its members were under thirty, although Kameneva was keen to recruit older members who would 'be involved in activities leading to the creation of VOI'.[111] *Iskra* was not a secret organization – indeed it sent the first issue of its newsletter to the borough party committee for approval (which it received)[112] – and it was mentioned in a national newspaper in 1983.[113] *Iskra* as a whole was said to support the idea of a VOI.[114]

Kameneva tried to make contact with *Prometei*; she and Zagvozdina had mutual friends.[115] It seems that the *Prometei* model was viewed as an appropriate one by many disabled activists. *Prometei* and *Iskra*, like *Korchaginets* (see below) were to a large extent women's organizations, which may have been significant. Did such organizations survive because disabled women were considered even less threatening to the system than men?

There was a thin line between the activities of a Golubev or Zagvozdina and those of the dissident participants in the human rights movement. Perhaps the most important difference was that Zagvozdina and the others were working only within the Soviet context: raising consciousness among disabled people and badgering the authorities, but never appealing over the heads of those authorities to international opinion.

8) The Action Group to Defend the Rights of Disabled People (USSR)[116]

However, disability was also a cause within the dissident movement. In early 1978 the Moscow Helsinki Watch Group sent a proposal for the founding of a VOI to the Supreme Soviet and three international organizations. In May three disabled people – Yurii Kiselev (who had been involved in the 1956 protests), Valerii Fefelov and Faizulla Khusainov – set up an Action Group to Defend the Rights of Disabled People, and the Helsinki group expressed its support. A VOI was the Action Group's ultimate goal. Their founding declaration stated that only disabled people could defend their own rights; *Minsobes* was an 'indifferent protector'. The Action Group's declaration was within the mainstream of the disabled people's movement in that it stated their intention to lobby the appropriate Soviet authorities. It was outside the mainstream in its declaration to appeal to world public opinion if the Soviet authorities did not cooperate. Moreover, the Group stated its intention of seeking links with international disabled people's organizations.[117]

This was exactly how the Group proceeded. First it declared its loyalty to the authorities and engaged in the type of lobbying of official Soviet institutions at which many other non-dissident activists excelled. However, the Action Group subsequently appealed to the CSCE governments, international human rights organizations and foreign radio stations, without result.[118] The Group managed to survive

1985: Society in Crisis

and continue its activities through the 1980s, despite the emigration of Fefelov.[119]

The Action Group, according to Fefelov, did not at first regard themselves as dissidents. They were treated by the authorities as if they were. As a result, they soon joined the dissidents. Sakharov and Bonner, herself disabled, were particularly supportive of the disabled people's cause. The Group went as far as to co-author, with the Helsinki group, a document on disabled political prisoners.[120]

How was the Action Group regarded within the mainstream disabled people's movement? The answer to this question would shed some light on what remains one of the enigmas of Soviet history: the impact of the dissident movement on the population at large. One might assume that by rooting itself in the human rights movement the Action Group had distanced itself from mainstream disabled activism. It had chosen its ally, and that ally was not *Prometei*. The choice was no doubt personal but was perhaps also based to some extent on geography. The human rights movement was centred in Moscow and Leningrad. Kiselev was a Muscovite, and in the 1970s other disabled activists were mostly provincial, and widely scattered: Zagvozdina and Karev in their remote Urals towns, Gus'kov in Saratov *oblast*, Vyatkin in the Crimea, Golubev in Ivanovo, Häkkelä in Voronezh, and so on. Moreover, the Action Group was, not surprisingly, regarded with suspicion and caution, by Zagvozdina among others. On the other hand, there were links. The Action Group tried to keep in touch with disabled people and publicize abuses: Kiselev claimed to be receiving about two letters a day from Soviet disabled people in 1979. Even in remote areas, disabled people did know of the Group's existence. For example, the signatories of the letter to Brezhnev mentioned above used the argument that if he created a VOI this would cut the ground from under the feet of the dissidents and their Western allies.[121] The Group had some existence outside Moscow, at least initially, since Fefelov was from Vladimir *oblast* and Khusainov from the Tatar ASSR. Moreover, some of the non-dissident activists seemed to sympathize. Gus'kov and Gennady Golovatyi (a respected disabled poet) were ready to resign from *Prometei* to express their support for the Group, and Iskra seems to have circulated a questionnaire on the Group's behalf.[122] Karev corresponded with Fefelov – an action which got him into trouble with the authorities.[123]

1980–1985

Despite the occasional persecution encountered by disabled activists, their organizations were not liquidated. They survived the period of the 'Second Cold War', from 1979 to 1985 – a time when the dissident movement was almost suppressed. In the circumstances, one strategy was to wait for better times, in the meanwhile preparing the paperwork for the future Society. In July 1983 five activists, including Golovatyi, Gus'kov and Karev, met in Moscow to begin work on the society's charter.[124] Subsequently a number of alternative versions were produced.[125]

Meanwhile, new organizations were springing up in various locations in the first half of the 1980s. Perhaps among the disability groups one should mention *Levsha*, a society of left-handed people, which was set up in 1982.[126] In autumn 1984 an Esperanto club run by and for disabled people was founded in Latvia and soon acquired many members from elsewhere in the USSR.[127]

1) Korchaginets

The *Korchaginets* Club, founded in 1981, became the largest organization of disabled people since the closure of *Promkooperatsiya*.[128] The club was open to anyone with mobility problems, uniting disabled people at home and in residential care. It existed USSR-wide and had about 400 members by October 1985. Most were in their twenties. Some of its activists played a leading role in campaigning for creation of an official national society. By March 1985 there was sufficient contact between *Iskra* and overlapping membership for the organizations to discuss merger; however, they remained separate.[129]

Led by Ol'ga Burkova of Sverdlovsk, a group of disabled young women had originally decided to found a penfriends' club. It soon ceased to be an entirely women's organisation; Gennadii Loginov and Anatolii Tkachenko were particularly active members. In March 1983 they issued their first *samizdat* journal; soon they were producing two and organizing a range of hobby clubs by correspondence as well as other activities such as correspondence with sick children in residential homes (against the opposition of their teachers), a flourishing lonely hearts column, quizzes and a lottery in aid of the Peace Fund.

The immediate objective of the *korchagintsy* in the mid-1980s was to break their isolation and acquire some purpose in life and a sense of worth. However, for many members – the majority, according to Burkova – the ultimate objective was the creation of a VOI. As a first step towards this, as well as to make its own work more efficient, those members of the club who were concerned about efficiency tried to set up a hierarchical structure, establishing local sections, a Central Council and a Bureau of the Central Council. All 'meetings' were conducted by letter.

2) Sporting Associations
In the early 1980s disabled people adopted a new and successful strategy. They began to focus on improving disabled people's access to sport. The ultimate goal remained: new sporting organizations were a means to an end, since they were generally intended to pave the way for a VOI. The ingenuity of this approach lay in the fact that it was possible to bypass *Minsobes*. There were also fewer financial implications for the state than would be involved in the creation of a VOI. The Baltic republics, as so often, led the way. In Estonia the *Invasport* club – established unofficially in 1980 – was by 1984 headed by no less than the Minister of Social Security. Estonian disabled people had their own television programme and officially sponsored sports competitions.[130] In Leningrad, *Ortsport* was founded in 1979.[131] *Feniks* followed in 1984 as a branch of the car enthusiasts' association, a ploy to 'deceive the authorities' about its real purpose (VOI).[132] It also organized literary and other non-sporting activities, drew up a draft charter for a VOI and petitioned *Minsobes* to allow its creation.[133] The Latvian sports club *Optimist* was established in 1983. Unlike the Estonians, the Latvians found the local authorities unhelpful, and television shy of touching on a 'delicate issue'. By 1987 *Optimist* members were said to have given up expecting support from the authorities; they

tried to be self-reliant.[134] In Bryansk in 1985 a group of disabled people, having unsuccessfully petitioned the authorities to permit the founding of a more general disabled peoples' organization, decided to bide their time and created a sports club instead.[135]

3) Official Policy towards Creation of a VOI, 1984
The ultimate objective of most of the disabled people's clubs seemed to come a little closer to realization on the eve of Gorbachev's accession. In October 1984 the union republican ministers of social security, with other senior officials, discussed the issue of pensioners and one of their recommendations was that four republican ministries should investigate the desirability of a VOI along the lines of VOS and VOG. Only the Belorussians came out officially in favour in 1985. Although the Russian academics who conducted the investigation had come to the same conclusion, they were induced by the Minister to say the reverse. For the time being VOI was on hold.[136]

INDEPENDENT SELF-HELP GROUPS AND CHARITIES: PARENTS' ORGANIZATIONS AND NETWORKS

A significant section of the voluntary sector under Gorbachev united parents with various types of need: people caring for disabled children, whom the state did little to help; bringing up children on their own; or with 'multi-child' families of three or more. In some cases there is evidence that parents with similar sets of problems were already cooperating before 1985. For instance, in the 1970s Moscow parents of children with cerebral palsy became involved in a project to build a rehabilitation centre where children could receive training which was not available from the Soviet welfare state. The centre was finally opened in 1990.[137] In Leningrad, the Maternal Glory society was set up in 1979 and actually registered 'around' 1980. It seems to have been a genuine self-help group and was said to have been the precursor of the many borough organizations for large families which sprang up in Leningrad during *perestroika*.[138]

As Chapter 2 suggested, another area of concern was the

plight of children in children's homes and their fortunes after they left residential care. The Pedagogical Search (*Pedagogicheskii poisk*) Association was created in 1984 to help such children and young adults. It achieved registration only in 1991.[139] An alternative approach was to pull children out of residential care. In Akademgorodok, Novosibirsk, Zoya Borodaevskaya was allowed, by informal arrangement, to foster thirteen children on a short-term basis, feeding and nursing them back to health only for them to fall ill on their return 'home'. Borodaevskaya decided to set up her own official children's home. She lobbied the local education authorities from the late 1970s, without success, but her efforts were to bear fruit and be widely imitated under Gorbachev.[140]

INDEPENDENT CHARITY: THE ROLE OF THE CHURCH

Since it was illegal for the Church to organize charity between 1929 and 1990, it is naturally difficult to find evidence of charitable activity. Van der Voort cites anecdotal evidence of giving by individual clerics; of beggars congregating by church doors until they were moved on by the militia; and of unofficial organized giving by groups of parishioners who met under of the pretence of tea parties to discuss the distribution of financial help to local people in need.[141] One example of a parish organization which existed from 1979 and emerged as a charity under perestroika was that attached to the Church of St Nicholas the Miracle-Worker in Leningrad.[142] The organizers of the Radonezh Society, an early *perestroika*-era charity, had been active in voluntary work before Gorbachev – educating children, distributing *samizdat* and restoring churches.[143]

CONCLUSIONS

There was no officially recognized independent voluntary sector before 1985. 'Voluntary work' or 'voluntary organizations' were supervised by the CPSU. Voluntary – often involuntary – work by citizens was used as evidence of the regime's legitimacy, to control people's spare time and to substitute for gaps in state provision. However, it seems that by 1985 citizens were increasingly reluctant to participate in this type of activity. An exception were the voluntary societies of blind and deaf people, which had meaning for their members despite their links to the party. Other disabled people were anxious to create an equivalent organization for themselves, a Society of Disabled People or VOI. They appealed to officials in person and by petition and used the press energetically to pursue their cause. They found allies among certain journalists and achieved a measure of success in that, despite the Ministry of Social Security's attempts to make VOI a taboo subject, it did break through into the press on several occasions. Each article about the subject was greeted by a flood of welcoming responses from Soviet disabled people.

Moreover, disabled people, especially women, corresponded among themselves and created networks which in the 1970s and 1980s became nation-wide societies with organizational structures and producing *samizdat*. The organizations were viewed as precursors of VOI, as were groups attached to institutions in Voronezh and Omsk. Although the Action Group to Defend the Rights of Disabled People was a dissident organization, the others were neither dissident nor official. From 1979 additional embryonic branches of VOI were established, now masked as sports clubs, and these sometimes achieved official status, especially in the Baltic republics and Leningrad. At the same time, parents' self-help organizations were emerging, uniting parents of disabled children or with large families. Meanwhile, despite the law forbidding charity by the Church, charity continued, to some extent in organized form.[144]

The evidence about informal organizations presented in this chapter shows that the post-1985 voluntary sector had roots in society before Gorbachev's accession. The CPSU was already beginning to lose its monopoly. Moreover, it is likely that the groups discussed here form the tip of an iceberg. The phenomenon of informal self-help groups and charities was almost certainly both broader and deeper. This chapter has dwelt on the two chief types of self-help group which formed before and after 1985, but one can see further evidence of activity if one looks at other groups. Veterans of the war in Afghanistan, for example, were already beginning to organize before Gorbachev came to power, as in Novosibirsk. (See Chapter 6.) Moreover, if one examined more personal correspondence and conducted interviews one would almost certainly uncover many more disabled people's and parents' groups. Most probably had no organizational structures. However, the fact that some did, and that reasonably strong independent but non-dissident organizations could be built under the Soviet regime, is surely significant.

4 *Perestroika* and the Immediate Causes of the Voluntary Sector's Emergence

'We have met cases of death from starvation. That's 45 years after the lifting of the blockade [of Leningrad].'[1]

'The charity movement...is a [psychological] necessity for Soviet society.'

D. Granin[2]

INTRODUCTION

Chapters 2 and 3 surveyed the socio-political problems in the areas of welfare and 'voluntary' work which contributed to the sense of impending crisis by 1985. The creation of a voluntary sector was a response to these, but it could not have come into being without Gorbachev and *perestroika*. This chapter discusses factors characterizing the Gorbachev period which promoted the emergence of voluntary organizations after 1985.

Since welfare and voluntary work issues were part of the general crisis of the system, it was not surprising that Gorbachev and his team intended them to be tackled in the same way as other problem areas, 'activating the human factor' by encouraging *glasnost* and democratization. *Glasnost* opened up discussion, while the policy of democratization provided the environment in which voluntary organizations could emerge. Economic reform also provides part of the context for the emerging voluntary sector, since commercial, service-providing ventures began to emerge, engaging in welfare provision in competition or cooperation with non-profit organizations.

There were also more specific factors which contributed to the development of the voluntary sector. The first factor was a negative one. Attempts to revive and extend the welfare state proved unsuccessful, and their failure only exacerbated negative attitudes towards the welfare state which had already been growing before 1985. The failure of reform prompted public attempts to revive, as an alternative, a culture of philanthropy and genuine volunteering. A parallel process was the development of a culture of self-help.

Resources were released by the abolition of *nomenklatura* privileges and new voluntary organizations could benefit from these. Unfortunately the influx of foreign aid in 1990–91, while providing some short-term relief, had a generally harmful effect on the voluntary sector. On the other hand, foreign charities also began to work at helping Russian charities establish themselves. The impact of this foreign help is discussed in the final section of the chapter.

STATE FAILURE

In some respects Gorbachev's programme was initially more state interventionist than that of his predecessors – for example with regard to quality control of industrial goods, or anti-alcohol legislation.[3] Hence there was no inevitability about the emergence of an independent voluntary sector. Spending on health and social security both grew. The abolition of party privileges also released services and institutions into the general state welfare system. The beneficiaries of increased expenditure now more often included those non-workers who had been neglected in the past. With proper funding, ideas for modernizing the welfare state – some of which had been stored in desk drawers during the stagnation years – might be put into practice.

However, attempts to reform the welfare state were often unsuccessful. Shortage of money remained a key factor. Also crucial were reasons connected with the nature of the party-dominated bureaucracy. Soviet officials were too formalistic, too shy of taking responsibility, too afraid of devolving power, too secretive and sometimes too corrupt to be able to improve services significantly. In addition, they often had a hostile and contemptuous attitude towards the non-working population which all the new talk of 'charitableness' and 'caring' could not disguise.

The years 1985–7 saw several initiatives designed to encourage older and disabled people to join the workforce and ease the labour shortage in Russian industry. At the same time, the new policies reflected both a more general concern with the needs of these disadvantaged groups, and also input from the older and disabled people themselves. In particular, they recognized that pensions and benefits had slipped in value, failing to match increases in the cost of living and providing a below poverty-level existence for many recipients.

A decree of May 1985 initiated a cautious reform of the pension and benefits system, as well as proposing measures to address some of the problems outlined in Chapter 2, such as the state of residential care.[4] The five-year plan approved at the twenty-seventh CPSU Congress in 1986 envisaged small improvements in social security by the year 2000.[5] These were both clearly inadequate and also not speedily implemented: the lack of progress on pensions and benefits was to be a main topic of debate at the first Congress of People's Deputies (CPD) in 1989. Later in 1989 the Supreme Soviet raised minimum pensions to 70 rubles, in anticipation of more serious reform of the pension law. However, the poverty of the state was demonstrated yet again. Even this small rise was opposed by the Ministry of Finance and in a bizarre effort to collect the money, a number of *non-state* organizations, headed by the communist party and including VOS, VOG, trade unions and the Peace Fund, contributed a further 1.6 billion rubles to the 1989 budget.[6] The new pension law appeared in draft form in November 1989 – prompting half a million letters from Soviet citizens to the Supreme Soviet – and was signed in May 1990. The provisions of the new law were to be implemented only gradually, up to July 1993.[7]

Another step towards addressing the needs of older people was the establishment in December 1986 of an organization for all pensioners, not just war veterans: the Soviet Organization of Veterans of War and Labour.[8] It was apparently conceived entirely as a 'transmission belt'. That it was used as a pool of support for the CPSU was indicated by the fact that all but one of its 75 delegates to the USSR Congress of People's Deputies were communists. It should probably be viewed as the final offshoot of the spurious voluntary sector, rather than the first shoot of the genuine one.[9]

Only after Gorbachev's accession, in May 1985, were local social security departments ordered to keep lists of pensioners in special need; this was followed by the experimental provison of home-help services in the Baltic republics.[10] The USSR-wide *Zabota* (Care) campaign in 1987, conducted by local authorities, veterans' organizations and other official voluntary agencies, revealed the primitive state of official knowledge about the scale of problems by once again setting as a target to locate all older people in need of services. Although some home-help and other services were provided as a consequence of the campaign, it was also criticized for turning into just another example of official shamming.[11] Moreover, home-helps were paid so little that few people wanted to do the job.[12] In the city of Ufa, for example, there were only 27 home-helps in December 1987.[13] Social services departments also tried to reforge contacts between pensioners and their former workplaces – creating a typically Soviet vicious circle of evasion of responsibility. Another development was the creation of day-care centres. Moscow City Soviet, for example, decided to establish one in every borough by 1991.[14] By 1990 the Minister of Social Security was suggesting, in a yet more radical shift towards care in the community, that the state must improve benefits for carers as an *alternative* to building expensive residential homes.[15]

In 1986 people disabled from childhood received assurances of help in a further decree issued by the Central Committee, Council of Ministers and Central Trade Union Council.[16] That this resolution appeared at all was thanks partly to the lobbying of disabled people, but they found it disappointing. The final version was apparently less radical than Politburo discussions of the subject: *Goskomtrud*, the State Committee for Labour, was said to have 'done everything to emasculate' it.[17] Moreover, it was not implemented.[18] The state also tried to improve the situation of children in care. Resolutions issued in January 1985 – just before Gorbachev's accession – and July 1987 did not, however, display rethinking about any of the premises of existing provision.[19]

Meanwhile, the responsibilities of enterprises and collective farms in the field of welfare services were extended in 1987 and 1988.[20] Some factories organized their own 'charities'. In 1990, for example, the *Elektrosignal* Factory in Novosibirsk established a 'fund' to coordinate the efforts of workers to help large families; mothers and widows of soldiers killed in Afghanistan; and former employees receiving low monthly pensions.[21]

Where party control remained strong, the CPSU was able to force local enterprises to contribute to charity even in the last year of *perestroika*. It did so successfully, for example, in Lugansk.[22] With the weakening of party control elsewhere, however, enterprises were less clearly obliged to engage in charity and, given the context of economic reform, presumably felt less inclined to do so. By 1991 the press was reporting that 'donations to charity are falling dramatically...State enterprises, the church and collective farms have become stingier'.[23] Fund-seekers had to find other, non-party routes for exerting pressure on state enterprises. In Novosibirsk, for example, in June 1990, a (state) hospital used the local press. It appealed to enterprises to give hard currency, so it could purchase equipment for treating bladder stones. In exchange, workers at those enterprises would be able to jump queues at the hospital.[24]

Cook suggests that the pattern is of 'deterioration in the state's provision of social services despite increasing allocations'. She suggests as the economic causes 'uncontrolled inflation, severe shortages and black market control of scarce goods (including medicines), and labor unrest.'[25] As suggested above, the heart of the problem was political – the weakening of the party-state. Another factor, which contributed very directly to the perception of need for a voluntary sector, was the *increased level of demand* for state aid. When faced with new challenges such as a refugee problem, state agencies often proved too inflexible and uncoordinated to respond effectively.

Disasters

The state's failure to cope was most visible and tragic when it was confronted with natural and man-made disasters. The years 1986–9 were marked by a string of disasters. The accident at the nuclear power station in Chernobyl occurred in April 1986: only one year into *perestroika*. At this point the public had no choice but to give their donations to official agencies. They collected over 550 million rubles for victims of Chernobyl. Although foreign help was officially refused, nearly three million dollars had been donated by September 1989. Over three million rubles were also donated by the churches in the USSR – a fact which the government finally admitted in November 1987. The money was divided between the Peace Fund, Red Cross and a special account in the State Bank.[26] Other official agencies also helped out. For example, trade unions elsewhere in the USSR took children away from the accident zone for holidays in their pioneer camps.[27]

However, the state soon lost its monopoly over dealing with the consequences of the accident. There were 600,000 people involved in the clean-up after Chernobyl. Known as 'liquidators', they came from, and returned to locations all over the USSR. Chapter 6 describes how, in the face of mounting health problems and official indifference, they felt compelled to set up self-help organizations. Moreover, the state lacked credibility as a *problem-solver* because its nuclear power programme, shoddy safety standards and the callous behaviour of party leaders were seen as the *problem*.

The Armenian earthquake of December 1988 once again brought the state into disrepute, since it became clear that loss of life would have been much reduced had state housing been more solidly constructed. By 1988 foreign help was acceptable, and the disaster also drew Soviet volunteer rescuers to the scene, where they were shocked by the lack of organization on the part of the official Soviet rescue effort and by the superior equipment of Western rescue teams.[23] One amateur mountain rescue team from Kharkov reacted by determining to professionalize their operations – to invent their own equipment to match the Americans' and to seek official registration.[28] A grassroots movement of amateur rescue teams began to form and in November 1989 they gathered at Balashikha, outside Moscow, to create a Soviet Association of Rescue Teams, which would be ready to assist the state authorities in case of future emergencies.[29]

In June of the same year, the shoddily built and poorly monitored gas pipeline which crosses Bashkiria had exploded near Ufa, derailing trains on the parallel Trans-Siberian railway and leaving many people dead or seriously burned. Once again state agencies were clearly to blame. By 1989 the Peace Fund, Red Cross, Children's Fund (1987) and Charity and Health Foundation (1988) were ready to step forward to organize aid.[30] The Funds operated under considerable difficulties, many caused by state agencies. For example, the Red Cross hotline for relatives used the ordinary telephone network and possessed no system of cooperation with the Ministry of Defence or local hospitals.[31] The government incurred resentment when it confiscated donations to the Funds, despite the fact that they were all little more than state 'transmission belts', on the grounds that it would be better to pool resources.[32] Moreover, not only did the officially recognized charities apparently feel that they were better qualified than the government to spend 'their' money, but tension also arose when a third party – the victims themselves – claimed that *they* had the right to distribute the money collected. The national newspaper *Sovetskaya Rossiya* even suggested that it was immoral for anyone except the victims themselves to allocate the money.[33] In Novosibirsk, a Society of Ufa Disaster Victims was founded in March 1990 to defend the interests of survivors and relatives and organize a memorial train journey to the disaster site.[34] Members described their main emotion as 'anger' at the negligence and refusal to accept responsibility of the state organizations involved.[35]

Ethnic Conflict

The increased ethnic tension and related outbreaks of violence which marked the Gorbachev era led to the displacement of hundreds of thousands of people and created a nexus of associated problems which the state attempted, but failed to solve. By the end of 1991 ethnically-based violence had created about 100,000 refugees in the RSFSR alone. A roughly equal number of people had left their homes because of discrimination on ethnic grounds or concern about pollution.[36] The refugees tended to congregate in Moscow or other big cities, or border areas such as the Krasnodar and Stavropol regions.[37] This meant that a few places – often those where housing was least available – were subject to greatest pressure. Official attempts to distribute the refugees more evenly and in particular to settle them in depopulated rural areas enjoyed only limited success. In general, the government was slow to acknowledge the seriousness of the problem. It was only in early 1990 that a special service for migration and resettlement was established under the auspices of *Goskomtrud*. This was followed by a decree whose main purpose was to encourage refugees to return home; in so far as the decree also made back-up provision for refugees who remained in Russia, these were in the form of recommendations only to local authorities who often found it hard to cope with the burgeoning problem.[38] In a separate but related problem area, the number of homeless people in the USSR was increasing: it was estimated at 280,000 to 300,000 by January 1990 and this was considered likely to be an underestimate.[39]

Economic Reform and Poverty

One effect of *glasnost* was to increase awareness of the existence of poverty. By the end of the 1980s 43 million Soviet people (of a total population of 285 million) were said to live below the official poverty line, on under 75 rubles a month. If one adopts a more realistic poverty line of 100–110 rubles, as suggested by some officials, this number would rise to about 105 million.[40] Even if one chose the more conservative yardstick, almost half of pensioners fell into this category.[41] There were said to be 23 million pensioners and disabled people receiving less than 60 rubles a month in January 1989.[42] The Children's Fund[43] suggested that by January 1990 there were more than 40 million Soviet people living in *families* with a per capita monthly income of below 75 rubles. About half were said to be members of 'large' families.[44]

Although the social problems associated with the transition to a market economy became acute only after January 1992, Gorbachev's economic reform led to the beginnings of inflation and with it, increasing poverty. One charity activist, from North Ossetia, identified inflation as the main factor causing the revival of charity after 1989.[45] Another, a lone mother from Moscow, attributed the emergence of her group to the mothers' sense that they must club together, because the sharp drop in living standards made mutual aid a necessity.[46] Self-help groups devoted many of their energies to winning special favours from the local authorities, favours which would do at least something towards alleviating the poverty of their members. Concessions such as reduced prescription and public transport charges could mean a lot to pensioners and large families.

Moreover, the shortages which marked the last years of *perestroika* had a significant impact on the emerging voluntary sector. The new organizations competed with one another, lobbying local authorities for access to special shops and other sources of goods in short supply. On a national level, different interest groups tried to win special treatment in the new pension law. More and more groups were trying to divide up an ever smaller pie. Hardship, antagonism and envy were the results, with many voluntary activists experiencing resentment that other groups had secured advantages they had been unable to obtain. Many groups also transformed themselves into agencies for distributing charity, including foreign aid. This also led to fragmentation and hostility within the voluntary sector.

Unemployment was a further outcome of economic reform. Although slow to materialize among the population at large, it had a serious impact on disabled people. In 1990–1 more than 100,000 were made redundant.[47] Other groups were also affected and, like disabled people, often sought their own solutions within the new voluntary sector rather than rely on the state for help. Women were a notable example, although most of their self-help organizations were created after August 1991.[48] A smaller and less well-researched group were factory health and safety officers: they sometimes found themselves the first to be laid off by enterprises in difficulty. To protect themselves against poverty in unemployment was one motivation for founding their own professional organization in 1990.[49]

Public and Official Opinion

A vicious circle was at work, since state initiatives which

failed, contributing to public loss of faith in the welfare state, were themselves sometimes doomed to failure by pre-existing lack of support. Anti-reformers did mount some defence. For example, when in 1987 French television showed a film highlighting the misery of Soviet disabled people, this provoked an angry article in *Izvestiya*. In return, Soviet television showed a film about the dissident disabled activist Fefelov, accusing him of being an agent of the NTS, the émigré conspiratorial organization. A Bryansk newspaper published an article by a local disabled person reviling Western welfare provision and describing *inter alia* the depression experienced by British people resident in converted Victorian workhouses.[50] However, the radical journalists had the greater impact on public opinion. Whatever the accuracy of their articles, they painted such a depressing picture that previous assumptions about the paternalistic state and problem-free society were overturned: their mirror image seemed more believable. Research also substantiated the impression that the state could not cope.[51]

Many influential intellectuals and policy-makers did not see much in that state which was worth saving.[52] Naturally politics were involved as well as principles, since the new leadership was trying to distance itself from the past. Minister of Health Chazov claimed that his main achievement during his period in office (1987–90) had been to inform the government and public about the crisis in health care.[53] Both Chazov and Kaznacheev, Minister of Social Security from 1988, talked about the need for a complete rethinking of existing services and were ready to take up the concept of charity with enthusiasm.

CREATING A CULTURE OF PHILANTHROPY AND VOLUNTEERING

State-sponsored Charity and Voluntary Action

A culture of philanthropy seems to have emerged easily, once 'bourgeois' concepts were no longer unmentionable. Now, within the official political culture, there was no longer any shame attached to giving to or receiving charity. Charity had been written back into the official lexicon. Moreover, encouraging public donations was a rational policy when, in the early years of *perestroika*, the working population had spare rubles under their mattresses. There was also a willingness to give: a willingness vividly illustrated by the immense public response to the Chernobyl appeal in 1986.

Since officials in effect already considered social security for non-working citizens to be a form of charity, it was not so difficult for them to actually label as 'charitable' existing types of work or new but equally paternalistic forms. They also made no secret of their need for extra resosurces. In 1989 Minister of Health Evgenii Chazov declared with a disarming display of helplessness: 'We accept any kind of help from state or non-governmental organizations, as also personal donations from citizens'.[54] The Minister of Social Security also appealed for money from any quarter.[55] In April 1989 the Ministry opened special bank accounts to which citizens could send money to help residential homes, poor people living alone and Afghan veterans. In August 1989 it initiated a six month 'Charity Campaign' to raise money for 'especially needy' individuals, with the help of its own 'charity firms'. It collected more than 50 million rubles in contributions from 'nearly all Russian enterprises and millions of citizens' for 'particularly needy people'.[56] Not only the Ministry in Moscow, but also local social security departments were involved in such official 'charity'. In Sakhalin, for example, a district social services department organized a Charity Day which included the auction of a three-room flat.[57] In Novosibirsk, a palace of culture held an event which raised 450,000 rubles for the borough's social services, while another borough was able to raise money to provide fifteen people with regular free dinners.[58] The CPSU joined in the campaign, for example by mobilizing young people to deliver meals to Moscow pensioners, meals paid for out of a borough 'Charity Fund'.[59]

Money for charity was insufficient on its own. For the voluntary sector to develop, there had also to be *volunteers*. To some extent, the pre-1985 official culture of 'volunteering' provided a base for the development of charitable organizations during the Gorbachev period. It might seem that the easiest part of 'activating the human factor' – the basic premise of *demokratizatsiya* – would be to impart real meaning to existing opportunities for public participation. The *Komsomol*, for example, with its traditional role in providing 'voluntary' work, could occasionally be revamped: the Sverdlovsk *Komsomol*, in particular, was held up as a model for organizing a range of charitable services through its 'Youth Service' centre. The centre was flourishing by the end of 1987, and subsidizing its services to local housebound people by organizing discos and repairing flats.[60] From 1986 the *Komsomol* also sponsored the creation of clubs of veterans of Afghanistan.[61] However, it was likely to be hard to entice people to work in a new semi-official voluntary sector, when before 1985 people were already 'exiting' from the official one.

The Intelligentsia and Moral Revival

Gorbachev envisaged all of society 'in motion' but initially his policies were directed mainly at members of the intelligentsia. It was they who took the lead in exposing issues and suggesting the opening of new areas for independent action. To many organizers of charity, both its official and unofficial forms, the stimulus to action was a perception of moral crisis in Soviet society: a problem with public behaviour which they defined as being connected to, but more profound and serious than simple lack of faith in the political system. Callousness, selfishness and irresponsibility were understood to have threatening implications for society – and perhaps the Russian nation – as a whole, not just the authority of the political elite.

Early *perestroika*-period analyses of Soviet problems, focusing blame on Brezhnev, gave such intellectuals a chance to speak out more openly about their concerns, since they could imply that the decline in public morality was a result of the Brezhnev system. By 1987–8, blame was being focused further back, in the Stalin period, but this was still relatively unthreatening to present-day authorities. The more positive attitude adopted officially towards NEP, the New Economic Policy and more liberal conditions of the 1920s, did however promote the expression of enthusiasm for building civil society. For example, disabled people's organizations of the

1920s were praised in the press.[62] The authorities felt more threatened if people calling for the revival of charity were implying that the moral crisis in Soviet society had its roots in 1917, as became the increasingly widespread view in 1989–91 – among people in the voluntary sector as among the wider public.

Probably the most influential argument for a moral crisis appeared in March 1987 in *Literaturnaya gazeta*. Still more crucial, for the voluntary sector, was the conclusion drawn. Leningrad writer Daniil Granin's seminal article 'Charity' ('*O miloserdii*') discussed the demise of charity in Soviet life. By 'charity' Granin meant kindness, compassion and a sense of responsiblity for others. He argued that these were natural human qualities and that pre-revolutionary Russian literature in particular was replete with examples. It was only when people were forced to act abnormally and denied the freedom to exercise compassion that callousness became the norm. Kindness had disappeared with the arrival of Stalinism. People became too terrified to display compassion for the persecuted, and obligatory optimism created the impression that 'unhappiness and suffering were not Soviet characteristics'. Under Brezhnev, the prevailing atmosphere of hypocrisy, deceit and arbitrary rule had increased immorality. For example, divorced women began to refuse care of their children, and society began to accept this behaviour as normal. Granin hinted at the crumbling of the welfare state by describing his stay in a Leningrad hospital ridden by rats, where one auxiliary nurse served ninety patients. The false values of the period were indicated by the fact that young people were sent off on grandiose building projects like BAM[63] rather than using their time and energy where it was really needed, tending to the sick and lonely people whom the welfare state had failed. Granin argued that Russians needed to engage in charitable activities on a small-scale or individual level. Their action would supplement state help. He hinted that a new Fund for charity would be appropriate.[64] Granin's article provoked a flood of reader's letters and its impact was intensified when it was read aloud on national radio.[65] It inspired the creation of many grassroots charities, discussed in Chapter 5. Granin himself was regarded highly by Gorbachev and his significance was indicated by the fact that he was one of the hundred parliamentary deputies chosen directly by the CPSU in 1989.

COOPERATIVES, PHILANTHROPY AND SELF-HELP

As early as 1986 the Law on Individual Labour Activity permitted 'services for single elderly and disabled people and other people incapable of working'.[66] The development of the cooperative sector had even greater potential: cooperatives could provide new money for charity, offer job opportunities and produce goods which in the state sector were in short supply and of poor quality, such as prostheses and wheelchairs.

Local authorities pressurized cooperatives to donate money to the Children's Fund and other official charities.[67] They also used cooperatives' profits to fund their own new 'charitable' projects, such as providing free meals for local pensioners.[68] It is difficult to assess how much overall cooperatives contributed financially to independent charities and self-help groups. My questionnaire evidence suggests rather little. Journalists writing in 1990 were probably correct when they asserted that 'the charity movement in the Soviet Union increasingly resembles a man unable to take a deep breath. Why? Because, to continue the metaphor, it lacks a lung, that is the rich.'[69] The situation was complicated by the connections between cooperatives and crime. 'Charity' offered opportunities to dishonest cooperatives, opportunities which were inflated in popular rumour. Since both the public and many local authorities had a negative and suspicious attitude to cooperatives, their association with the voluntary sector, honest though it sometimes was in reality, did much to damage the reputation of charity.

Cooperative leaders who did have a genuine interest in philanthropy, such as Konstantin Borovoi, often preferred not to give to charity but instead to organize their own charitable activities. Borovoi's cooperative adopted clients of the local social security and education departments and provided directly for their needs.[70] MIKO,[71] the Moscow Disabled People's Cooperative Association, made its money by translating and publishing activities and used its profits to run an employment agency, which was free of charge to disabled people.[72]

Cooperatives, being small and flexible operations, could provide employment for those, such as mothers of disabled children, or disabled adults, who had found it hard to get jobs within the confines of the command economy. MIKO's employment agency, for example, was itself staffed by people with disabilities. VOI had 250 cooperatives Russia-wide by summer 1991. In all, the VOI's enterprises offered employment to 10 633 disabled people.[73] This achievement was offset by the fact that, with the advent of *khozraschet* (cost-centre accounting), disabled people were often the first to be dismissed from regular enterprises, and in 1990–1 more than 100,000 were made redundant.[74]

Disabled people's cooperatives were generally not among the first to be established, not surprisingly, in view of the immense difficulties involved. In Moscow in mid-1988, for example, there was said to be just one, out of a total of roughly two thousand cooperatives, the vast majority providing household services or food.[75] By autumn 1989 disabled people's cooperatives in Leningrad had set up the *Opora*[76] Union of Disabled People's Cooperatives, which, despite official discouragement, was able to organize a conference of about sixty cooperatives, half from the city itself. In all fifty towns were represented.[77]

One of the most important functions performed by new cooperatives was to produce items for disabled people – from wheelchairs to simple household aids – which were too individualized or too innovative to have been successfully provided by the command economy. This was a type of co-operative activity which the authorities were ready to approve, particularly in the case of cooperatives making prostheses which enabled otherwise healthy young disabled Afghan veterans to return to normal employment.[78]

A further function of the cooperative sector could have been to provide private medicine, but medical cooperatives were so heavily restricted and penalized that they were unable to even begin to compete with the state health service.[79]

It was equally hard to make money out of enterprises such as producing prostheses. As one activist put it, 'we're far behind the kebab-sellers'.[80] However, the main focus of disabled people's cooperatives was on self-help and/or charity, and they featured in directories of Russian 'charities'.[81] Some even bore the title 'charitable cooperative'.[82]

In general, cooperatives were under constant pressure from the state authorities, by whom they were barely tolerated. Disabled cooperative workers suffered harassment in the same way as did kebab-sellers. For example, the MIKO cooperative, having been released from taxes by the local borough soviet in 1990, suddenly found that decision rescinded and faced bankruptcy as a result.[83] Under such circumstances, it was unsurprising that cooperatives did not play a particularly large role in supporting the emerging voluntary sector.

THE EXPANSION OF SELF-HELP

The Soviet system never destroyed – and in some respects officially encouraged – a culture of self-help which also provided an important basis for action after 1985. Moreover, and perhaps even more significantly, there was a strong reaction against paternalism which made independently organized self-help an attractive alternative. Many differerent types of Soviet citizen belonged to self-help organizations. The mushrooming of such groups showed that eventually not just the intelligentsia, but also society as a whole was truly 'in motion'.

The pre-85 official voluntary sector had incorporated organizations such as VOS and VOG, which could be loosely classified within the 'self-help' category. Yet, apart from their employment function, they were not very different from other organizations which grouped together social categories such as youth, women or workers in a particular branch of industry. All were 'transmission belts' for party policy, although this did not entirely deprive them of practical significance – it just made them less helpful to their members than they could have been had those members really been in control of their own affairs.

The pre-1985 unofficial voluntary sector, on the other hand, provided an alternative and more valuable model. It also provided a core of committed activists for all three main types of participant in the self-help sector: parents, disabled people and Afghan veterans. Such pre-1985 activists were known locally and, in the case of disabled networks, sometimes also nationally. They possessed already existing projects and had thought out the issues. The disability movement, with its particularly strong roots in the era of 'stagnation', was the major strand of self-help during *perestroika*. More generally, the existence of this unofficial heritage, together with the more widespread phenomenon of 'informal' activity indicates the maturity of Soviet society and the fact that there were people already well-prepared to take the lead in genuine, grassroots voluntary work under Gorbachev. However, participation was always difficult and sometimes dangerous. It was not an activity to be undertaken lightly, as the evidence in Chapters 6–8 suggests. Often members of self-help groups were pioneers operating without allies, and this required a considerable degree of courage and enterprise.

THE ABOLITION OF PRIVILEGES

A facet of the moral crisis was the criticism of immorality among the ruling elite. Privileges were one of the main topics of *glasnost*-era journalism and 'democratic' politicians exploited the issue to pursue their own agendas and further their careers. Yeltsin made a powerful speech at the Congress of People's Deputies in 1989, linking the problems of poor and disabled people to the privileges of the elite, and issues of poverty and disadvantage were thoroughly debated at the Congress.[84] From 1989 a series of official resolutions abolished party privileges. In October 1989 the Fourth Directorate of the Health Ministry was closed and the special medical institutions transferred. In February 1990 special food supplies were diverted from the party and other state and social organizations to orphanages and hospitals.[85] The establishment of USSR and Russian Supreme Soviet commissions on privileges in 1989[86] was followed by similar investigation of privilege at a local level. Novosibirsk city party committee, for example, set up a Commission to

Investigate Benefits and Privileges. These developments offered considerable opportunities to voluntary organizations hoping to benefit from the redistribution of property involved.

THE IMPACT OF FOREIGN AID

As late as 1989 Soviet citizens, for all their problems, were still able to feel in a position to help foreigners in trouble, and in December 1989 and early 1990 Moldavian and Ukrainian Red Cross organizations collected and transported aid for Romania in what were described as 'bridges of solidarity' to a 'fraternal nation'.[87] By 1990, however, the tables were largely turned. The Soviet government was rethinking its own foreign aid programme and Western 'humanitarian aid', from governments and voluntary organizations, was beginning to flow into the USSR.[88] The central and local governments attempted to control the distribution of aid as far as possible. For example, from March to December 1991, Moscow City Soviet supervised the distribution of 415,000 food parcels to families in the capital.[89]

However, the influx of food parcels in the winter of 1990–1 also had an impact on the developing Russian charitable movement. Although it is difficult to generalize about many of the late *perestroika* charities, one frequent characteristic is their involvement in distributing humanitarian aid. It seems that some charities were created only in order to distribute aid.[90] A survey of Moscow charities in early 1992 discovered 44 organizations which had distributed foreign aid, although only 27 of these had done so on a large scale, to more that 500 families.[91] The aid was normally food, often clothing and less frequently medicines and medical equipment.[92]

Only three respondents mentioned that they had problems ensuring that aid reached its intended recipients.[93] Nevertheless, the problem of voluntary organizations siphoning off aid was one which tended to be highlighted in the press and in rumours spreading among the population.[94] The accusation of failing to distribute aid fairly not only spoiled the voluntary sector's image in the eyes of the general public, but also soured relations between voluntary organizations and between the organizations' leaderships and their members: in this sense the aid had a destructive effect on the sector. Moreover, in so far as Russian organizations did distribute aid effectively, this turned many organizations which had possessed a strong self-help focus into poor-relief agencies. Almost all the groups who responded to the 1992 Moscow survey, for example, were small self-help organizations.

However, some Western voluntary organizations also tried to widen and support a self-sufficient Russian voluntary sector. The Cultural Initiative Fund and the International Foundation for the Survival and Development of Humanity were joint Russian-American organizations, largely funded by American millionaires George Soros and Armand Hammer respectively. In 1989 the Rockefeller Foundation ran a seminar for Russian voluntary organizations.[95] The American charity United Way opened a Moscow office in August 1990 and began to promote the development of the local voluntary sector through its training, publications and advice. In early 1991 it began to provide consultation on the draft law on charity.[96] Several British ventures started in 1989. Victor Zorza and Leonard Cheshire initiated the hospice and Cheshire homes movements in Russia, and Jill Braithwaite, the wife of the British Ambassador, began to encourage contacts between Russian and British voluntary organizations: collaboration which was to lead to the official founding of the BEARR Trust[97] in early 1992.[98] Charity Know How was to be founded in November 1991. In the post-Soviet period understanding was to grow quite quickly, among British charities at least, that training and advice were generally more helpful than handouts.

To Russian voluntary organizations, struggling to survive, partnership with westerners seemed a sensible survival strategy. The MIKO cooperative for disabled people, for example, after its assets had been illegally seized by the local authorities, decided to change its status to an international society and became a member of Mobility International.[99]

Russians were therefore presented with rather different models of Western voluntary organization. Many, especially outside Moscow, saw Western organizations only as relief agencies, but a few activists, particularly in Moscow, began to use information about practice in Europe and, especially, the

United States, to help themselves think more analytically and comparatively about what they were trying to achieve in Russia.

CONCLUSIONS

Gorbachev's programme included greater investment in the welfare state and state agencies adopted a number of strategies to tackle accumulated social problems. However, shortage of resources and imagination helped render the state's efforts ineffective. The state proved no better at meeting *new* challenges. Moreover, the public, academics and ministers anxious to distance themselves from their predecessors were all inclined to blame the state for creating problems in the first place. It seemed the state could do no right: alternatives had to be sought.

Privatization of welfare services was attempted only cautiously under Gorbachev. The cooperative sector provided useful supplementary technology for disabled people and some employment for especially disadvantaged social groups but otherwise did little directly to bolster state welfare. More ideologically attractive to almost everyone was the creation of a voluntary sector. Ministers could encourage charity and try to revive the official cult of volunteering as a prop to the crumbling welfare state. The intelligentsia, driven by a sense of moral crisis, called on Russians to create genuine grassroots voluntary organizations and recover their sense of caringness and community responsibility. The disadvantaged people whom the welfare state had most failed in the past used the new, more liberal political climate to build on the pre-1985 traditions of official and unofficial self-help. The influx of foreign aid from 1990 partly stunted the development of the Russian voluntary sector, since it brought charities under suspicion of dishonesty and often turned self-help groups into charities. On the plus side, the availability of foreign aid encouraged the formation of yet more voluntary organizations and towards the end of the period Western charities began helping their Russian partners to conceptualize and organize the Russian sector more effectively.

5 Charities

INTRODUCTION

The culture of volunteering was revived, from 1987 onwards, by a diverse array of charities, most of them new. This chapter examines their emergence (or restructuring) and development. It begins with the most 'official': those created from above, according to the standard Soviet organizational model. The extent to which an organization was controlled by the CPSU was for many purposes its most important characteristic. However, as *perestroika* progressed and party control weakened, 'official' became increasingly difficult to define.

Chapters 5 and 6 are not intended to provide a comprehensive guide to charities and self-help groups, nor are the activities of most groups described in detail. The focus is, instead, on seeking to explain certain key issues: when and why voluntary organizations emerged, their ethos, their relation to the party-state, the projects undertaken and the organizations' degree of success.

PARTY-APPROVED, NATIONWIDE CHARITIES

One might assume that the official charities would form the most successful section of the voluntary sector. They could establish a nationwide network of branches without meeting obstruction, and they enjoyed both direct financial support from the state and also media coverage which helped them to raise money from the public.

However, the political environment was in many respects unfavourable to the creation of new CPSU-supportive institutions. (One might compare the relative lack of success of the new, officially-sponsored workers' movement.) The public might be expected to volunteer more enthusiastically to work in charities which had a more authentic grassroots base. Moreover, the economic reform also made for an unhelpful situation, since the party could no longer expect the state to finance 'transmission belts' as it had in the past. Enterprises sometimes resisted party requests that they subsidize its protege 'voluntary' organizations. A memorandum written within the Leningrad *oblast* party apparatus in about 1990 suggests that such behaviour was common. 'At present a number of the public organizations and movements which support the CPSU find themselves in a difficult position. The CPSU used to give orders and put pressure on various organizations and communist factory directors to help these CPSU-supportive organizations. This included material help. But today we cannot use such methods.' Instead, the memorandum listed sums which were to be paid directly from CPSU coffers to keep the voluntary organizations alive.[1]

The official end of the charity spectrum was represented by four nationwide charities – sometimes referred to as 'the Funds' by Soviet writers. The Red Cross dated from the nineteenth century, the Peace Fund from the Khrushchev period. The Charity and Health Foundation[2] and Children's Fund were *perestroika* creations.

The Union of Societies of the Red Cross and Red Crescent[3]

The Russian Red Cross, founded in 1867, had survived the whole Soviet period. (However, the Political Red Cross, an officially-recognized organization which looked after the needs of (ex-revolutionary) prisoners, was banned in 1938.)[4] The Red Cross performed emergency work during the early 1920s and in the Second World War. Later, it concentrated on activities such as running first aid courses, collecting blood donations and – at local level – helping victims of natural disasters. From 1960 the Red Cross funded district nurses (*patronazhnye sestry*), who sometimes performed home-help as well as medical services. At first they looked after war veterans; later their clients included other elderly and disabled people. By 1986 4,344 nurses had 110,000 patients USSR-wide. The Red Cross also ran clinics for pensioners. The Red Cross was funded by 30 kopeck membership dues collected at schools and workplaces. Its employees had a plan to fulfil and were expected to achieve almost 100 per cent membership in educational establishments, although under

Gorbachev the Red Cross found it harder to 'drum out' contributions. By 1990 membership of the Soviet Red Cross had fallen to 109 million.[5] The formalistic nature of membership was indicated by a 1989 nationwide survey. Two thirds of members failed to mention the Red Cross when invited to name familiar charities they knew.[6]

The Red Cross restructured and expanded under Gorbachev. It extended home-help services fourfold by 1992, as well as responding to emergencies by mobilizing resources on a national level. Now that the national press publicized accidents, natural disasters and ethnic conflicts, the Red Cross could draw voluntary donations and found itself with plenty of work. One-third of people polled in Armenia and Georgia in 1989, after the Armenian earthquake of 1988, knew someone who had been helped by the Red Cross.[7] However, the Red Cross could not on its own engender a new voluntary sector, just as the CPSU could not be reshaped to provide the basis of a multi-party system. The Red Cross's agenda, though broad, could not encompass the whole spectrum of need. Moreover, the Red Cross was tainted by its association with the old regime, leading to suspicions of dishonesty and inefficiency.

The Peace Fund[8]

The Peace Fund was the other major charity of the Soviet period, but its activities had a more international focus. The Fund seemingly lost its rationale once the Cold War ended. It did maintain an interest in peacekeeping, with some ideological reorientation. For example, it contributed 2.5 million rubles towards the restoration of Optina Pustyn monastery, as the 'centre from which the idea of non-violence spread throughout Russia'. However, the Fund now spent most of its money on more practical projects and its restructuring involved an 'abrupt turn to social problems'.[9]

Its public position was that it was not an arm of the party-state, but rather a partner, supplementing state activity. However, its greatest contribution to the new voluntary sector was probably in providing money for projects run by other official charities. A particularly large sum, 120 million rubles, was given to the Children's Fund to improve children's homes. The Fund also subsidized the creation of home-help services run by local social security departments. However, from 1988 donations to the Peace Fund – no longer in effect compulsory – dropped sharply and the Fund began to engage in commercial activities. In 1990, for example, the Fund received 49 million rubles in donations and made a further 50 million from 'economic activity'.[10]

The Charity and Health Foundation (FMZ)

'One has the impression that a new ministry has been created, a Ministry ... of Charity.' (Odessa charity activist, 1988)[11]

1) Origins and Leadership
The project to establish a major new charity 'from above' presumably had the backing of Gorbachev, as a – second choice – alternative to his earlier idea of a charity headed by Granin and based on existing grassroots groups (see below). In 1991 Gorbachev was said to be still supportive of the FMZ.[12] The Foundation was the brainchild of heath minister Petrovsky and its original brief was to raise funds to supplement the under-resourced health service.[13] It was headed in turn by two leading reformers. Eminent eye surgeon and entrepreneur Svyatoslav Fedorov was appointed chairperson (*predsedatel'*) of the FMZ. On his suggestion the Foundation expanded its agenda and became a *Charity* and Health Foundation. Fedorov realized that health could not be isolated from more general social issues. In 1990 Fedorov resigned, disillusioned, and was succeeded by his deputy, Vadim Men'shikov. Gorbachev's colleague Aleksandr Yakovlcv – following political fashion – took on a new post of *Prezident FMZ*.[14] However, despite the radical stance of Fedorov and Yakovlev, Men'shikov was in many respects an old-style functionary and the FMZ did not always operate as a vanguard of reform.

2) Aims and objectives
The FMZ took up many of the themes of Granin's pathbreaking article. At its founding conference, the Foundation's primary aim was described as: 'to promote morality among Soviet people, develop a caring and charitable ethic, and

increase a sense of responsibility for maintaining and improving citizens' health.'[15] Most of the FMZ's work concentrated on more practical objectives. In 1989 it listed its potential clients as:

- Over 23 million pensioners receiving pensions of under 60 rubles a month.
- 10 million pensioners, elderly people and people with disabilities who had no relatives to care for them.
- 7 million disabled children.
- 700,000 people in need of 24-hour care.
- 400,000 residents of older people's homes.[16]

The deputy chair of the Penza branch pithily defined the FMZ's goal as 'help [for] those who received insufficient or no aid from state structures'.[17]

The FMZ, sometimes collaborating with state organizations, established soup kitchens and meals on wheels services, distributed free second-hand clothes, repaired flats and residential homes, sponsored the design and production of better wheelchairs and other items for people with disabilities and supplied state hospitals with medicines and equipment. It helped establish private medical establishments and nursing agencies, with free treatment for the most disadvantaged patients.[18] Local branches throughout the provinces were encouraged to seek accommodation for elderly and disabled Russian-speaking refugees.[19] The actual work of each branch varied: in some the focus was more on social services, in others on propping up the health service. Some locations had specific problems: for example, branches in Bryansk *oblast* had to cope with the effects of radioactive contamination resulting from the Chernobyl accident. Leningrad tried to address the needs of drug addicts and AIDS sufferers, not groups usually mentioned by provincial organizations.

The FMZ was able to help large numbers of individuals. For example, during 1989, the FMZ aided more than 100,000 pensioners and disabled people.[20] It claimed to be especially successful in providing medical assistance, placement in residential homes and changes of disability category. It was least successful in helping people jump queues for flats and telephones or getting residence permits.[21]

Although the FMZ leadership realized that they had not solved even a 'thousandth part' of the overall problem, local FMZ branches sometimes expressed Brezhnev-style complacency about their performance. In Voronezh, for example, it was said that by 1991 free dinners, home-help services and wheelchairs had been provided to all in need.[22]

3) Power Structures and Personnel
The founding conference of the USSR FMZ was in September 1988. It was already too late for the establishment of a Union-wide organization: the analogous Latvian and Estonian republican organizations were unwilling to be included within the national Foundation on the same terms as the other thirteen. The relationship between centre and republics had to be renegotiated to allow greater republican autonomy in January 1990.[23] Local and national boards (*pravleniya*) of the charity were set up according to predetermined lists, in accordance with the principle of *nomenklatura* appointment.[24] The boards often included representatives of the local authorities and party committees as well as of the women's councils, the Red Cross and other 'transmission belt' organizations.[25] The Orthodox Church was also represented, although in Novosibirsk at least the priest was included without his prior permission.[26]

A hierarchical network of branches was established. This was hardly surprising in September 1988. Fedorov criticized the FMZ for its typically Soviet bureaucratization, claiming that 'charity cannot emerge from organizational meaures'.[27] By January 1990, however, democratic centralism was on the wane. Branches no longer had to subsidize the centre.[28] The Tula branch, for example, could claim 'no relationship' with the centre.[29] The Ulan-Ude branch stated it was 'independent'.[30] By March 1991 Men'shikov was publicly worrying that the local branches mistrusted the centre.[31] There was local satisfaction with the centre's hands-off approach. In Pskov, for example, the FMZ valued the fact that central office adopted the role 'of coordinator, never dictator'. They prided themselves on their ability to respond directly and efficiently to local needs.[32] However, supervision from the centre could be replaced by supervision from the local authorities: in

Kostroma, for example, the city soviet was said to have monitored the FMZ closely.[33]

Local branches were headed by an unpaid local notable, usually from the medical or social security establishments, and administered by a paid deputy chair and assistant. Nearly half the deputy chairs (in the RSFSR) were women.[34] According to one, 'From the very start, salaries at the Fund were small...so on the whole the staff was female.'[35] There were possiblities for friction between the chairperson and the sometimes less establishment-oriented deputy. In one branch, for example, the deputy disliked the fact that the chairperson spent so much time asking for advice from higher up 'in order to prove his loyalty'.[36]

4) The FMZ's Niche within the 'Welfare Establishment'
The FMZ was set up to supplement existing organizations with responsibilities for social security and health. It was intended to tap different resources: public goodwill and money. It did not really have different *problems* to solve, although to some extent it did promote the interests of citizens whose needs had not previously received adequate recognition, such as people with diabetes or recently released ex-prisoners. The FMZ was ambitious and competitive: this reflected Fedorov's style. He wanted it to prevent social problems from happening by providing proper pensions, disabled access, and so on, rather than to paper over cracks.[37]

The FMZ had five representatives in the USSR CPD, to which it was allocated seats as an official 'public' organization. Deputies were chosen from a shortlist of five by the FMZ board.[38] In addition, there were 36 other CPD deputies who sat on various boards and commissions of the FMZ. They seem to have been regarded by the FMZ leadership as a kind of parliamentary charity elite, promoting FMZ projects to the nation. Men'shikov and other FMZ leaders, as experienced Soviet officials, knew the value of informal contacts for getting things done and prized the fact that this charity elite included a number of influential people (including Granin).

The FMZ's leaders hoped that, on a local level, the 10,000 members of FMZ boards and audit committees stretched across the country would act as a force for change on both state and public.[39] However, since many of these members sat on the boards *ex officio* it was not realistic to hope that they would all be active.[40] 'Unfortunately, the mutual understanding and cooperation [with other bodies] which characterize the central office are often absent at the local, and even republican level. This leads to dissipation of effort and resources.'[41] Presumably much depended on the clout of the branch's chairperson. Yaroslavl, headed by the deputy chair of the *oblast* administration, seems to have been a particularly flourishing branch.[42]

The whole creative intelligentsia was expected to promote the FMZ. The Foundation aimed to 'attract scholars and those involved in the arts to educate the public and create a more caring society'.[43] The national board included nineteen leading writers and performers, as well as heads of the intelligentsia professional organizations – the 'creative unions' – and representatives of the clergy. Lecturers in the *Znanie* Society – the communist mass political socialization agency – were expected to give lectures on charity; the Orthodox church asked its priests to do the same in their sermons.[44]

Resources

The FMZ needed both human and economic resources. Volunteers were crucial and might be hard to attract, given public scepticism about volunteering. It took time to establish a volunteer network, perhaps because of public scepticism, but by 1990 the FMZ claimed more than 60,000 volunteers and 2,500 'auxiliary commissions' (*komissii sodeistviya*).[45] By March 1991 there were about 4,000 commissions.[46] One is instinctively sceptical of Soviet statistics, but it does seem that the Foundation won a certain legitimacy in public eyes. By spring 1991 children and young people throughout the USSR were said to be widely involved in voluntary work, chiefly as amateur home-helps, under the FMZ's aegis. Female pensioner volunteers were seldom mentioned in official publications – presumably because their participation was not a source of official pride in the same way as that of workers or young people – but questionnaires indicated that they played a significant role.[47]

Material resources were inadequate: the FMZ, ambitious as it was, found that its aspirations outran its funding. Fedorov gave up the struggle, deciding that the FMZ was simply patching holes in a rag which was bound to come to pieces.[48] By mid-1990 it had collected 75 million rubles. However, only six million were donations from citizens.[49] As inflation bit, donations fell. Inhabitants of Vladimir donated 295,000 rubles in 1989, 150,000 rubles in 1990 and nothing in 1991.[50] Fund-raising was a skill Soviet charities lacked. In the past, the Red Cross and Peace Fund had been able to rely on compulsion. Now the FMZ began to display considerable imagination: activities ranged from a charity rugby match in Krasnoyarsk to an auction of tractors and pianos in Vladimir.[51] Lotteries succeeded even in hard times. In Astrakhan, for example, the FMZ used a lottery to raise 200,000 rubles for disabled people in 1990.[52] Performers at all levels were encouraged to provide shows and concerts. They included the popular Alan Chumak, whose psychic powers imbued jars of tap water with healing properties.[53]

Business was an auxiliary source of income. At first the FMZ found it difficult to set up businesses, partly because it was initially exempt from tax and therefore of no interest to local authorities. However, in the first half of 1990 its enterprises made 909,000 rubles. There were about 400 by October 1990.[54] They varied in nature: one of the more exotic was a firm in the Volga town of Rybinsk which supplied magical healing magnets.[55]

When humanitarian aid began to flow into the Soviet Union in winter 1990 the FMZ was one of the chief distributors of goods in kind from Germany and other Western countries. Men'shikov, however, cautioned against developing a long-term reliance on aid: 'foreign aid comes and goes, but our problems remain with us'. Accordingly, the Foundation tried to develop long-term links with foreign organizations, for example to train Soviet doctors.[56]

The Church also donated to the FMZ. Although the FMZ had an apparently close relationship with the Orthodox Church, it was not always happy to see too heavy a reliance on income from religious organizations, especially non-Orthodox. The Novosibirsk branch was chided in spring 1991 for depending too heavily on such sources – particularly the Adventists – rather than building up closer relations with the 'Soviet authorities'.[57]

Most FMZ resources, however, came directly from state

enterprises and other official organizations.[58] Even Adventist Novosibirsk, back in spring 1990, had received a donation of 100,000 rubles from the city's soviet executive committee.[59] The Voronezh organization was proud of acting as 'the initiator in drawing forth resources from other public organizations'.[60] At the national level, too, the FMZ could not have managed without the initial capital provided by its sponsoring institutions. VOS donated three million rubles and the Peace Fund and the Health Ministry 1.5 million rubles apiece.[61]

A paradoxical situation had therefore arisen. The FMZ's mission was to tap extra funding for the Soviet welfare state; in fact, it served mostly to redistribute money within the state system. Its ability to somewhat revive the official cult of volunteering may have been a more significant achievement.

The Lenin Children's Fund[62]

The Children's Fund revived an eponymous organization which had been abolished in 1938, ostensibly because all abandoned children were safely in state care.[63] The Children's Fund was as closely connected to the establishment as the FMZ and Peace Fund. In one sense – its adoption of Lenin's name – it even outdid them. Gorbachev attended its founding conference in October 1987.[64] Its top six posts were on the *nomenklatura* lists.[65] Like the FMZ, it sent five deputies to the Congress of People's Deputies. It too was created according to a decree of the Council of Ministers and counted a range of official organizations, such as the Peace Fund, among its sponsors. It created the usual hierarchy of regional and local offices, headed by local bigwigs. Its ideology, like that of the FMZ, repeated the 'caring' and moralistic sentiments of the new thinking. Since in many ways the Children's Fund was similar to the FMZ, it will be discussed in less detail. There are interesting contrasts, however.

In fund-raising, the Children's Fund was even more successful than the FMZ. As in any society, it was not hard to raise sympathy for the plight of children. The Fund amassed more than 220 million rubles in its first two years of existence, 102 million of which were gained in the January 1990

Christmas telethon.[66] The Children's Fund telethon was probably the single most successful Soviet charitable fundraising event of the period.[67] Donations came from state institutions as well as individuals. Leningrad city soviet, for example, gave 100,000 rubles, while a big Saratov factory donated 60,000.[68] The Fund was also able to create a highly popular weekly newspaper, *Sem'ya* (Family), which had a print run of five million in 1990.

For all its official attributes, the Children's Fund was not an entirely a 'top down' institution. Unlike the FMZ, it had roots in the pre-Gorbachev period and put out its first branches thanks to *glasnost* and the efforts of a leading member of the intelligentsia. Albert Likhanov, editor of the *Komsomol* magazine *Smena*, had for some years been raising public concern about children's homes and the fate of children abandoned by their parents. In the early 1980s he organized, through *Smena*, the collection of one million children's books from readers to create libraries in children's homes. Likhanov's analysis was squarely within the 'moral crisis' framework. He believed that 'modern orphanhood is rooted in the growth of social selfishness, moral crassness, complacency and a reluctance to see our moral and social ills'.[69] In particular, women were blamed for the problems of children.

Now, partly thanks to Likhanov, with the advent of *glasnost* readers and viewers were overwhelmed with horror stories about the plight of many Soviet children.[70] The Fund analysed the chain of events: 'At first this [true information, supplied by embryonic Children's Fund] led to shock, but then there occurred a reversal in public attitudes concerning children's issues and a public movement formed to save the children.'[71] As well as generating public pressure, Likhanov lobbied energetically in high places.[72]

Likhanov hoped that the Fund would improve the lives of children in state care and protect the interests of all Soviet children by a mixture of advocacy and practical help. Unlike the FMZ, the Fund perceived itself as a lobby for a specific social group, and approached the party-state authorities in this spirit. Like the FMZ, it also responded to individual appeals; helped local self-help groups – usually of parents, or former inmates of children's homes; and designed mass programmes of action. Sometimes these programmes had a specific regional focus, as when the Fund sponsored doctors to tackle the tragedy of child mortality in Central Asia. However, most programmes were nationwide. Disabled and sick children were often targeted but children's homes remained the Fund's most important cause.

The Fund's money improved conditions in state residential care, but the Fund wished to do more and bypass the state. Many, perhaps most voluntary organizations dreamed of establishing independent institutions. The Children's Fund was sufficiently wealthy to partner local educational departments in setting up a network of small homes, each run by a single couple. It considered these as being among 'its' most significant achievements. However, since the initiative often came from the parents, the homes will be considered later in the chapter, as independent charities.

The Children's Fund, like the FMZ, varied considerably from branch to branch. In some places it limited itself to implementing programmes conceived in Moscow. The Chelyabinsk branch, for example, refused to help a family with children living way below the poverty line, justifying their refusal by saying it was not part of any of the Fund's programmes.[73] Such organizations often confined their work to the holding of isolated fund-raising activities like bazaars. Elsewhere, the Fund was much more involved in the life of the local community.[74] Its popular agenda allowed it to mobilize local public opinion. 'The mini-organization, with its three employees, is instantly surrounded by sympathizers – parents, lawyers, doctors, policemen – and begins to form public opinion. And this is a force capable of breaking down the walls of the most impenenetrable and deaf departments and offices.'[75]

The more active branches included those which established enterprises to provide money when donations dried up in the late *perestroika* period. In Penza, for example, such a factory was said to have been the branch's salvation in 1991.[76] According to a Fund journalist, the feminization of the Fund's bureaucracy was an issue. 'Who, in general, works in the local branches? Women. Former teachers, trade union, party and *Komsomol* employees, most of them trained as teachers too. Many of them haven't a clue how to organize economic activity.'[77] Lack of clout was no doubt part of the problem. In successful Penza, it was perhaps significant that the female deputy chair had got herself elected to the local soviet in 1990.[78]

In 1990–1 the Fund suffered considerable negative publicity, originally resulting from the discovery of cruelty to children by employees of the Leningrad branch, followed by protests, including a hunger strike, on the part of other staff and former employees angered by the branch's authoritarian management style and wasteful spending.[79] The Fund may not have been any worse than other Soviet bureaucracies, although it is perhaps significant that in Leningrad it was the only one of the big funds to be mentioned in the party memorandum on special support for loyal organizations (see above).[80] It was in a sense unfortunate – compared to the other Funds – in that the timing of the Leningrad scandal led to its becoming a particular scapegoat for people seeking to attack the communist party indirectly. Now the *Lenin* Children Fund's name became a liability.[81]

Conclusions: Old Wine in New Bottles?

The Funds, despite their differing origins, were formed entirely within the traditional mould – to imitate party structures and be susceptible to party control. However, they tried to present themselves as truly *public* organizations. They did this partly by somewhat distancing themselves from, and contrasting themselves with the *state* and its unsuccessful endeavours. (The decreasing need for what one Fund employee termed a 'backwards glance at the *party*' was implied rather than explicit, but was an important factor in the last years of *perestroika*.) In addition, successful local branches adopted a *local* identity, in keeping with the decentralizing fashion of the times.

On the other hand, it was often hard work to build up small local branches of the Children's Fund and FMZ. They tended to be run by people such as former teachers without much influence on powerful local officials and factory directors. Moreover, in so far as resources were raised successfully, relatively little of this money came from the Soviet public, either as donations or via the Funds' business activities. State organizations, plus VOS and VOG, were the chief benefactors. In addition, there was a sense in which the large funds were each other's competitors. The head of the Soviet Red Cross, for example, was convinced that the arrival of the FMZ and Children's Fund had just halved the money available to the Peace Fund and Red Cross.[82]

The Soviet Cultural Fund and Pushkin Society
Finally, mention should be made of another new official charity, the Soviet Cultural Fund,[83] which was credited by Gorbachev with having 'returned the notion of philanthropy to our lives'.[84] The Fund enjoyed the support of both Gorbachevs and was headed by the respected non-communist literary scholar Dmitri Likhachev. Although its cultural focus distinguished it from the other Funds, it shared the same mission of addressing Russia's 'spiritual crisis'. Under the Fund's auspices Likhachev revived the Pushkin Society, which had been liquidated in 1952. Local branches – sometimes pre-dating the national society – sought to motivate and inspire young people and develop provincial culture.[85]

SEMI-OFFICIAL NATIONAL CHARITIES WITH INTERNATIONAL LINKS

The Foundation for Social Innovations: a 'Pressure Cooker of *Perestroika*'[86]

'No one has yet been able to paste the word "official" on Gennadi Alferenko and make it stick.'[87]

The label 'pressure cooker of *perestroika*' could not be applied without qualification to the FMZ or Children's Fund. It fits the FSI, although the latter may also be considered a pressure cooker of postcommunism: its most important venture was to finance Yeltsin's trip to America in 1989, a trip which seems to have done much to persuade Yeltsin of the merits of the market.[88] The FSI was a protégé of *Komsomol'skaya pravda*, which, despite its links to the *Komsomol*, was one of the most radical of publications in terms of *glasnost* about social issues. However, the character of the FSI was determined chiefly not by the newspaper, but by the Fund's creator, Gennadii Alferenko. Like the Children's Fund, the FSI was an intelligentsia creation. Unlike the other funds, it had provincial roots. In Novosibirsk, Alferenko, a scientific researcher, had set up an independent dance company in 1970, believing with Dostoevsky that 'beauty will save the world' and hoping that the dance company could survive independently, untarnished by the surrounding Soviet reality. In 1985 he fulfilled another dream when a Fund for Youth Initiatives[89] was created under the aegis of the Novosibirsk *Komsomol* to help young people – from electors to dog owners – organize clubs. *Komsomol* sponsorship should be seen within the context of official concern about the 'exit' of young people from officially-sponsored leisure pursuits. The national *Komsomol* borrowed the idea and set up 250 similar Funds in other towns as a means of supervising informal organizations.

Alferenko's natural entrepreneurship helped him exploit the opportunities offered by *perestroika* to their limits. Alferenko first moved forward by using the national press. In 1986, after an article in *Komsomol'skaya pravda*, he was contacted by Gorbachev, who asked him to set up a national fund promoting social innovations. In 1987 Alferenko established the FSI at *Komsomol'skaya pravda*, as a readers' voluntary association. More than 30,000 imaginative ideas were received in the first year alone. Readers were asked to send money to put the best projects into practice. Some promoted citizen diplomacy, others focused on domestic social problems. For example, 9.7 million rubles were collected for the programme 'Duty' (*Dolg*) to build a rehabilitation centre for veterans of the Afghan war. Another project reunited American and Soviet Eskimos who had been separated by the closed border since 1948. Despite some obstruction from the *Komsomol* Central Committee, Alferenko perservered. He had contacts in the CPSU Central Committee apparatus and also forged links forged links with large American and European foundations. By January 1989 about half of FSI projects involved American participation. In 1989 it established an American branch, with an sub-office in Alaska. This was a dream survival strategy which must have been the envy of many another Soviet organization.[90]

The FSI seems to have avoided some of the odium which attached to the big funds. This may have been partly because of its somewhat international and theoretical focus. In addition, the FSI probably benefited from having avoided creating a typically Soviet bureaucratic structure. Indeed the Fund and its member societies were only registered by the Russian Ministry of Justice in July 1991.

The FSI's charter named its main goal as 'social renewal'.[91] Elsewhere this was more precisely formulated as 'turning Russia into an open civil society'. The FSI was proud of its role in sponsoring the creation of dozens of new organizations, such as the Union of Chernobyl liquidators.[92] Another of the societies existing under FSI auspices was the 'Folk Warriors'[93] Association of Social Programmes, which originated as a physical education society under the auspices of the Coal Mining Ministry, although relations with the Ministry were sometimes strained. Folk Warriors had a working class focus: despite its diversification into people's diplomacy and other areas, it maintained an interest in helping miners and their families.[94]

World without Violence

The World without Violence[95] movement was another national organization, at least nominally, although it was smaller in scale than the Moscow-based Funds. Despite being – eventually – registered, it was located at the 'unofficial' end of the charity spectrum. It seems appropriate to mention it after the FSI in view of its international and 'peace' focus. The inspiration was Lev Tolstoi rather than any Soviet directive. The movement, based in Tula *oblast,* forged international links which gave it some base for survival. It organized 'peace marches' in places associated with Tolstoi and publicized an ideology of non-violence. For example, it worked in a local school. None of the organizers was a communist or establishment figure. By occupation they were the head of a cooperative (the chairperson); the director of an 'astrology school'; an ecologist from a House of Science and Technology; an official of the Mendeleev Chemists' Society; and a sociologist.[96]

JOURNALISTS' CHARITIES

The importance of links between journalism and the emerging voluntary sector has already been mentioned. Moreover, there were charities which were specifically attached to particular periodicals.

One of the largest and most prestigious was Anti-AIDS (*Anti-SPID*), founded in June 1989 at the offices of the radical magazine *Ogonek*. Its list of patrons included many of radical intellectual elite, such as Tat'yana Tolstaya, Gavriil Popov, Garry Kasparov, Svyatoslav Fedorov and (in Germany) Vladimir Voinovich. Famours donors ranged from Yeltsin and Sakharov to the Borodin Quartet. The charity presented itself as emanating entirely from this intelligentsia milieu, stressing that it was not a *nomenklatura* creation. 'There were no state officials among the initiators of the Fund ... and no one [connected with the organization of the Fund] ... was appointed by a state official.'[97] It was a rich organization, with foreign as well as Soviet donors – demonstrating the effectiveness with which the radical cultural/political elite could mobilize resources.[98]

The Mariya Fund[99] was created in summer 1989 at the women's magazine *Rabotnitsa*. The partial success of the Mariya Fund illustrates, as in the case of *Komsomol'skaya pravda* and the FSI, the media's potential for locating people in need of help, volunteers and donors. The Fund tried to help women who had survived Stalin's camps. It appealed to readers' sense of daughterly duty by reminding them that women prisoners had passed their childbearing years behind barbed wire and hence failed to realise their 'womanly destiny'. Readers were asked to in effect adopt a mother. 'We who are the right age to be their daughters should consider it our duty to take on the role of their children and meet their requests as if they were our mothers'.[100] The former prisoners wrote in with their many requests, such as 'I'd like to be readmitted into the party, which I joined in 1919. I'd also like a telephone'.[101] One ex-prisoner, for example, received 157 letters offering help and support after *Rabotnitsa* printed her story.

Yet another charity founded by a journalist, though not attached to specific journal, was Mother's Right,[102] a fund created in 1990. Mother's Right was the brainchild of a student journalist, Veronika Marchenko. Marchenko started trying to publish material about the deaths during peacetime service in the army in 1988, but *glasnost* widened sufficiently to allow the article's publication (in *Yunost'*) only in June 1989. Marchenko's article provoked a 'flood' of responses. Mother's Right emerged as a fund and publicity-raising organization to help parents of soldiers who had been murdered or committed suicide while performing their regular military service. The volunteers were motivated by 'a desire to help unfortunate people', so this was not a self-help group, though it collaborated with the committees of soldiers' mothers which are discussed in Chapter 6. The cause proved to be a popular one: 'a mass of unknown people, anxious to help us, made donations'. The media also collaborated.[103]

LOCAL GRASSROOTS CHARITIES WITH A CATCH-ALL CHARACTER

Miloserdie[104]

The *Miloserdie* societies complemented and competed with the FMZ. They tended to exist within the informal sector, although there was a variety of political orientation within the *Miloserdie* movement, with links both to the *Komsomol* and to non-Orthodox Christianity. The Leningrad society, which achieved official registration and party secretary Gidaspov's perhaps somewhat hypocritical blessing, was one of the most official.[105] The head of Moscow *Miloserdie*, also registered, considered his organization to be an official-informal hybrid.[106] By contrast, the leader of Voronezh *Miloserdie* styled herself a *neformal* in her article for a national newspaper.[107] Provincial organizations were usually unregistered and were often more clearly 'informal' in other respects than their equivalents in Moscow and Leningrad.

Urban suggests that a characteristic of the informal movement in the early and middle years of *perestroika* was 'an orientation toward addressing one or another specific social concern by means of pragmatic, remedial measures...not directed against the Soviet system but toward various lacunae evident in its capacity to solve social problems... It pertained mainly to three clusters of concerns: the socialization and development of young people; the defence of cultural and historic sites; and environmental protection.'[108] Although Urban does not mention charity, his description is equally applicable to the *Miloserdie* groups.

Even before Granin's 1987 article 'Charity' was published, small groups had been operating in Leningrad, mostly attached to schools and colleges. They provided basic medical and housekeeping assistance for pensioners and disabled people. The oldest group, of trainee teachers helping blockade survivors, dated back to the early 1970s. There were also disabled people's organizations, notably the *Feniks* club mentioned in Chapter 3. Under Granin's influence, more groups formed. The energetic *Komsomol* secretary of a technical college, Aleksei Lushnikov, was the leader of one such 'brigade'. The more general Christian Democratic organization *Chelovek* was the most politically significant of the groups which in October 1987 came together to form the *Miloserdie* Society 'Leningrad'.[109]

The local and national media presented the views of officials opposed to the project alongside sympathetic descriptions of the society as the acceptable face of informal activity: a model of citizen involvement in furthering the aims of *perestroika*. For example, an article in *Izvestiya* described it as being *run* by Granin, emphasizing the good Soviet principle of one-man leadership, and pointed out its links with the social security departments and Red Cross.[110]

Komsomol secretary Lushnikov, as vice-chair, was responsible for the society's administration. Granin became the first chairperson and was invited by the Politburo to turn *Miloserdie* into an nationwide charity. The combination of mass grassroots involvement and leadership from the intellectual elite promised to be a winning formula for an NGO, as was already indicated by the early popularity of both the Children's Fund and *Memorial*. Presumably too the party elite was hoping to control the new movement by incorporating it into the establishment. Annoyingly for the Politburo, Granin refused to cooperate, on the grounds that such a society ought to be created on the basis of grassroots

activity and work on a local level, as in Leningrad, and not take the form of a traditional party-led Soviet institution. He characterized the special feature of the existing society as being that its activity 'comes from below, not by directive'.[111]
The society enjoyed good relations with the city *Komsomol*, social security department and veterans' organization.[112] However, it encountered obstruction and public attacks from other sections of the local authorities. *Miloserdie* finally secured official registration only in April 1988 after Gorbachev telephoned Leningrad city council at Granin's request. At this point Gorbachev again requested Granin to set up a national charitable organization, but Granin again declined.[113]
Despite its 'official' features, size – 5,000 volunteers by April 1988 – and rapidly increasing scale of activities, *Miloserdie* clung to its 'informal' image. Granin's wish was to 'create an organization which would give maximum results with the minimum of meetings, speeches and papers'.[114] As Chapter 7 suggests, this was not so easy to achieve. The Politburo had failed to coopt the charity, but the Leningrad authorities had a strong motivation to incorporate the large and active society into the *local* bureaucracy.
Moscow *Miloserdie* was established in 1987 independently of 'Leningrad'.[115] The founders were two doctors, A. Verbitsky and S. Gladyshev. They were lent a room three evenings a week at the editorial offices of *Komsomol'skaya pravda's* weekly supplement, *Sobesednik*, which publicized their activities. *Sobesednik* took credit for the organization, but *Miloserdie*'s activities were determined by its energetic leaders and volunteers. The limitations to *Sobesednik*'s patronage were demonstrated by *Miloserdie*'s problems in achieving registration. It finally registered thanks to the intervention of a prominent acquaintance of one of the founders.[116]
Despite achieving registration and embarking on an ambitious range of projects, the Moscow society retained an informal character. This was perhaps partly thanks to the different political atmosphere in Moscow, which allowed *Miloserdie* to evade party control; Verbitsky's hippy-like appearance no doubt contributed to the 'informal' image. When Moscow *Miloserdie* finally gained premises they were modest and the charity operated in a democratic and unbureaucratic fashion.

Although there was no central *Miloserdie* organization, the *Miloserdie* movement was a nationwide phenomenon. Groups emerged spontaneously in dozens of towns, inspired by Granin's article and by the example of Leningrad and Moscow. Kazan, Belgorod, Rovno, Kuibyshev, Kolomna, Ivanovo, Voronezh and Novosibirsk were among the Russian towns where *Miloserdie* societies were created in 1988. By spring 1988 there were at least seventeen in the USSR as a whole.[117] In June 1988 leaders of *Miloserdie* groups from fourteen towns gathered in tents – another 'informal' feature! – outside Moscow. In December 1988, representatives of 53 towns met in Leningrad. Again there was a marked absence of 'official' faces: this was a gathering of informals. The volunteers decided to set up an All-Union *Miloserdie* Association, not to control the movement, but to act as an umbrella organization which would be able to register individual *Miloserdie* societies under its aegis. This came to nothing, since Granin thought better of the idea: a mistake, considering the sufferings endured by unregistered provincial groups. However, after the creation of the FMZ, with its own brief to sponsor and control the emerging voluntary sector, it is hard to imagine that a nationwide *Miloserdie* could have succeeded. Despite this setback, the informal provincial charity movement continued to grow and by May 1989 87 towns contained *Miloserdie* activists.[118]

The *Miloserdie* societies and associations shared many features. Their activists were in general not part of the Soviet establishment, and sometimes were on the margins of society. They tended to be either young or elderly. In Voronezh most of the two hundred volunteers were under 25, a characteristic which their slightly older leader regarded as indicating a comforting idealism among the those achieving adulthood under *perestroika*. (The Voronezh volunteers liked to 'philosophize' and discuss the many dimensions of the concept of charity.)[119] Some activists were religious: in Novosibirsk, for example, two leaders were Lutherans, while the other volunteers were mostly Baptists. Two of the Novosibirsk activists had spent time in psychiatric hospitals, one for conscientious objection and the other for sheltering a group of 'punks' in her home.[120]

The volunteers were committed to small-scale, person-to-person help, independently of state structures. They would, for example, help out in hospitals and children's homes or do housework and shopping for elderly housebound people. During its most successful period in the Gorbachev era, 1990–1, the Moscow association ran a canteen and provided meals on wheels for fifty clients. In the more primitive conditions prevailing in Belomorsk, a small town, the tasks were described as 'fetching medicine, food, water and firewood; cleaning and making repairs; accompanying people to the bath house and polyclinic.'[121]

The *Miloserdie* societies worked together with self-help groups, for example, of disabled people, and contained members with disabilities, but they were service-providing organizations. Many of their members, of both religious and secular outlook, were driven by a general desire to do something useful for society, rather than by concern about the particular plight of a defined group of people. A powerful motivating factor was their sense of shock at discovering the conditions in which elderly and disabled people frequently existed. Sometimes this was compounded by moral outrage, directed, for example, at the children of people living in squalid residential homes.[122] After the initial burst of enthusiasm the number of volunteers tended to decline, and those organizations which could became more professional, employing permanent staff. Leningrad *Miloserdie* apparently had no paid staff as late as August 1989, whereas three years later it employed 64.[123]

Since the Leningrad and Moscow organizations were registered, they could in their turn found other organizations. For example, in Leningrad, where house fires were a daily occurrence, the society joined forces with the local fire brigade to revive the pre-revolutionary society for aid to fire victims.[124] One can only speculate as to how the voluntary sector might have developed had the provincial *Miloserdie* societies also achieved official status and been able to sponsor other charities and self-help groups in their turn. The absence of registered status was an immense handicap. The practical achievements of groups existing in a limbo of semi-legality or – if they had been categorically refused registration – illegally was nevertheless impressive.

MISCELLANEOUS CATCH-ALL CHARITIES OF THE LATE *PERESTROIKA* PERIOD

Although commercial organizations encountered many difficulties when they attempted to become involved with the voluntary sector, a number of quite large charities emerged in the new climate of the years 1990–1, with links to commerce and branches in several towns. They form an interesting contrast both to the small-scale, idealistic provincial *Milioserdie* groups and the party-sponsored official charities of the mid-*perestroika* period. The World and Man Charitable Fund[125], for example, was created in February 1990 and registered a year later. It possessed two profitable enterprises and spent 500,000 rubles on charity in 1991–2, putting it nearly in the same league as Leningrad *Miloserdie*.[126]

SMALL CHARITIES CONCENTRATING ON SPECIFIC CAUSES

Family Children's Homes

The Children's Fund presented the growing network of small independent children's homes as its own project. The Council of Ministers approved them with a resolution of 17 April 1988, 'Children's Homes of the Family Type' and a follow-up 'model statute' on 8 September 1989.[127] By May 1991 there were 237 in Russia.[128] The Children's Fund originally had an 'organized' concept of the scheme: the homes would be clustered in 'children's villages', modelled on the Austrian Kinderdorf. In December 1988 *Pravda* appealed to readers to contribute towards funding this project. However, this attempt to organize the initiative resulted in the creation of only one Russian 'village'.[129] A local authority attempt to organize small children's homes occurred in Novosibirsk, where the *city* administration, aware of the queues of would-be adoptive parents, favoured the scheme, despite the headaches it caused for *borough*-level authorities. In 1988 it decided to sponsor a programme of family children's homes: one was planned for each borough. This was not enough to satisfy all the couples who expressed an interest, but was one too many for most borough education departments.[130]

However, despite some involvement from the authorities and the active interest of the Children's Fund, 'top-down' appearances were usually misleading. Family children's homes (or 'guardian families' as the Children's Fund began to call them) seem to have been the result of a largely grass-roots initiative. The homes operated as scattered individual ventures, following roughly the same pattern but not conforming entirely to the requirements of the 'model statute'. They were only partly supported by the state, and one of the participants claimed the state 'hadn't provided as much as a spoon'.[131] Women were the main participants, sometimes the only ones, despite the official requirement that a married couple be involved. The foster mother was paid only a meagre salary, and the women and couples who created the homes sank their savings as well as their entire time into the project. Often from reasonably comfortable middle-class backgrounds (commonly teachers), the mothers found themselves plunged into poverty: only thorough-going altruists could persist.

Would-be organizers faced a host of problems with local officialdom on whom they were dependent for permission to foster the children, salaries, housing – a major problem in the Soviet context – and transport. Local education departments often resented the implied slight to state homes. Members of the public could not understand why anyone should be paid for being parents. Some neighbours expected the children to be 'hooligans' and tried to prevent the location of homes 'in their backyards'.[132]

Overall, the project was a disappointment. Only about 2,000 children had been placed by spring 1990.[133] The system was conceptually flawed and insufficiently monitored.[134] However, some homes survived successfully into the post-1991 period and provided good parenting for the children concerned in spite of all the hardships.

Organizations for Refugees

By late 1991 there were said to be 208,000 displaced people in the RSFSR, of whom about half were refugees from ethnic conflict. When the problem first emerged, with the events in Nagornyi Karabakh and Sumgait of February–March 1988, it was the big Funds who attended to refugees: the Children's Fund, Peace Fund, and in particular, the Red Cross. Only two years later did the state attempt to address the problem, without, however, using the word 'refugee' or facing up to the full implications of the problem.[135]

In fact, neither the Funds nor local authorities were able to cope with providing for the refugees. A number of charities therefore emerged to help them. In Leningrad, for example, KOESKYU (the Committee for Extending Economic, Cultural and Legal Help to Refugees)[136] provided wide-ranging help to integrate refugees into their new communities in the city. In Moscow, the Committee of Russian Refugees[137] attempted to lobby for their rights. It tried both to provide for refugees and encourage them to relocate in depopulated rural areas. Another voluntary organization, the Civil Cooperation Public Committee on Refugee and Internal Migrants' Affairs[138] was headed by Lidiya Grafova of *Literaturnaya gazeta*, and founded by journalists, *Memorial*, the Soviet Sociological Association and the Union of United Cooperatives. Elena Bonner and Galina Starovoitova were associated with this organization, which also had connections with foreign charities. It operated on a fairly large scale, participating in the construction of housing for refugees in 25 provincial locations and distributing 10,000 parcels of German food aid. All three of these refugees' organizations were registered in 1990.[139]

Telephone Helplines

The initiative for founding helplines came from a journalist, Anatolii Rubinov, as far back as 1979. After considerable bureaucratic deliberation, helplines were set up as part of the state health service in four boroughs of Moscow. They employed not only doctors, but also sociologists and lawyers.[140] During *perestroika*, other helplines were created, some in association with Befrienders International (the Samaritans). For example, in Voronezh a helpline was set up under the auspices of the FMZ. It was open every night and was staffed by paid psychologists and psychiatrists; most of the clients were elderly women living on their own. The most common topics of discussion were listed as 'crises resulting from drug and alcohol abuse, problems of loneliness and serious illness, job-related issues and existential musings'.[141] In Perm, a helpline registered in 1988 particularly targeted adolescents, disabled people and people contemplating suicide.[142]

Animal Charities

According to Granin, Soviet citizens had been encouraged to poke fun at the Western craze for animal charities, but during *perestroika* it became clear that they were no less popular with Russians. In 1988 it was claimed that 'talks have been going on for twenty years about introducing legislation on criminal liability for cruelty to animals' but had always been unsuccessful because of the attitude that 'there are too many really important problems to bother about cats and dogs'. In 1988 a Russian Supreme Soviet presidium decree was finally passed, after a campaign supported by many prominent intellectuals including Likhachev and Rasputin.[143] Nevertheless, the economic hardships of *perestroika* meant food shortages and callous treatment not only for ordinary pets, but also for zoo and circus animals, whose often desperate plight became the subject of public concern and prompted the creation of a variety of NGOs.[144]

RELIGIOUS CHARITIES

The revival of charity overlapped with the revival of religion in Russia and religious charities are best understood within the wider context of religious revival, which is not the story of this book. Moreover, the early charitable work of the Christian churches (1988–90) has been quite thoroughly covered in another source.[145] The following section will therefore be relatively brief.

Christian Charities

Gorbachev's overtures to the Church and the welcoming of Orthodoxy into Soviet official life occurred in 1988. This welcome included, for example, the inclusion of Orthodox clergy in the structures of the FMZ. Clergymen were also placed on the boards of the Children's Fund – in other words, incorporated into the official charity movement as early as autumn 1987.

However, there were still battles to be fought before the churches could establish their full right to exist and function. Given that the permanency of *perestroika* seemed by no means assured between 1988 and 1990, and in the absence of a new law on religion, participants in Church-sponsored charity during these years were taking a risk. Church charity was technically illegal. Many Orthodox priests waited for directives from higher up.[146] It was only on 1 October 1990 that the new law on Freedom of Conscience removed the 1929 ban on charitable work by the Church; on the same day, a Commission for Moral Education and Charity was created at the Holy Synod.[147]

The constraints existing between 1987 and 1990 discouraged the establishment of many Christian charitable *organizations*, but *acts of charity* were performed openly with increasing confidence. As early as 1987 some believers had offered their services in Leningrad hospitals, in response to Granin's article and the creation of *Miloserdie*. However, this was forbidden, with a reference to the 1929 law.[148] The Church as an institution was apparently also wary of *Miloserdie*, as a creation of the Leningrad intelligentsia.[149] In Moscow in September 1987 clergy approached the city's health administration, apparently without immediate result.[150] In 1988 Patriarch Pimen brought the issue of church involvement in charity into the open when he suggested to an *Izvestiya* correspondent that the Church should become involved in charitable work in state institutions.[151] By April 1988 Orthodox clergymen and parishioners were already working in a Leningrad hospital and in June 1988 a Ministry of Health official gave the go-ahead to Christian volunteers who wished to work in state hospitals.[152] However, apparently many of the initiatives were shortlived, as volunteers' enthusiasm waned or they found that they could not cope.[153]

The official welcome awarded to believers who propped up state welfare services could be viewed as exploitation, since the Church was not in control of the initiatives and did not possess its own officially registered charitable institutions. Moreover, one of the reasons why Orthodox clergy were included on the boards of the FMZ and Children's Fund was presumably because the state hoped to tap the wealth of the Church – as it had done through the Peace Fund before 1987.

However, independent Orthodox charities did begin to emerge, at first within the 'informal' sphere and then, after church charity was legalized in 1990, as officially registered organizations. In September and November 1990 the first Christian hospitals were consecrated in Leningrad and Moscow.[154] In October 1990 a Union of Orthodox Brotherhoods was established.[155] By August 1991 there were at least 25 brotherhoods. They worked in state hospitals and residential homes and also set up orphanages and homes for elderly people. However, despite the expansion of the network not all churchmen were favourably disposed towards the brotherhoods.[156] In 1991 the brotherhoods were joined by a 'sisterhood' of secular women, established in Moscow.[157]

The Radonezh Society claimed to be 'the first religious public organization to receive official status'.[158] It was created as a 'religious cooperative' in 1987, registered as in December 1990 as a voluntary (educational) organization and eventually re-registered as a brotherhood. The Radonezh Society had links with the pre-*perestroika* period, since it was founded by ex-dissidents who had formerly spread *samizdat*, restored churches and given children religious education. Now they were able to operate six secondary schools and a teachers' training institute, as well as broadcasting religious radio programmes. They also helped poor parishioners and local 'large families' and opened a free canteen for children. Curiously, they claimed that their sources of finance were 'donations from state enterprises and organizations'.[159]

The St Panteleimon Brotherhood[160] was another Moscow society of sizeable proportions, with 96 members by 1991. Founded in June 1988, it claimed to be the first brotherhood in the capital. It arose from the desire of young doctors and other members of the intelligentsia to become involved in the charity movement. At the same time, its leader pointed out that it could be seen as a religious protest against state control of welfare. Its focus was largely medical: for example, it set up a charitable pharmacy and a nurses' college. Most of its income was said to derive from private donations. It registered only with difficulty, winning the battle in 1990 after a sympathetic deputy had raised the issue in the Supreme Soviet.[161]

Brotherhoods could be attached to monasteries as well as parishes. The Brotherhood of the Blessed Kseniya[162] was located at the Alexander Nevsky monastery seminary in Leningrad. Established in spring 1988 – hence at the very beginning of the official Orthodox charity movement – the brotherhood initially provided volunteer orderlies to work in state hospitals. They then persuaded the hospital administrations to let clergymen visit patients, at the latter's request. The brothers also helped in a children's home and with hospitalized prisoners. They did shopping and housework for elderly people and read them religious works. Volunteers included parishioners and schoolchildren. By April 1990 there were about a hundred members. My interviewee at the Brotherhood in 1990 was ambitious for similar charities to be established at every seminary and monastery throughout Russia.[163]

By 1991 the Patriarch could describe a wide range of Orthodox initiatives, concentrating particularly on hospitals but also mentioning children, drug abusers and victims of Chernobyl.[164]

The churches also donated money to independent secular charities and self-help groups. A directory of organizations published in 1992 lists many examples of such help.[165] In fact this may have been the Church's main contribution to the emerging voluntary sector, rather than the activities of specifically Christian voluntary organizations. Some secular organizations had close links with the Church. For example, the Rebirth Organization for drug abusers in Leningrad attempted, from 1990 onwards, to 'return patients and their relatives to the bosom of the Orthodox Church'.[166]

Non-Orthodox Christian congregations, being often unconnected with the Soviet establishment, had less to gain from caution in the middle stages of *perestroika* and quickly became engaged in charitable work. As early as 1988 Baptists became active throughout the USSR and they looked back on the year as a 'year of charity'.[167] Adventists also became involved in charitable work. In Novosibirsk, for example, Adventists 'adopted' a hospital.[168] The Adventists set up a national aid organization in 1990; its Moscow branch distributed humanitarian aid and tried to help a wide variety of people.[169] Tolstoyans operated the World Family Association[170] in Moscow, which tried to bring education, culture and morality to children in state homes and hospitals, partly by supplying them with foreign religious literature.[171]

Foreign churches and religious orders became involved in the Russian voluntary sector as early as 1986, when Mother Teresa visited Russia on the invitation of the Peace Committee and later worked in Armenia and Georgia.[172] After this, foreign religious organizations began to flock to Russia. Bristol-based Euroevangelism, for example, began working on charitable projects in Russia in 1988.[173]

Jewish Organizations

Soviet Jews had strong international links, for various reasons: because of the concern traditionally felt for their situation by Jews in the West; rising anti-Semitism, which heightened that concern; and the mass emigration of the *perestroika* period, which created special problems for Jewish communities who had to a large extent become Russified and wished to strengthen their sense of Jewish identity. However, there were also indigenous Jewish charities. 'Charity' is an imprecise label, since there was a strong self-help element to Jewish activities, which were perceived as benefiting the whole community through aid to individual members. At least one organization was styled 'charity and mutual aid society'. Some activities were directed towards the more specific needs of the Jewish community, such as preparing children for life in Israel, ensuring supplies of kosher food and performing circumcisions. Other volunteers provided services similar to those of the *Miloserdie* societies, but within the Jewish community, such as providing free dinners and childcare or offering medical help.[174] Jewish, like Christian organizations, were also involved in the wider charity movement. The Leningrad synagogue, for example, made donations to the *Miloserdie* society.[175] Help from Jewish charities was not restricted to Jewish clients.[176]

CONCLUSIONS

The four big Funds, incorporated into the *nomenklatura* system, were clearly very 'official' at the national level, but their local employees – especially the deputy chairpersons who did the day-to-day work – might feel and act as if they were less connected to the official establishment. It is even more difficult to place many of the charities mentioned in the rest of the chapter on an 'official-informal' spectrum. The FSI, for example, worked through the *Komsomol*'s official national newspaper, yet sponsored Yeltsin's visit to the USA when he was still in the political wilderness. Leningrad *Miloserdie* was a large registered organization, yet it remained in many ways closer in spirit to its provincial, unregistered sister organizations than to the FMZ, whose agenda was similar. Any organization connected to the Orthodox Church was *ipso facto* in an ambiguous situation as regarded 'officialness'.

Russian charities, like the wider public, experienced a learning process. They began with considerable idealism, determined that qualities such as caringness and imagination could be revived, and without a full idea of the whole scale of need. For example, single pensioners and alcohol abusers were the subject of early attention – not surprisingly, given their prominence on the official agenda – while homelessness was not.[177] The years 1987–9 were particularly notable because of the role of the *Miloserdie* movement. *Miloserdie* did much to enact the programme outlined by Granin in his article 'Charity'. The years 1990–1 were marked by the emergence of a host of other charities, both before and after the October 1990 legalization of religious charity and the new law on associations.

The charities represent an impressive achievement: the vigour and variety of the charitable sector by 1991 contrasted strikingly with the almost total absence of charities in 1985. Charities often raised substantial quantities of money and helped hundreds of thousands of Russians. However, as they often recognized, with frustration and disillusionment, they were only scratching at the surface of social problems. Self-help organizations, the subject of Chapter 6, were in some respects better placed to reach beneath that surface.

6 Self-Help Organizations

'There are many of us, and together we are a force.'[1]

INTRODUCTION

The distinction between charity and self-help is of great significance. Nevertheless, it is impossible to classify all voluntary organizations precisely. Chapter 4 suggested that one impact of both the economic crisis and the influx of foreign aid in 1990–1 was to turn erstwhile self-help groups into distributors of charity. Moreover, there were a number of organizations which from the outset embraced both aims. The overlap created the potential for tension and misunderstanding, although it could also be productive to bring together professionals and clients or different generations in a collaborative effort. The 'hybrid' organizations which most clearly straddled the charity/self-help divide are considered at the beginning of this chapter.

HYBRIDS

Medical and Educational Organizations

A number of organizations were created jointly by professionals – doctors and teachers – and clients, both patients and relatives. Such groups often had a self-help ethic, with participants aiding one another to create a more equal and trusting doctor-patient relationship.

The Centre for Curative Pedagogics,[2] for instance, was established in Moscow by a group of teachers and mothers of children with learning difficulties. It emerged in spring-summer 1989: a time which seems to have been particularly favourable for independent Moscow charities. For a while it was attached to *Miloserdie*. The Centre tried to help children 'whom the state had not been able to help' and facilitate their social integration, for example by educating them alongside children without special needs.³

The Human Soul Fund⁴ emerged as early as December 1987. It united doctors, relatives and people with mental illnesses, providing help with jobs, legal aid and other forms of emotional, medical and financial support.⁵ Another hybrid was Second Life,⁶ which provided support for people who had undergone transplant surgery. It was founded in spring-summer 1990, apparently as the joint initiative of doctors and patients, and had a fluctuating membership of 50–500. The 'declining influence of the bureaucratic system' was mentioned as a prerequisite for the society's creation.⁷

Memorial⁸

Granin's article in March 1987 had mentioned the need to honour the memory of Stalin's victims, as a facet of the revival of Russian charity. *Memorial* sprang from the same sense of moral obligation and was founded later in 1987, in Moscow and Leningrad. Russian provincial branches mostly emerged in the second half of 1988 or in 1989. There were up to 5,000 provincial activists.⁹ *Memorial* was unambiguously a non-official organization. Its original aim, to campaign for a memorial to victims of the Terror, soon widened into a more general campaign for de-Stalinization. Although best-known for its political activities, *Memorial* also developed into a self-help/charitable organization, working to improve the lives of surviving victims.

Typically, activists belonged to the local intellectual elite, such as headteachers, newspaper editors or museum curators.¹⁰ In a number of places *Memorial* took the lead in forming a local informal movement, suggesting once again the intelligentsia's crucial importance as the mover of *glasnost* and liberalization in the early and middle years of *perestroika*.

Memorial contained both elderly 'victims' and younger political activists and historians. In some places – particularly Moscow and Leningrad – this led to tension, with younger members suspected of using *Memorial* as a springboard for their political careers.¹¹ However, conflict was not the inevitable outcome of generational difference; the opposite result, a healthy learning process, was also possible and in many local areas the situation was more harmonious.

Memorial lobbied local authorities to give former prisoners improved housing, free public transport, medicines and other goods and services. (A Russian 'Law on Rehabilitation', making such provision universal, did not appear until October 1991.) One aspect of *Memorial*'s historical research involved searching for information which could help members claim various forms of compensation. *Memorial* also provided medical aid; its medical section was created up in 1989 as a separate organization and widened its brief to include help for abused children.[12]

Memorial turned to the state-sponsored FMZ for material aid with varying success. In Karelia, a FMZ employee was on Memorial's board and responsible for welfare issues. On the other hand, when radical Lipetsk *Memorial* asked for help from the Foundation it was refused with the words: 'you and your organization were called for interview at the KGB'.

In addition, *Memorial* provided emotional support. In many places this was a case of former prisoners and their descendants socializing informally. In Gorno-Altaisk, for example, 'We help each other . . . emotionally, by talking over our lives'. *Memorial* activists were also concerned to restore the social standing of former 'enemies of the people'. This was not just a question of honouring the dead and helping the survivors, but also of tending to the moral health of society in general. The goal was to 'inform the people about all the horrors of the prisons, camps and psychiatric hospitals, in order to help restore a feeling of sympathy with other people's sufferings, empathy and dignity – a feeling which had been almost forgotten.'

Branches could often see encouraging evidence of success in changing attitudes among the local community. Other successes were the identification of, and creation of support networks among the 'victims'. However, the latter were not necessarily materially much better off, despite 'privileged' access to goods in short supply and other concessions.

SELF-HELP GROUPS

Second World War Survivors

People who had been in Nazi camps as children also joined together in 1988, when the Union of Former Young Prisoners in Fascist Concentration Camps[13] was created under the auspices of the Children's Fund. (The Union's leader had been pursuing the cause since 1965.) By spring 1991 there were 28 branches of the Union throughout the USSR. In May 1993 it had 165,000 members. Although the Children's Fund was officially credited with taking the initiative, this was an 'authentic' organization, not one created top-down. Some at least of its members were careful to keep a distance from the veterans' organizations, which they regarded as 'the offspring of the CPSU'.[14] In 1989, as a result of lobbying, the government decreed that the approximately 3,000 survivors were entitled to various benefits, such as priority installation of telephones and reduced prescription charges. However, the Children's Fund had to pay for these, at least 'temporarily'.[15] The local branches performed an investigative and monitoring role. Novgorod, for example, helped members search for documentation to establish their rights to benefits – sometimes a difficult task – and monitored the local authority's fulfilment of its obligations according to the 1989 decree.[16]

A Jewish equivalent of the Union was the Association of Soviet Jewish War Veterans, Partisans, Concentration Camp and Ghetto Inmates and their Children.[17] The Association was established in 1989 and officially registered as a Moscow organization in August 1990. The Association helped sick and housebound members and also engaged in anti-fascist activity.[18]

Organizations for survivors of the blockade of Leningrad, although officially sponsored by the party-state, nevertheless sometimes possessed an authentically grassroots character and organized practical activities. For instance, one borough branch of Inhabitants of Blockaded Leningrad[19] set up comrades' courts to resolve arguments in communal flats. (The society's chief financial outlay was on battles with the rats which inhabited its office.)[20]

Older People

The official veterans' societies were ostensibly self-help organizations, and, in so far as they were run by senior nomenklaturists for their own benefit, they fulfilled this role. However, of course these benefits did not necessarily trickle down to ordinary older people, despite officially expressed hopes that 'the Veterans' Organization will play a great role in facilitating the development of mutual aid and support among pensioners'.[21] Many self-help activists tended to be dismissive about the veterans' organizations. Nevertheless, there were places where they created a framework for genuine volunteering and self-help. For example, the Charity Fund Committee[22] of the Novo-Zavidovo Settlement Soviet (Tver *oblast*) was a highly active, very practical and localized organization set up by the Organization of Veterans and run by pensioners. They helped repair dwellings and wells, fetched fuel and medicines, accompanied housebound people to visit graves of their relatives at the local cemetery and delivered a range of other services. Since most of the users were elderly, 'self-help' would have been a more appropriate label than 'charity'.[23]

Parents[24]

A massive group in any society are the informal carers. There were millions of Soviet citizens struggling to look after family members at home. They needed part-time and home work but it was not generally available, despite the provisions of government decrees. Grassroots, usually very localized parents' groups were to form a substantial part of the new voluntary sector. The big voluntary organizations – the Children's Fund, VOI and the FMZ – were able to act as umbrellas for small self-help groups, sometimes as their official sponsor. Some groups, however, preferred to avoid the shelter of the such umbrellas, considering VOI and the Children's Fund to be too 'official', but until October 1990 such collaboration was often essential in the interests of achieving registration.

Parents involved normally fell into one of four categories: parents of servicemen; 'large' families; lone parents; and parents of disabled or chronically ill children. Not all organizations were open to both parents: many were specifically for women.

1) Soldiers' Mothers

Soldiers were among the most vulnerable of social groups. Abuse, drunkenness and poor safety standards contributed to high rates of injury and even mortality among conscripts. In the years 1986–90, for example, 15,000–20,000 soldiers and officers were said to have died 'noncombat-related deaths', many violent.[25]

The committees of soldiers' mothers originated in June 1989 as a pressure group to enforce a decree permitting students to defer military service. The mothers' picket resulted in the demobilization of 170,000 conscripts, despite the opposition of army commanders.[26] The Moscow committee continued its existence, expanding its activities. These included monitoring conditions in the army: the committee claimed that 'Mother's careful and loving eyes see everything that army officials wish to hide'.[27] In September 1990 the first national congress of servicemen's parents met in Moscow: the Moscow mothers had inspired the creation of numerous provincial mothers' committees. Their major success, on a national level, was in convincing Gorbachev to issue a decree implementing many of their suggestions.[28]

Committees of soldiers' mothers shared some common origins with organizations of parents of Afghan veterans and on occasion they collaborated.[29] Bereaved veterans' families often experienced difficulty in obtaining pensions and benefits to which they were entitled and, before *glasnost* led to greater public awareness of the truth about Afghanistan, suffered from lack of public understanding of their situation. Mothers, who often became acquainted in the graveyards, began to form self-help groups to address these problems.

Parents of the approximately 300 soldiers who were missing in action – initially stigmatized for breeding 'traitors' – founded Hope, the 'people's committee for the liberation of Soviet servicemen'.[30] The Hope movement existed in a number of Soviet towns: Moscow, Leningrad, Togliatti, Volgograd and Vladimir. It collaborated with the Foreign Ministry, the Red Cross and the American-based International

Committee for the Rescue of Russian Prisoners of War in Afghanistan. However, the parents had their own approach to solving the problem: the collection of donations for ransom money from the public. There was no evidence that the rebels would be bought off.[31] However, eliciting widespread public sympathy and support was important in itself, as was the sense of solidarity created among the parents.

2) Large Families

'If a mother with a large family comes into the shop, people hiss, "They breed like rabbits, then they jump the queue."'[32]

Associations of large families became a widespread type of self-help group. Once again, *glasnost* had been a significant factor in facilitating their emergence. The so-called 'large' (literally 'multi-child') family did not necessarily enjoy public esteem – as the quotation suggests – but had traditionally been favoured by the pro-natalist state. Stalin established the status of 'heroine mother' during the drive to replenish the Soviet population after the war; Brezhnev extended privileges, widening the definition of 'large' to three or more children. This special state protection had been symbolized to the general public by notices in shops allowing mothers of large families to jump queues. In fact, state benefits and housing provision were often inadequate, but the taboo on discussing poverty meant that it was only with *glasnost* that parents could make the public aware of their poverty and the humiliations inflicted by state officials at every turn.[33]

Once again, a 'top-down' national organization was created to deal with the issues. The Soviet 'Large Family' Fund[34] displayed its political orthodoxy in rather original ways: it numbered the KGB among its sponsors and also featured a profile of Lenin's mother and her 'large' family in the first issue of its newspaper.[35] The Fund had an ambitious programme, including courses to teach business skills, but soon got into trouble when its head was prosecuted for embezzlement.[36]

The Fund does not seem to have succeeded in controlling the large families movement. It was succeeded by an Association of Russian Large Families, but the local organizations were essentially grassroots societies. They mushroomed during *perestroika*, addressing the material needs of large families, but also trying to improve public and official attitudes, 'raising the prestige' of families who considered themselves to be eminently respectable.[37] Some organizations were societies of 'multi-child *mothers*' only.[38]

3) Lone Parents
Lone parents organizations, too, were often restricted to either mothers or fathers. In Moscow, for example, 'Only Mummy'[39] was created in January 1991 and united about fifteen families, who helped one another materially and emotionally. Their main outside helper was the church.[40] Moscow 'Mummy-Daddies'[41] was a fathers' association which provided both material and moral support. It also tried to publicize the special plight of lone fathers and provided free legal aid to fathers who had been denied access to their children following divorce.[42] Societies for lone parents also existed in the provinces. Perm, for example, had its own club for single fathers, existing under the auspices of the Women's Council.[43]

Lone parents' organizations were less numerous than those for large families, and seem to have been both smaller and less often officially-sponsored. This was perhaps surprising, given that, if one includes divorcees as lone parents, there were more lone parent families than 'large' ones. By the mid-1990s one-fifth of Russian women were bringing up children alone.[44]

4) Parents of Disabled and Chronically Ill Children
Probably the most widespread type of parents' organization united the parents of children with illnesses and disabilities. They emerged for reasons similar to those existing in Western societies, where there are hundreds of similar organizations. There were also specifically Soviet reasons, connected with the inadequacies of the health service and the exceptionally limited opportunities for part-time and home working, leading to the enforced unemployment of mothers with disabled children; declining living standards under Gorbachev provided another impulse. This was true in Mytishchi (Moscow *oblast*), where a quarter of the 200 local families with disabled children were living below the poverty line.[45] More positively, the registration of VOI and its local

branches in 1988 meant that organizations of and for disabled people had been officially recognized and that they could in their turn sponsor others. Some parents' organizations arose as sections of the local VOI. For example, in Novosibirsk a mothers' soft toy cooperative was established as early as 1989.[46] To some extent, however, parents' organizations arose because of the perceived inadequacies of VOI. The emergence of organizations for deaf and blind children suggested similar dissatisfaction with VOG and VOS. In Leningrad, for instance, the Association of Parents with Blind Children compiled a database, provided medical help and music teaching, distributed foreign aid, organized leisure activities and tried to find job placements.[47]

In Leningrad, parents had their own umbrella organization, the City Association of Public Organizations of Parents with Disabled Children,[48] founded by fifteen organizations. Some organizations were fairly large and financially successful: one borough organization, for example, spent 70,000 rubles a year on 'charitable goals' and had a constant source of income from a local lottery.[49] Other groups seem to have focused more on mutual emotional support. Most frequently, physically disabled children were the object of attention. However, there were also groups of parents of children with learning difficulties.[50] Save the Family, for example,[51] was a city organization in Leningrad which had good connections with foreign charities, the media and the churches, through whom it received humanitarian aid. Its members mostly had autistic children, for whom they organized education at home; they also planned a music therapy centre.[52]

In addition, parents' groups were founded for children with particular diseases. For example, despite the mushroom growth of societies for adults with diabetes, it seemed necessary to some parents to establish separate groups;[53] Moscow possessed a Fund for the Protection of Children with Epilepsy;[54] and there were a number of organizations for children with cancer.

Disabled Adults' Organizations

1) The VOI Campaign, 1985–8
Chapter 3 charted the efforts of disabled people before 1985

to found a USSR Society of Disabled People: VOI. They never succeeded. However, a Russian Society of Disabled People (also VOI) was officially founded in August 1988.[55] Gorbachev's accession in March 1985 allowed the disabled groups which had been founded in the 1970s and 1980s to operate more freely. They were soon joined by new, local groups, for example in Novosibirsk (1986), Gorky, Kemerovo,[56] Leningrad and Moscow. These embryonic local branches of VOI were able to emerge thanks not just to the more liberal atmosphere of *perestroika*, but also to the foundations laid by the *Korchaginets* and other Brezhnev-era clubs, which had created some basic networks and a degree of organizational confidence. *Korchaginets* itself adopted the role of an umbrella organization and by early 1987 could describe itself as 'becoming increasingly a federation of local disabled people's associations'.[57]

Minsobes and the State Committee on Labour and Social Issues maintained their opposition to a national society of disabled people until spring 1988, creating the impression that it was 'almost a matter of honour to obstruct disabled people in every way possible'.[58] There was also opposition within the CPSU Central Committee.[59] VOI was an organization which senior officials may have feared the state was unable to afford: disability was such a massive and multifaceted problem. Moreover, one suspects that those appointed in the Brezhnev era, such as the minister of social security, Komarova, found it hard to accept the reversal of roles implied by the creation of the society. Disabled people would no longer be objects, to be divided into working hands and 'ballast', but in control of their own affairs and perhaps able to monitor the ministry itself.

Despite continuities running through the mid-1980s, 1985 was also a watershed. Chapter 4 discussed the increased official attention to disabled and elderly pensioners after 1985. In this context, the *Komsomol*'s role deserves mention, suggesting the need to slightly qualify generalizations often made about the organization's moribund condition. Before 1985 the *Komsomol* had had no official responsibility for dealing with disability issues. However, as early as March 1985, the *Korchaginets* club was encouraged by the fact that youth newspapers and *Komsomol* committees seemed to be adopting a more sympathetic approach towards them.⁶⁰ In 1987 the *Komsomol* Central Committee ordered local organs to 'improve' their work with disabled members.⁶¹ The *Komsomol*'s new concern with the problems of Afghan veterans was one reason for this involvement. Funds for Youth Initiatives (see Chapter 5) could also sponsor disabled activists and charities helping them. In Novosibirsk, for example, the disabled people's club which was created unofficially, and met in a park, in 1986, had by mid-1987 become associated with the Fund for Youth Initiatives and the city *Komsomol* committee had helped it organize the first local disabled people's sports festival.⁶² In Sverdlovsk, where by the mid-1980s Burkova, the founder of the *Korchaginets* Club, was a non-paid employee of the city *Komsomol* committee, the committee was equally helpful in establishing a city disabled people's organization.⁶³ In Serpukhov the *Komsomol* in 1987 published a brochure about the Club calling for the establishment of a VOI.⁶⁴

Glasnost was an essential element in the development of the disability movement, even though many problems had been discussed openly even before 1985. Now, however, the real squalor of residential homes was exposed and the existence of various interests and needs within the disabled community was acknowledged. *Komsomol'skaya pravda* was especially active in this respect.⁶⁵ The somewhat simplistic and moralistic approach often adopted by journalists and activists in the charity movement did not always facilitate adequate understanding of the issues. However, the accent on exposing examples of callousness suited the disabled people's cause, since one of their main concerns was to publicize violations of their rights. As Chapter 3 suggested, disabled activists had a history of linking up with journalists to advance their cause.

The chief factor leading to eventual success in early 1988 was the energetic campaign conducted by disabled activists.⁶⁶ In December 1985, for example, members of the *Korchaginets* Club and Moscow *Iskra* sent a letter to the Central Committee of the CPSU, raising the issue of a VOI.⁶⁷ The new sporting organizations too tried to take advantage of the new atmosphere of *perestroika* to win official recognition. Disabled sport was an issue which did not concern *Minsobes* and quickly ceased to be a taboo subject. It was here that disabled people made their first breakthrough. Despite official reluctance to invest money in the new venture,[68] in summer 1987 the Soviet Federation for Disabled People's Physical Culture was founded, to be followed in February 1988 by an RSFSR Federation for Disabled Sport.[69]

Meanwhile, during 1987 letters supporting the creation of VOI flooded into editorial offices and 'petitions rained on the Moscow authorities.'[70] *Komsomol'skaya pravda* arranged for a question to be asked about the founding of a VOI in the Supreme Soviet. In Moscow, where Yeltsin was first party secretary and the informal movement was more advanced than elsewhere, disabled people busily set up borough organizations and in December Moscow soviet approved the establishment of a city society for people with spinal and motor disabilities.[71]

In February 1988 'victory' was finally achieved on a national level: an organizing committee for a Russian Society was set up by *Minsobes* and in March 1988 the minister, Komarova, resigned.[72] Some provincial activists were convinced that the authorities had succumbed to pressure from regional action groups.[73] Muscovites stress that they played a particularly important role. Possibly the fact that one of the Muscovites had an influential connection was a significant factor; this seems to have been essential in securing the registration of many other voluntary organizations.[74]

2) The Creation of VOI as an Official/Grassroots Society

Joy that the campaign of so many years had been crowned with success quickly gave way to anxiety. References to 'our' society[75] were succeeded by the recognition that it was still necessary to fight to make sure it did not become 'theirs'. The use of 'we' and 'they' did not only make the normal Soviet distinction between the public and officialdom, but also between disabled and non-disabled people. It became clear that, to the ministries, VOI would be just like the veterans' organizations or the big funds – a *nomenklatura*-led, hierarchical organization. The new minister of social security, V. Kaznacheev, was soon speaking, to VOI representatives and in public, of the need for voluntary help to *prop up* state social services.[76] Voluntary, but not independent: it was pointed out in March 1988 that VOI was to be 'observed and monitored' by *Minsobes*.⁷⁷ *Minsobes* clearly viewed the society as 'its' new voluntary organization, perhaps making a comparison with the Health Ministry's FMZ, which was established one month later than VOI. However, the official rhetoric of VOI was in tune with the disabled people's own demands. The emphasis was on self-determination. The two organizations stood in curious contrast, reflecting one of the paradoxes of *perestroika* and the complete confusion now afflicting official ideology. The FMZ's basic premise, that disabled people were objects of compassion, was in direct opposition to VOI's main goals of 'facilitating the wide involvement of disabled people in public life'.⁷⁸ Both were radical and conservative in their own ways. The Fund had abandoned the old Soviet assumption that 'pity humiliates', while downplaying disabled people's desire for self-determination; VOI did the opposite.

By the time of its founding conference in August 1988 VOI already had 376,000 members in local branches and primary organizations.⁷⁹ 'Elections' to boards at various levels were according to lists of members prepared in advance, but nevertheless genuine activists did manage to merge their informal groups into the new organizations. Contrary to the expectations of disabled activists, the first president of VOI was not one of them, but A. Deryugin of the RSFSR Organization of Veterans. Presumably a *nomenklatura* appointment, he was 'elected' by the VOI Board in contravention of the Society's charter. Deryugin seemed to be committed to VOI's aims, but was not as active in pursuit of their cause as many would have liked. His appointment was perceived by some disabled activists as the first step – of many – to pack VOI with veterans and nomenklaturists.

Although where local disabled people's groups already existed these formed the basis of the VOI branch, many of the local and regional founding conferences were organized directly by social security departments. There were tensions between grassroots activists and bureaucrats. In Novosibirsk, for example, the society was said to be split between maximalists and gradualists in 1989.⁸⁰ The society's founder was a typical informal activist, whereas the official head of the Novosibirsk *oblast* organization, Petukhov, was a former party official. However, the presence of people like Petukhov was not necessarily a disadvantage. Petukhov had an excellent managerial style and established connections which he used skilfully in the interests of VOI members.[81]

Unlike many activists in the new voluntary sector, who were already suspicious of 'centres' in any form, most of the disabled people who helped set up VOI in 1988 were convinced that it had to exist on a national level. (Initially, they were disappointed that a USSR society had not been created. However, with the gradual disintegration of the USSR this concern decreased.) A Moscow office was needed to exert the kind of influence on government that was required to get to the heart of disabled people's problems. Specifically, this meant new legislation on a range of issues plus the 'return' of enterprises which disabled people perceived to have been stolen from them when *Promkooperatsiya* was closed in 1960.

3) VOI: Achievements and Identity Crisis

VOI soon found that attitudes in *Minsobes* were well-entrenched, despite the change of minister. However, thanks to the effects of the new political system and the efforts of disabled people, in 1989 official policy began to shift in the direction of recognizing disabled people's rights.

The spring 1989 USSR CPD, with its debates on poverty and privilege, presented the first opportunity for a breakthrough. The Congress sped the introduction of the new pension law — which contained some improvements for disabled people[82] — and set up a Supreme Soviet Committee on veterans' and disabled peoples' affairs with VOI-sponsored deputy Zaslavsky in charge of a working group on disability issues. The group set about producing a law on disabled people.[83] The law appeared in December 1990 as 'Basic Principles of Social Protection of Disabled People in the USSR'. The definition of disability was widened, discrimination against disabled people was stated to be illegal and a comprehensive programme of improvements was set out.[84] With the onset of the 'war of laws and parliaments' a USSR law was not very useful. The USSR law was adopted on a temporary basis in Karelia[85] but seems to have had little impact in the rest of Russia. VOI's first three priorities at the end of 1990 were to make the provisions of the USSR law effective by getting through an equivalent Russian one and local-level resolutions; to draw up a programme for protecting disabled people during the transition to the market economy; and changing the RSFSR electoral law to establish a quota system for disabled people, so their election to the parliament would be ensured.[86] However, the electoral law was not changed and the Russian law on disabled people failed to progress beyond a draft before the August coup.[87]

The other main goal of the society – financial independence – was addressed by a February 1990 Council of Ministers resolution 'On Means to Improve Social Services for Disabled People in the USSR', which offered incentives to enterprises which transferred to the jurisdiction of VOI. However, by July 1991 only 12 enterprises had been transferred. Neither local authorities nor factory workers were easy to persuade that it would be to their benefit. VOI stepped up its campaign to retrieve all the enterprises 'stolen' under Khrushchev, with a vain appeal to soviets at all levels.[88] Also by July 1991, the society had only 549 specially created enterprises and 250 co-operatives, very unevenly distributed across Russia: this was a basis on which 12 per cent of VOI organizations at most could hope to become self-financing.[89]

However, legislative change and economic achievements were not the only criteria by which one could judge success. VOI's membership had increased to 1,100,000 by autumn 1991.[90] This numerical expansion was initially accompanied by enormous optimism. It is impossible to overestimate the importance to their members of emerging from their previous isolation. To make contact with other disabled people was for many a novel experience. The entertainments and tours organized by VOI gave a new dimension to the lives of people who had formerly been housebound. Also, immediately after VOI's creation, local soviets felt obliged to issue resolutions offering concessions to disabled people and including recommendations for vital changes to town planning and architecture. Unfortunately, as in the case of USSR and RSFSR legislation, many of these provisions remained on paper only. However, in a situation of acute shortage, even temporary access to goods and services – from bibles to swimming pools – was a welcome small-scale gain.

Despite such successes, many VOI activists were beset by pessimism as many of their initial expectations remained unfulfilled. As one Moscow disabled leader commented in January 1991, 'It has turned out that on paper the disabled people's cause is doing well, but in real life it's pretty hard.'[91] Increasingly, bitterness and divisions at the local level reflected divergent attitudes towards the role of VOI.

There was sometimes a sense of division between disabled people who lived in their own homes and those in residential care. In general, VOI catered mostly for the former, although there were also branches which attempted to address the needs of people in residential homes.[92] Perhaps more divisive was the issue of whether VOI was primarily a self-help group or a charity. VOI's official statements stated that it was the former, as, for example, its president Deryugin made plain on a number of occasions, including in a letter to Gorbachev.[93] However, as the economic crisis deepened in 1990–1 the society began to recognize the need for charitable funds. In Novosibirsk, president Petukhov specifically forbade the distribution of individual aid. He created antagonism by doing so, since many ordinary members of VOI perceived the organization to be a charitable one. It was said that in Nizhnii Novgorod the society's membership doubled as soon as local branches gained access to small stocks of deficit goods, while a Moscow survey revealed that 86 per cent of members would not have joined VOI had the shops been full of goods.[94]

In the worsening economic situation, many disabled people increasingly felt they needed charity; yet many disabled activists lamented the loss of sight of long-term goals and the transformation into a poor-relief agency. It was not just an issue of wrong priorities. When VOI became a distributor of goods in short supply, the atmosphere in local societies soured: by definition, not everyone could receive the shortage goods. Local organizations became paralysed as ordinary members began to regard the management as 'they', not 'us', and to suspect that they were only working for VOI out of greed.[95]

A further problem for VOI was the perception of many local activists that the central apparatus was not achieving enough, for example because it had not pushed through the Russian law on disabled people, and because, unlike VOS, it did not try to get special concessions for physically disabled people written into the new pensions and benefits law.[96] They complained that it was ineffective because it had absorbed the traditional Soviet bureaucratic habits. Such accusations were not entirely fair, but they were founded not only on knowledge or rumour about what VOI actually did. Perhaps more important than any connection with the actual facts about VOI was that such perceptions were a manifestation of the general tendency throughout the USSR towards localism and mistrust of the 'centre' in the last years of *perestroika*.

4) Other Groups Uniting People with Disabilities and Illnesses
It was almost inevitable that under these strains the disabled people's movement should fragment, just as so many voluntary organizations and other independent associations did during the *perestroika* years. In particular, parents of children with disabilities, young people and people who had disabilities other than spinal-motor ones often left, disillusioned to set up their own associations. As the founder of the USSR Association of Young Disabled People's Organizations[97] explained, 'We need independence, because young people have their own specific problems.Without the direct involvement of young people no one will try to solve them.'[98] The Association was established 'to fulfil the functions which are not performed by the social security departments or by VOI (which has now become more or less a service-providing organization).'[99] A number of the new organizations, more outward-looking in some respects than VOI, cultivated and benefited from links with international organizations. This was true in particular of the young people's organization *Apparel*', which had good connections with Mobility International.[100]

The mushrooming of new associations had begun to take place even before VOI fragmented; indeed, the constant proliferation of new groups was typical of the voluntary sector. Some of the new associations were formed on a national level. More often, they were local, sometimes deliberately so.

The most widespread organizations for people suffering from a particular illness were societies of people with diabetes. While diabetes in developed Western countries is regarded as a manageable disease, in the USSR people who developed diabetes in their youth were often regarded as disabled and few expected to live to old age. There were an estimated 600,000 to one million insulin-dependent Soviet people with diabetes in 1990. Hence this was a serious problem both in scale and nature. Moreover, it was a problem which intensified as economic reform brought disruptions in the supply of insulin and sucrose-free food items. The situation was particularly acute for people living in rural areas and small towns. For example, in the small town of Svetlyi, Kaliningrad *oblast*, there was said, supposedly because of the absence of specialist doctors, to be no attempt to regulate the diet of people with diabetes, leading to high mortality rates. Nor was it even possible to perform the simple test for diabetes without travelling many kilometres to the city of Kaliningrad. 'Understanding that the state was incapable of resolving the problems of people with diabetes, they felt forced to unite within a Society of People with Diabetes'[101] in December 1988. The Svetlyi activists realized that in fact relatively simple measures could have a big impact: they improved the supply of diagnostic strips and acquired a British video informing people about how they themselves could manage the illness. The Svetlyi group numbered 400 by September 1990.[102]

In big cities membership could be very large. For instance, in Leningrad/Petersburg, membership grew from 50 in 1989 to 10,000 by October 1993. The societies seem to have been extremely active, an activity which can be partly explained by the fact that parts of the solution, such as spreading information, were relatively easy to organize.[103]

As already mentioned in connection with parents' groups, not just VOI but also VOG – as a long-standing, official society – was now under competition. On a national level, the Russia Charitable Association of Deaf People was founded in Moscow in August 1991[104] and an independent Russian Chess Federation of Deaf People was created in Sverdlovsk.[105] Local branches of VOG sometimes experienced a corresponding decline: in Pskov, for example, the society had 171 volunteers up to 1990 but only 26 by the time of coup.[106] One of VOG's problems, mirrored in VOI, was that it was perceived to neglect the interests of people who were profoundly disabled. This was illustrated by VOG's traditional lack of interest in promoting Russian sign language – a deficiency which profoundly deaf activists now attempted to remedy.[107]

Afghan Veterans and Chernobyl Liquidators

The veterans of the war in Afghanistan and the conscripts who helped clean up after Chernobyl may be considered to form a single category. They were politically significant, since their problems were the result of the two major Soviet disasters of the 1980s, disasters which were in the public mind directly linked to the failings of the old-style Soviet regime and provoked powerful emotions. Not only were Afghanistan and Chernobyl caused by massive miscalculations, but also their consequences had been at first concealed from the Soviet public, so that the veterans of both had a crusading task, in which they were helped by journalists, to whom the Afghan and Chernobyl stories often had more appeal than the problems of people with diabetes or rural pensioners.

There was also a similarity in that members of both groups were almost exclusively male, and usually young. This meant that they could normally have expected to play a more active role in public life than the mothers who constituted the members of many other self-help groups. In the case of both types of veteran disability was widespread. 18,000 people were disabled as a result of the Afghan war. The liquidators, too, increasingly developed health problems. On the other hand, many Afghan veterans were physically healthy and able to set up flourishing organizations which enjoyed a commercial success not attainable by many other self-help groups. (Success presented its own dangers, in terms of connections with crime.) Both liquidators and *afgantsy* had a strong sense of collective identity engendered by the horrors they had experienced. This promoted the creation of self-help organizations.

Afghan veterans began creating their own informal groups in the early 1980s, long before the authorities tolerated open discussion of the war. It was only in 1986 that the *Komsomol* began to pay serious attention to the Afghan veterans and encourage the creation of veterans' clubs. During the *perestroika* period numerous organizations emerged on both local and national levels. Altogether, by July 1991, the main Soviet Union-wide organization, the Union of Afghan Veterans, claimed to represent more than 300,000 veterans.[108]

To some extent, the disabled veterans' cause was the same as that of other disabled people. For example, since many of the veterans were amputees, their plight helped focus public attention on the wider problem of the inadequacy of state-produced prostheses. Many articles in the national press emphasized the seriousness of the problem and publicized the attempts of charities and cooperatives to tackle it. However, some Afghan veterans tended to remain aloof from other organizations, even those of disabled people. This was partly because of alienation from society in general, a phenomenon sometimes described as 'Vietnam syndrome'.[109]

Nevertheless, their organizations performed many functions similar to those of other self-help groups. The Penza branch of the Union of Afghan Veterans,[110] for example, was simultaneously a social club, a charity offering help to veterans and their families and a society devoted to honouring the memory of fallen comrades.[111] The Novosibirsk society had several additional goals, including military training of children and the acquisition of housing for members, the most urgent problem for many Soviet young people.[112] Military education also featured in the programmes of Afghan veterans' groups elsewhere.[113]

In 1986, the year of the accident, the Chernobyl liquidators were officially praised to the skies. However, this did not assure them more permanent attention. Within a few years, throughout the Soviet Union they were experiencing a 'mass of [interconnected] medical,... social and practical everyday problems'.[114] The liquidators were angry that records of the levels of radiation they received had been deliberately and systematically falsified and that they were denied disabled status.[115] They were offended and disturbed by the way the government handled the Chernobyl funds. The money placed in the State Bank was used to compensate the state for the clean-up operation, while there was considerable secrecy about how the rest was spent. The liquidators were offered special privileges and concessions as compensation by the government only in March 1990.[116] However, by then they had decided that the only way forward was to unite within their own organization, the Chernobyl Union.[117] One of the Union's objectives was to create an association of independent lawyers to defend the liquidators' rights.[118]

CONCLUSIONS

Self-help groups formed the major part of the Russian voluntary sector. Although they began to emerge in substantial numbers at about the same time as did the charities (1987–8) they increasingly overtook them. There was also a sense in which they were perceived as having greater validity and right to speak for disadvantaged people. The self-help groups were also significant because they addressed the needs of so many Soviet citizens. VOI, the largest society, had a membership of over a million. Often self-help group members were people who had been totally outside public affairs in the past and for whom the experience of forming a voluntary group was extremely significant in itself as a personal experience. Moreover, the groups addressed issues of pressing concern: forming a self-help group was a rational course of action in the economic climate.

In general, the organizations were locally based, out of necessity but also because this was desirable in the climate of 1990–1, with the 'war of laws and parliaments' making local authorities the people to lobby. Local branches even of VOI were closely linked to their local community, rather than branches of a national organization, with whom they often found it hard to identify.

Within the new voluntary sector, disabled groups and charities concerned with the needs of disabled people occupied a prominent place. For example, disability was the sole or partial focus of two-thirds to three-quarters of organizations created before the coup, according to one Moscow survey.[119]

Self-help group members would often have agreed with the analysis presented in Chapter 2: their most serious handicap was that they were not part of the working population

Self-Help Organizations 139

and therefore denied full citizenship. Creating jobs for unemployed members was the aspiration of many organizations: a difficult objective, despite the creation of a number of cooperatives. In the circumstances, mutual emotional support plus energetic lobbying of local authorities for extra benefits were more common and successful activities.

7 The Communist Response

'It's already a Soviet axiom that any novelty can only be pushed through by waging battle. Unfortunately this applies to many socially beneficial projects... Today [September 1989], the creation of each [charity]... can only be achieved after overcoming a mass of bureaucratic impediments, bizarre and manipulative official regulations.'[1]

'What new... political circumstances made it possible to create your organization [in 1990]?'
RESPONDENT A: *'A [temporary] warm spell in the political weather.'*
RESPONDENT B: *'The fact that people started to feel sure that they themselves could actually change something.'*[2]

INTRODUCTION

This chapter and Chapter 8 will discuss issues connected with the erosion of party power as the voluntary sector evolved in 1985–91. After examining how officials and volunteers often thought in zero-sum terms – assuming a gain for one side was a loss for the other – Chapter 7 analyses the reactions of communist authorities, Chapter 8 the organizations' role in building political and civil society. It assesses how much ground the communists had lost by August 1991 and discusses who was to blame – or thank – for this outcome.

EXPECTATION OF CONFLICT ON BOTH 'SIDES'

The purpose of the Soviet system as it existed until 1989–90 was to maintain CPSU power. Although the system was not totalitarian, party policy was totalizing in aspiration, aiming to control the entire society. Any transformation of the system represented a threat to the power of the communist party. Substitution of the Soviet welfare system by informal organizations and direct attacks on the CPSU over welfare issues (for example the healthcare and pension privileges of the elite) are part of the same process of eroding party power. Even when the issues addressed by charities and self-help groups seemed non-political, the principle of maintaining party control was at stake. Leningrad officials 'categorically refused to register [the apparently inoffensive *Miloserdie* Society] because they did not want to accord recognition to a society which would not have to obey anyone's orders'.[3] At a moment of truth, the first day of the August 1991 coup, a leader of the new welfare movement was informed by a local council official that he expected *all* independent organizations to be liquidated.[4]

Since the party's monopoly of power could only suffer, not benefit from the establishment of a real voluntary sector, attempts to create one were a zero-sum game. As the voluntary sector grew, so the party lost. Conversely, the party's successful assertion of its power to rule in the old manner represented a loss for the voluntary sector. Advocates of a middle ground found that ground cut away from under their feet. Compromises *were* made between voluntary organizations and 'the authorities' – otherwise the organizations could not have survived – but often the two had opposing interests. The party was attempting to coopt the NGO, while the NGO compromised only to ensure its survival and was resistant to any hint of cooption. Compromises which allowed organizations to survive even partly independently were *ipso facto* a loss to the regime.

The double failure of hardliners to prohibit the voluntary sector and of party reformers to create a middle ground is illustrated by the story of *Miloserdie* and the Charity and Health Foundation, FMZ. In 1987–8, as *Miloserdie* societies sprang up at grassroots level, the party lost control of charitable initiatives. Hence the panic displayed in Leningrad at the formation of *Miloserdie*. In autumn 1988 the CPSU gained a temporary victory with the establishment of a rival institution, the FMZ, which was granted a monopoly on charity. *Miloserdie* societies were told they had no reason to exist and refused registration. Yet the party had not won the battle. *Miloserdie* continued to operate. Moreover, the FMZ could not be moulded into an organization acceptable both 'above' and 'below'. FMZ, a typical child of *perestroika* – half 'Ministry of Charity'[5] and half NGO – was not a viable institution. The two halves went separate ways. On a national level, the FMZ was maintaining the Soviet system, run by nomenklaturists, working 'according to plan', its parliamentary deputies even defending the integrity of the USSR. On a local level, the FMZ less effectively propped up the system of party rule and even undermined it as local branches sought autonomy from the centre. The usual *perestroika* momentum was at play: the seemingly irreversible trend was away from party control and towards local autonomy.

The political environment and, more specifically, the decline of CPSU legitimacy were crucial factors in determining this dynamic of decreasing control.

In 1988, when the FMZ was created, both CPSU reformers and non-party critics could agree on a 'moral crisis' analysis of social problems to which official approval of charity seemed an appropriate response. Official rhetoric could still be believed by grassroots activists, who were able to equate *perestroika* from above with *perestroika* from below. This was nicely illustrated at the founding conference of VOI, also in 1988. Minister of Social Security Kaznacheev presented the creation of VOI as an opportunity for disabled people to leave the 'roadside sward and take to the high road of full participation in *perestroika*' and excited delegates swallowed the official line and voted for the pre-prepared resolutions and charter. Later they explained their failure to push through their own more radical drafts with the words: 'We came from far away, where we had never managed to win any of our struggles. And here we were promised everything.'[6]

In 1988, at the Nineteenth Party Conference, the ruling elite had adopted Gorbachev's programme of democratization, which entailed both party reform and the introduction of multi-candidate parliamentary and local elections. However, elite commitment to genuine change was often far from wholehearted. This soon became apparent in all spheres. The gap between words and deeds was also experienced by members of the voluntary sector who wished to translate promises of pluralism into reality. By 1991, after several years of constant struggle between independent groups and authorities of all types, the NGOs were often less trusting than they had been in the middle years of *perestroika*. They expected to achieve nothing without a battle. Moreover, thanks to the radicalization of *glasnost*, there was much greater willingness among activists, as among the general public, to see social problems as systemic, i.e. rooted in the overall political problem of CPSU power. Correspondingly, action independently of the party seemed more attractive and voluntary organizations which were independent of the CPSU often had greater legitimacy than the big funds. However, independence from CPSU supervision frequently went hand in hand with increased dependence on handouts from the local soviets in 1990–1.

A Range of Typical Perceptions, Official and Unofficial

1. *'I personally am against the creation of a Miloserdie Society... [Granin] isn't properly informed about our work. Look at our annual reports. Our house is in perfect order'. (Leningrad social security official, 1987.)*[7]
This was the archetypal pre-1988 *Minsobes* response. The state *alone* could provide welfare services. The proof was in the official statistics: a typical conflation of paper with reality. Groups who suggested otherwise were told that 'they should not exist'.[8] Although the appointment of Kaznacheev as Minister of Social Security in 1988 led to different official rhetoric and to permission for VOI, nevertheless the *sobesy* were still active at a local level in thwarting voluntary organizations.

2. *'Charity has become a widespread phenomenon of Soviet society. We can only welcome this fact. However, to a certain extent charity has become ungovernable.' (Minister of Social Security, Viktor Kaznacheev, 1990.)*[9]
Kaznacheev was appointed in 1988 but his statement – admittedly in *Pravda* – betrays an old-fashioned impulse to divide phenomena into two opposite categories: 'uncontrollable/unwelcome' and 'controllable/good'. Kaznacheev went on to remark that the only way in which all social needs could be met would be by 'a ministry, professionally engaged in charity'. This confusing concept had a basis in reality – the

establishment in March 1990 by *Goskomtrud* of the All-Union Association 'Caringness and Charity' (*Gumanizm i miloserdie*).[10] The new association was apparently supposed to be the umbrella or reins of the new voluntary sector. If the Ministry was still engaged in this type of controlling activity as late as March 1990 – the same month that the party's leading role was written out of the constitution – conflict with the uncontrollable grassroots organizations was only to be expected.

3. 'Extremists... are aiming to seize the leading positions in the [Memorial] movement, which... could lead to the formation of a new socio-political organization in conflict with party and state authorities... They are attempting to create a society with a brief to supervise and direct the process of democratization'. (Secretariat of the CPSU Central Committee, secret resolution, November 1988.)[11]
In this confidential document, the party officials showed that their thinking was based on assumptions of 'ideological struggle', not Gorbachevian 'pluralism of opinions'. They believed that *Memorial* members could be neatly divided into friends and enemies of the regime. *Memorial* foes were viewed as a mirror image of their communist opponents. Rather than supposing that *Memorial* might be *different* – genuinely committed to the ideals of democracy – the Secretariat thought that *Memorial* shared the officials' view of democratization as something to be controlled. *Memorial* supposedly wanted to exercise its own monopoly on democratization. It was also attributed with 'intolerable' pretensions to a monopoly of discussion about Stalin's Terror.

Fish describes the 'utter inability and/or unwillingness of power holders to deal seriously and imaginatively with autonomous political actors'.[12] His generalization is equally valid with respect to the semi-political actors of *Memorial* or the Soldiers' Mothers committees, and to a large extent also to apparently non-political activists.[13]

4. 'The newly created [Charity and Health] Foundation is hardly likely to be able to compete with individual, spontaneously created societies, uniting people for whom charity is a calling and a spiritual gift.' (O. Kutateladze, Odessa charity activist, 1988.)[14]
Activists' perceptions of the moral superiority of grassroots action was also a factor promoting polarization. In similar

vein, a visitor to Leningrad *Miloserdie* in 1989 was convinced that it was 'nourished by the living spring of popular initiative'. She saw this as an *antidote* to 'infection by the disease of bureaumania'. The use of opposing metaphors – healthy nourishment versus disease – reveals the same 'conflictual' expectations. Like Kutateladze, the journalist believed – having chatted to volunteers about their motivation – that 'real compassion, unofficial ("informal") and non-organized, brings enormous satisfaction'.[15] By implication, official and organized compassion (as sponsored by the FMZ) was not worthwhile.

5. '*We thought that the local authorities would be gladdened by our endeavours, but the opposite turned out to be the case. Unofficial charity became viewed as 'alternative' and therefore dangerous.*' *(E. Bokova, leader of Voronezh Miloserdie.)*[16]
'*We were always in favour of a constructive approach but the authorities never reciprocated.*' *(S. Kropachev, Krasnodar Memorial.)*[17]
Both Bokova and Kropachev suggest that the expectation of conflict stemmed from the authorities, who in turn created a conflictual situation. This was probably usually correct, though the conflicts sometimes evolved out of a pre-history of personal antagonism. Bokova, for instance, having gained entrance to the founding conference of the Voronezh FMZ, was disconcerted to see on the platform a local official described by Bokova in a newspaper article – which cost Bokova her job – as 'merciless'. It was difficult to believe in the FMZ as a potential middle ground where all official and informal charity activists could unite when they had to overcome such bad memories, dating from a more repressive period.

6. '*The Miloserdie Society is like a reproach, a challenge to the state apparatus*'. *(N. D'yachenko, Leningrad 'Miloserdie', 1989.)*[18]
'*The local social security agencies, whose activity loses its meaning when set beside that of Lyubutka [a society which exposed misclassification of children with learning difficulties], are in a state of undeclared war with its members*'.[19]
D'yachenko's comment on the phenomenon to which she referred elsewhere as 'trial by charity'[20] brings us full circle to quotation 1 and state officials' sensitivity to criticism. The

volunteers by their deeds embarrassed the bureaucrats, who reacted by waging war. D'yachenko pointed out that, in the public debate on the *Miloserdie* society, opposition to the society's founding was expressed most vehemently by senior officials from local state agencies who *should* have been coping with the problems Granin exposed.[21]

Uncomfortable comparisons could be made. Publicity about the terrible living conditions of people who had been persecuted by the regime inevitably provoked comparison with the privileges of their persecutors: comparisons which can hardly have put officials at their ease. A *Rabotnitsa* reader, commenting on the magazine's plans to set up a charity for victims of the Terror, suggested that the charity should be funded from the purses of party officials. 'It's time to strip people who murdered, informed, crippled and interrogated of their inflated pensions...handouts and benefits. It is they who should be the main contributors towards compensating people who suffered.'[22]

With attitudes like these, conflict between state and voluntary organizations was likely to be widespread. Of course, reality is always complex and nuanced: conflict would sometimes be accompanied by compromise.

THE RANGE OF OFFICIAL RESPONSES

Butterfield and Weigle suggest a typology of relations between unofficial organizations and the authorities – up to 1990 – consisting of five categories of state response: cooperation, benign tolerance, attempted preemption, attempted cooptation and complete antagonism.[23] This provides a helpful starting point, though it is hard to accept Butterfield and Weigle's suggestion that 'benign tolerance' was the most common response. Perhaps their judgement was made a little too early. By contrast, Urban suggests that 'neglect and repression remained the predominant response'.[24] Aggression, in the form of responses 3–5, seems to have been more frequent than cooperation or tolerance. All three responses – preemption, cooption and manifestations of outright aggression – were often employed at once, together with attempts to plant party reliables to supervise the NGOs.

In general, the authorities attempted to control the new movements by using 'the whole arsenal of methods at their disposal', to employ a standard Soviet metaphor. At the same time, they could appear inconsistent, helping one month and obstructing the next. As the following account suggests, there were many paradoxes and inconsistencies arising from 'the splintered, multi-agency, multi-level nature of the state itself'.[25]

In addition, the pattern of response changed over the years, as *perestroika* passed through successive stages. In general, the charities experienced the same responses from the authorities as did more political organizations, though this was not always the case. Up to 1989 both sides trod cautiously, although there were local instances of greater tolerance by the authorities (such as in Moscow under Yeltsin's tutelage from 1985 to 1987). The attitude of the central party authorities hardened towards the non-official organizations during the election campaign of early 1989,[26] but it would seem that some exception was made for charities. In Novosibirsk, the directors of houses of culture were warned not to offer their premises to any non-official organizations – except the local *Miloserdie* Society.[27] In general, independent groups of all kinds found it easier to operate after July 1989, when Gorbachev instructed the Central Committee on the need to cooperate with them. Moscow *Miloserdie*, for example, found its path much smoother from the second half of 1989.[28] Another Moscow-based association claimed that 'in the summer of 1989 such organizations got registered easily and in large numbers'.[29] However, Moscow was not representative of all provincial towns, where politics often changed more slowly.

With the rewriting of Article 6 of the Constitution in March 1990 and the law on associations of October 1990, registration should have become more straightforward, but of course communist officials did not necessarily accept the end of their monopoly and both local and nationwide organizations continued to experience obstruction.

Elections also changed the political environment. The 1989 USSR Congress of People's Deputies, in its role as a motor of *glasnost*, brought poverty unequivocally onto the public agenda. In those few places where 'democrats' controlled local councils after March 1990, this aided cooperation with NGOs. Moreover, commissions for charitable and other voluntary organizations were set up in the Supreme Soviet and most local soviets.[30]

Cooperation

Cooperation was a more likely response from 'democratic' authorities who themselves had an interest in undermining party rule. For example, in Moscow's radical-controlled Oktyabr borough, the (disabled) chairperson, Il'ya Zaslavsky, was able to help the *Invachess* Association for disabled and non-disabled chess players.[31] Mayor Popov and his democratic colleagues in Moscow were helpful to the Pushkin Society, whereas the more conservative *oblast* authorities were sometimes obstructive, despite the society's official status.[32] *Memorial* branches also found life easier from 1990 in some places, apparently because of improved relations with local soviets.[33] In Orsk, the head of the local VOI was impressed by the speed with which 'a group of new, democratically inclined deputies' took up the cause of physically disabled residential home inmates who were in danger of being reclassfied as 'psychiatric' patients. The deputies had cause to be helpful: they, with local journalists, were engaged in a battle to free the local newspaper from control by the city party committee. The paper's independence was ostentatiously demonstrated by its publication of a biting letter about the reclassification project – under a picture of barbed wire and searchlights, symbolizing the home's prison camp status. (However, direct criticism of the party committee and Ministry were edited out: the democrats' bravery had its limits!)[34]

In some places a democratic or semi-democratic soviet was at odds with a hardline executive committee. In Bryansk, one NGO contrasted the help they had received from the soviets with the unhelpful stance of the executive committee, CPSU and *Komsomol*. In Leningrad a similar contrast was experienced.[35]

A conservative local authority could be pressurized into co-operation by the more radical Kremlin leadership. In Lipetsk, a letter from Aleksander Yakovlev, enquiring as to the position of former 'enemies of the people' in the *oblast*, was followed by a reduction in persecution.[36]

Officials who had overwhelming practical problems to solve were sometimes more likely to accept voluntary help. One Moscow doctor, after describing staffing shortages at her hospital, characterized the help of local believers as 'an absolute godsend'.[37] The Leningrad police were willing to cooperate with the city's first informal group for drug addicts, perhaps because 'they were the people in day to day contact at the grassroots level with the issues and therefore better informed.'[38]

Conversely, distance from responsibility for a specific situation could encourage officials at the centre to be more tolerant than local bureaucrats who felt more under threat. The Leningrad drug addicts' group found the Moscow health authorities supportive[39] – and this enabled them to survive the hostility of the Leningrad health establishment.

Even within a single office there was unlikely to be monolithic unity, and successful NGOs were sometimes able to cultivate sympathetic individual bureaucrats. For instance, within the executive committees of two Moscow boroughs (Oktyabr and Lenin) helpful officials – acting, it was stressed, as *individuals* – aided a children's charity find premises.[40]

Occasionally cooperation by the authorities was attributed to admission of defeat, in the face of persistent lobbying. The Leningrad Society of People with Diabetes claimed that the soviet executive committee and CPSU had to give in to their badgering, because 'they recognized our determination'.[41] In Chelyabinsk, Lyudmila Rogova was able to establish a kindergarten for children with cerebral palsy thanks to her enormous persistence in pestering and successfully persuading local officials. Some of them, knowing that they would lose the battle of wills, would apparently avoid meeting her by taking refuge at a tedious meeting or distant outpost of their empire. However, they did not always escape.[42]

Finally, a one-off act of cooperation could be used to 'neutralize' a troublesome voluntary group. This is what seems to have happened in Samara, where a thousand-strong group of parents with large families was presented with allotments by the local authorities. The parents then had plenty to keep them busy, and stopped criticizing the authorities over other issues.[43]

Avoidance and Procrastination

'No one said "No" – those times had passed! – but neither did they say "Yes"'.[44]

Butterfield and Weigle class non-intervention as 'benign tolerance'; more often, 'unhelpfulness' might be a better label. Few, if any, organizations could manage entirely without help from the authorities. They needed premises and, if they were at all ambitious, they needed a bank account, which meant applying for registration. NGOs were not happy when, as the Petrozavodsk *Memorial* president expressed it, 'Nobody interferes, but nobody helps either'.[45]

Not surprisingly, in the early days of the voluntary sector – until about 1989 – local authorities were often bewildered about how to react to the emergence of unofficial charities. They sensed the absence of a 'common language with the alternative organization[s]'[46] and tended to keep well clear. Bokova experienced this in Voronezh in summer 1988. 'I went to the *oblast Komsomol* committee and asked them to help found a *Miloserdie* society like the Leningrad one [already registered]. They told me, "Try to do it [yourself] and if it works we'll help you". I turned to the new leadership of the *oblast* social security department. "It's not very likely to work," was their response. I telephoned the chair of the Red Cross. In reply: "What good is such a society to us?"'[47]

One might suppose that the authorities' hesitation would be particularly acute after the axeing of the Secretariat in September 1988. Ryzhkov and Ligachev, for example, both complained about how local officials felt lost without Central Committee guidance.[48] On the other hand, the creation of the FMZ, also in September 1988, made the situation clear at least with regard to *Miloserdie* groups: they were not to have a place among officially-sanctioned local charities.

As voluntary organizations grew in size, local authorities must have felt intimidated by the scale of need unmasked. Associations of large families, for example, could be several thousand families' strong. In 1991 the Perm Union of [nearly 5,000] Large Families was still requesting attention. A journalist suggested that the authorities' persistant avoidance resulted from their realization that such families had so many grievances that the problems were impossible for them to solve.[49] In Moscow, Leningrad and Voronezh large families' organizations had similar experience of local authorities' refusal to help.[50]

Avoidance of giving or receiving help could also stem from fears of 'trial by charity'. This presumably explains why, for example, the Leningrad Society of People with Diabetes paradoxically found it harder to get support from the organizations which had a direct welfare role – the trade unions and social security departments – than from the the communist party and local council.[51] When *Miloserdie* activists visited a residential home for elderly people they found the door locked. The administration seemed to suggest that they regarded it as a 'closed institution'.[52] Bokova, in her capacity as a journalist, had even been escorted from one Voronezh home by the militia.[53] Conditions in residential homes were so appalling and corruption and theft apparently so widespread that trial by charity might be followed by judicial trials.

The authorities might, conversely, be too complacent to admit that voluntary groups needed help.[54] The party committee in Elektrostal, Moscow *oblast*, did not offer financial help to the local *Miloserdie* group but, in 1991, was providing 'ideological help' instead.[55] Alternatively, charities and self-help groups might simply be too far down the authorities' list of priorities: they could be too preoccupied by more direct aspects of the power struggle to deal with voluntary organizations. The head of the Disabled People's Football Association believed that the authorities were too 'concerned with saving their own skins' to help his organization.[56] Similarly, Pskov VOG blamed the *Komsomol*'s indifference on its preoccupation with recruitment (to counteract the mass defections of the *perestroika* years).[57]

Being an officially-recognized organization was not necessarily a guarantee of state support. Rather the reverse: the party-state authorities might expect the organization to deal with 'its' clients singlehandedly. Pskov VOG was consistently refused aid from the CPSU and social security departments.[58] A Leningrad branch of VOI found that, far from helping VOI, the social security department expected VOI to 'provide for' disabled people the state could not help.[59]

Preemption

As already suggested, the party attempted to create or manipulate spurious 'voluntary' organizations to address the problems of the welfare state. These official organizations could be used to preempt unofficial organizations with the same agenda.

As soon as the FMZ was created in September 1988, local authorities began to make life difficult for the *Miloserdie* activists. In 'a whole series of towns',[60] including Voronezh, Novosibirsk and Moscow, *Miloserdie* societies were told that they would not be registered because they were now superfluous. In Moscow, the issue was promotion from 'association' to the status of 'society', with the right to sponsor the creation of other NGOs. This refusal to register was experienced despite the fact that as recently as the previous month the Moscow *gorkom* had instructed borough party committees to cooperate with the 'public' charity movement.[61] After they had been refused registration, the Moscow *Miloserdie* volunteers wrote a letter of complaint to Gorbachev and found themselves summoned to the *gorkom*.[62]

In Voronezh, *Miloserdie* activists unsuccessfully nominated Bokova for election to the FMZ board: a spontaneous challenge which threw the 'pre-decided' candidates into a temporary flurry. *Miloserdie*, refused registration, was allowed to continue as a 'group' but its inferior status was painstakingly and humiliatingly demonstrated.[63]

Although FMZ's national officials on several occasions stated that they welcomed cooperation with independent activists, in the circumstances it is not surprising that the activists adopted a somewhat sceptical attitude to the Foundation. They, and their independent groups, continued to exist, so the official attempt at preemption may be regarded as a failure, despite the fact that most *Miloserdie* groups remained unregistered.

Attempts to preempt *Memorial* began in autumn 1988. The Central Committee tried to turn *Memorial* into a fund, organized by loyal citizens who desired merely to build a memorial and help former political prisoners.[64] In 1989 a certain Numerov, widely regarded as a KGB plant, set up a breakaway society the revealing name of Moscow Association of

Victims of *Illegal* Repressions. (Repressions conducted by political leaders other than Stalin were by implication legal.) Russian, Soviet and provincial Associations soon followed. 'Suddenly, all at the same time, in different towns, alternative, fraudulent organizations emerged and succeeded in registering with incredible speed. They were showered with golden rain, in exchange for refusing [to adopt] political programmes.'[65] In Moscow they failed, however, to siphon off older and more conservative members of the movement. Although genuine separate organizations for victims and their families did emerge, *Memorial* remained supported by a cross-section of opinion.[66] In this instance, therefore, preemption was not a successful ploy.

Cooption and *kontrol'*

Cooption involved neutralizing an institution by drawing it onto the 'official' side of the battlefield. Since this was often done by packing the organization with communists, it seems appropriate to consider also in this section the related issue of *kontrol'* or party supervision.

One tactic for cooption was to force a declaration of loyalty to the regime. Members of voluntary societies were persuaded to denounce or expel dissidents and other 'anti-Soviet elements', thus displaying their own political reliability.

The authorites may have believed that they had secured a pledge of loyalty from Moscow disabled activists not to make a nuisance of themselves in December 1987, at the time when disabled people's lobbying for VOI reached its peak. That winter two articles in *Moskovskaya pravda* attacked dissident Action Group leader Yurii Kiselev and his Radio Liberty connection, partly through the mouths of Moscow disabled campaigners. They made clear that the 'anti-Soviet' Kiselev represented no one and that the Moscow Society of Disabled People would work closely with the party.[67] The device was perhaps not entirely effective. Members of the Moscow organizing committee were not genuinely committed to working closely with the party.[68]

In Novosibirsk, *Miloserdie* was told that it would only be given permanent premises if believers were expelled from the organization. Novosibirsk *Memorial* was refused registration unless it expelled members of the Democratic Union.⁶⁹

Cooption could also be achieved by permitting registration but packing the founding conference and/or the governing board of the new organization with CPSU supporters. They tended to be characterized – with somewhat ageist shorthand – as 'veterans' by volunteers. It was true that the veterans' organizations do seem to have been staffed by retired party and state officials, whose loyalty was not in question. The Central Committee's plans to pack the founding conference of *Memorial* mentioned the veterans' organization as the first pool of support; the Committee of Soviet Women, trade unions and *Komsomol* were also intended to send delegates.⁷⁰

VOI was particularly afflicted by 'veteranization'. Disabled activists worried about this even in 1988 – when VOI was presented 'from above' with a president from the Veterans' Organization. They were sceptical about the motivation behind ministerial offers of help. 'The energetic activity of the Ministry... can be explained by its aspiration to take VOI firmly under its control, to make sure the Society doesn't damage its institutional interests.'⁷¹ Their anxieties only increased as it seemed that VOI was being reabsorbed into the party-state establishment in 1990–1. Some seriously disabled activists – self-consciously outside this establishment – complained that local leaders were increasingly Category 3 disabled veterans, who had only become disabled recently and were on full pensions, thus having no understanding of the needs of the people for whom VOI was created.⁷² Such veterans, often assumed by disabled activists to be retired officials or factory managers, were easier for social security departments to work with, and their presence increased the perception of many activists that VOI was turning into an agency of the local security department, as just another dispenser of aid.⁷³

In Leningrad, the party's energetic rearguard action to stall the process of *perestroika* included trying to control the charity movement even in 1990. *Miloserdie* found that local communist authorities packed its management board with officials and attempted, unsuccessfully, to persuade the Society to set up a hierarchy of borough organizations, which implied incorporation into the *nomenklatura* system. The communists also suggested introducing membership cards and keeping accurate membership lists, the better to impose democratic centralism. Volya Fedorova, a retired *raikom* secretary of pre-Gorbachev vintage who sat on the *Miloserdie* board was particularly feared because of her power and connections in the local council apparatus. She was fond of repeating that she had been 'appointed to watch over' the volunteers.[74]

Since the society had thousands of volunteers, this was hardly a surprising response. The party must have felt anxious at the idea of such a large organization existing beyond its control. The attempted cooption was successful in distancing some of the more anti-establishment activists. Some of the Christian Democrats left to engage in their own charitable and political activities. Pressure from young charity workers in spring 1990 to hold elections to the Society's board and get rid of officials led to a struggle which resulted in the resignation of Granin himself. This proved only a temporary setback, and *Miloserdie* was able to renew and expand its activities.[75]

In Novgorod, survivors of Nazi camps were given the impression that the party authorities hoped to create a 'toothless and absolutely obedient' branch of their Union. Its leader was a CPSU-appointee. In 1990, however, one of the group of non-party survivors who had actually founded the branch took over, and from then onwards the party stopped interfering in the Union's affairs.[76]

Cooption could also take the form of an attempted takeover by a big, official charity of a small grassroots organization. For example, the Children's Fund apparently tried to absorb the 'Large Family' Association in Voronezh; the Chelyabinsk women's council tried to take over the Soldiers' Mothers' Association; while the Leningrad Red Cross made a similar attempt on a branch of VOI.[77]

Sometimes local party officials tried to enlist the support of voluntary organizations for communist election candidates. In Orsk, an official of the town's party committee suggested that VOI members should vote for the hardliner Makashev in the Russian presidential elections of 1991, but this pressure was resisted.[78]

Overt Opposition

Hostility on the part of the authorities was manifested in bullying and persecution. Activists could find themselves the objects of slander in the press[79] or alternatively denied access to the local media – access which was important to the organization's survival. *Glasnost* was often much slower to expand in the provinces and NGOs sometimes turned to the local unofficial press, such as the *Siberian Information Agency Bulletin* (1989–90). Refusal – or persistant postponing – of requests for registration was often experienced. In summer 1989, for example, an apparently harmless large families' organization in Novosibirsk found it impossible to get registered.[80] (A counter-strategy was to appeal over the heads of the local authorities. A Tula organization registered with the Russian Ministry of Justice after the Tula *oblast* soviet denied registration.)[81]

In Leningrad *Miloserdie* activists were threatened with fifteen days' imprisonment for collecting money outside the Kazan cathedral.[82] In the North Urals, *Memorial* activists were actually arrested and received procurator's warnings after an unsanctioned meeting.[83] Other *Memorial* activists also experienced persecution. No doubt *Memorial*, as a semi-political organization, was especially liable to meet with examples of outright aggression, particularly where its leadership was conscious of its political role.

CONCLUSIONS

Conclusions on the outcome of the struggle are presented at the end of Chapter 8. It is difficult to generalize on the more specific topic of how the authorities responded, given the varied nature of the sample. However, analysis is possible to an extent in the case of *Memorial*. There only two clear cases of enthusiastic cooperation with *Memorial* before 1990; both were in museum-centred branches which were particularly apolitical. From 1990, cooperation became more common.[84] Voluntary organizations without a human rights agenda were likely to encounter more positive treatment than did many branches of *Memorial*. Yet there is plenty of evidence to suggest the authorities' zero-sum perspective: they wished either to absorb or to hinder and destroy. Where they differed was in the degree of control they tried to exert over organizations they perceived as broadly sympathetic, and in the degree of their aggression to organizations perceived as hostile.

Even in 1991 the CPSU had not given up, as the example of drumming up support for Makashev in Orsk VOI suggests. In a quite different corner of Russia, Pskov, the local communists were still closely supervising the presumably innocuous VOG in 1991.[85]

8 Building Political and Civil Society

A. KUPRIYANOV: 'The Moscow Society of Disabled People was set up a year ago. Who runs whom? Do you run the society, or is it the other way round?'
S. IVCHENKO (head of Moscow social services): 'I wouldn't phrase the question so bluntly.'[1]

To some extent voluntary organizations were consciously building a civil society as well as trying to meet their more specific objectives. The FSI, for example, intended 'turning Russia into an open civil society'. It was proud of its role in sponsoring the creation of dozens of new organizations, such as the Union of Chernobyl liquidators.[2] Moscow *Memorial* also used the phrase. The concept of civil society was well-known, at least in Moscow political circles.[3] Even the CPSU declared in 1990 that its objective was building civil society.[4] However, perhaps the concept was less well-known in the provinces. The introductory letter to the questionnaire on which much of this book is based described the research focus as 'the process of establishing a civil society' (*khod stanovleniya grazhdanskogo obshchestva*). However, no respondents chose to engage in debate about the implied assumption that they were participating in this activity.

Engagement in politics, on the other hand, was a more comprehensible concept and an activity respondents were quick either to admit or deny. There was, of course, a range of politicization within the voluntary sector. The following account will consider some aspects of politicization, before discussing features of civil society: the cohesiveness and durability of the organizations, their degree of independence from the state, channels of influence on the party-state and NGO networks. The chapter then assesses the impact of the voluntary sector on public opinion, before drawing some conclusions about the extent to which the voluntary sector furthered the cause of *demokratizatsiya*.

ASPECTS OF POLITICIZATION

Some charities and self-help groups included political action in their charters, although probably this was only possible for those established in 1990–1. It applied, for example, to the Russian Fund for the Socio-Legal Defence and Rehabilitation of Disabled People[5] (whose founders included Mayor of Moscow Popov). The Fund's goals were to 'ensure observance of the civil, social, cultural, economic and political rights and liberties of disabled people'.[6] More often, the NGOs' charters said nothing about political rights; however, it was commonplace for them to present themselves as human rights organizations, defending the rights and liberties of their members or clients. Such rights could be understood generally, but they could also be specific, in which case the organization might clash with local authorities. For example, in Orsk, as already described, VOI fought a plan to redefine a local residential home for physically disabled people (and the inmates themselves) as 'psychiatric'.[7]

Some organizations had a particular focus on human rights violations; occasionally, they were directly descended from the human rights movement of the Brezhnev era. The 'Cooperation' Centre[8] in Moscow (1988) was one such charity. Run by Valerii Abramkin, a former political prisoner and Helsinki Group member, it dealt primarily with the human rights of prisoners and former prisoners. Abramkin attempted to reform the Criminal Code and at the same time help individuals. (In 1991 the charity spent about 20,000 rubles on this type of aid.)[9] In March 1991 the Nikolai the Miracle Worker Fund[10] was established to defend the victims of miscarriages of justice. The organizer's expectations of confrontation with the world in general may be gauged from the fact that she refused to allow the publication of the fund's address and telephone number in a directory of charities![11] Other human rights organizations included *Memorial* and the groups of soldiers' mothers.

Politicization would seem especially likely in the case of organizations with such a human rights agenda, although they were often reluctant to acknowledge participation in politics.[12] A typically complex case is that of the soldiers' mothers in Chelyabinsk, whose committee originated as an initiative by local Social Democrats, but who decided at the outset (1990) that they would stand 'outside politics', by which they meant that they would have no party affiliation. They claimed that 'we don't participate in political activities'. However, they also mentioned that 'we express our demands in pickets and by using radio, television and the newspapers. In 1990... we demonstrated together with the Democratic Union, Social Democrats and Anarchists...'[13]

In some groups experience of actual political activity could be disillusioning. This was true, for example of Mother's Right.[14] Futile demonstrations and unsuccessful election campaigns made them reluctant to spend more time on activities not closely connected with their more immediate targets. The prevailing mood of public apathy and disillusion in the late *perestroika* years contributed to the formation of such attitudes.[15]

So far this discussion has adopted the simple term 'politicization'. However, there were necessarily many shades of opinion – the split was not just between radicals and more passive volunteers. For example, the Orsk branch of VOI was said to be split between supporters of [moderate] *perestroika* and those of the radical Inter-Regional Group. Mother's Right contained members who looked to Gorbachev as a 'good tsar' and others who were more sceptical. A disabled people's club in Bryansk distinguished between their positive appraisal of Gorbachev and their critical attitude to the Bryansk local authorities. The Novgorod Union of Former Young Prisoners in Fascist Concentration Camps was created by a three non-communists; most of the members were classed as 'communists who turned themselves into democrats'.[16]

VOI, like *Memorial,* was marked by great differences of outlook: not surprisingly for such a huge organization. There was a wide spectrum of opinion about how closely to work with local authorities, and whether they were essentially adversaries or allies. The ambiguous position of VOI, straddling the 'official'–'non-official' divide, facilitated such divisions. Some disabled people stated that their mission was to monitor the work of the social security departments (especially the VTEK) and saw the relationship as a struggle for power.[17] Others were content not to challenge the existing system and to work for gradual change. In Leningrad,

Building Political and Civil Society 161

the 1989 election programmes of candidates for the post of president of the city society reveal very different views. Of the 'radicals', one candidate emphasized that VOI was a political organization committed to defending the human rights of all disabled people; another called for changes to VOI's charter to give local branches full independence, exclaiming 'No to the dictatorship of the Centre!'; a third wanted to abolish *Minsobes* – not the only disabled activist to express this view – and suggested that it should exist on a borough level only. On the other hand, two further candidates (one a party member) stressed the need to cooperate with local social security and health departments.[18]

COHESION AND FRAGMENTATION WITHIN ORGANIZATIONS

Like the authorities, the grassroots organizations displayed a 'splintered nature' which determined the range of their responses to the state and communist party. Yet cohesion was an essential characteristic of a strong organization, one which could withstand party pressure and carve out space for genuine autonomous action. Building a successful civil society was premissed on the overcoming of atomization and creation of a sense of solidarity. ('Solidarity' was the most apt of names for the 'self-governing trade union' which united so much of Polish society in the construction of civil society in 1980–1.)

One of the most successful aspects of the new voluntary sector was its ability to find and unite people who were suffering from the same type of disadvantage. It is true that some networks predated 1985, but these did not always remove the necessity for painstaking work to build up the membership of self-help groups. One account of a group of parents of disabled children described the process: 'Who knows whether they would have met, had our shops contained anything other than empty shelves? Standing in queues, as it turned out, had its positive sides. The parents in the society's founding families met in the shop. They decided that since they shared the same problems they should tackle them together. The most energetic united to form an action group, which sought out all the families with disabled children in the borough. They collected information literally crumb by crumb: in the borough health, education and social security departments.' Soon 'the families began to meet often and spend lots of time together, making friends with one another'.[19]

Solidarity among members had a significant impact, on the personal level, but more significant for the creation of a civil society was the solidarity which existed among the organization's activists and aided them in their public actions. There were certain consistent centripetal and centrifugal forces which promoted or, alternatively, hindered cohesion.

Overall, the organizations which completed questionnaires for this research tended to feel that work in their organization had *united* the activists. In fact, this was one of the questions which elicited the most consistent response. Of course, these are organizations which survived to 1993; frailer groups disintegrated. Yet the response is still significant, pointing as it does to the strength of certain centripetal forces. The continuation of unfinished business drew members together. Few organizations could claim to have finished their work: immense problems remained to be tackled. A sense of working for an important cause, against the odds, could also be a powerful unifying factor. This seems to have been the case, for example, in the North Ossetian branch of the FMZ – concentrating as it did on dealing with refugees – as well as for many self-help groups. 'Unity of Christian outlook' promoted cohesion in some cases. Good leadership was important in others. In addition, factors which might at first glance seem unfavourable, such as the presence of different generations, could be helpful in promoting unity. Some branches of *Memorial*, for example, benefited from the fact that children and grandchildren of survivors of Stalin's camps joined forces with the survivors themselves and dealt together with an issue which could have significance for all generations within a family.

In general, though, centrifugal forces were also strong. One *Memorial* respondent suggested that this was because of the 'usual reasons in such situations', in other words, a decline in enthusiasm, changes in personal circumstances, and so forth, which affect volunteers in any society. The fact that many self-help groups were run by sick or disabled people or exhausted mothers made activism harder to keep up, particularly in the economic crisis of late-*perestroika* Russia. For example, the chairperson of a society for people with diabetes in Lomonosov wrote that 'the people who wish to put the programmes into effect are ill and not in a fit state to carry out the endeavour.'[20] Furthermore, attempted co-option and preemption by the authorities created bad feeling between activists. In addition to political differences, 'different approaches to commercial activity' could also divide members.[21] Although many voluntary organizations were deliberately democratic, this did not imply that their members all supported the transition towards a market economy; indeed many agreed with the head of Leningrad *Miloserdie* that 'charity and money are incompatible concepts'.[22] On a more practical level, absence of premises was an obstacle to cohesion mentioned by one group, but probably experienced by many more, given that this was a common disadvantage, often resulting from lack of support from the local council.[23]

Poor leadership was a significant factor. This could derive from party attempts to control: the idleness of a president imposed 'from outside' by the local authorities caused dis array in one self-help group.[24] More generally, leaders lacked management skills and practice in democratic procedures. A Leningrad disabled journalist described what seems to have been a not unusual situation in VOI: "The conference was like the Congress of People's Deputies or Leningrad City Soviet. The same muddle and disorganization, endless votes and repeat votes, the non-fulfilment of decisions only just taken, queues at the microphone, mutual insults.'[25] Local VOI leaders often failed to convince members of their probity, efficiency and dedication. Personality conflicts assumed unnecessary proportions and members who expected total *glasnost* were often disappointed. The members themselves often had unrealistic expectations and irrational suspicions. All this mirrored the experience of other new organizations under *perestroika*, and the increasing pessimism and panic in society in the years 1990–1.[26]

A common problem was that societies contained too diverse an assortment of members, with quite different needs. For example, the representative of a Leningrad VOI branch wrote that 'our society is marked by too diverse a range of interests and problems. That's why we had, and still have to spend a lot of effort on keeping our organization together as single unit.'[27] VOI suffered everywhere from the problem of representing too diverse interests. In 1988, when it was founded, it had seemed crucial to establish big organizations with national structures. VOI splintered quickly in 1990–1.

With charities, the reverse process seems to have occurred, perhaps because of almost ubiquitous need resulting from the economic crisis in 1990–1, which prompted well-meaning attempts to avoid creating a hierarchy of need and address the needs of all groups at once. The FMZ had set a trend. The last years of *perestroika* witnessed the birth of many other miscellaneous and catchall types of charity. Two typical entries in a directory of organizations were: 'the fund undertakes all types of charitable activity'[28] and 'the association extends all types of help to citizens of all categories'.[29] Given the miscellaneous goals of many charities, it was not surprising if these too were not always effective.[30] In some cases ambition ran well ahead of practical achievement. The ambitiously named TransEXPO Voluntary Union for Supporting Transport, Ecology, Culture and the Solution of Social Problems[31] in fact sponsored sport at six children's homes and participated in restoring a church.[32]

EXTENT OF INDEPENDENCE FROM THE STATE

Western analysts writing about Soviet-type systems tend to view civil society as something quite distinct from the state, a sphere of autonomous citizens' activity, from within which citizens are able to exert pressure on the state. The distinction between two clearly defined entities, state and civil society, is central to the whole *raison d'être* of the concept. (A further, personal sphere may also be added.) In the case of the emerging civil society in Poland, the distinction between state and civil society is clear, since civil society tended to exist in conscious opposition to the state. With regard to Russia, analysts differ as to how rigid a distinction may be made.

Definitions which do not clearly distinguish civil society from the state are *conceptually* confusing.[33] However, empirical evidence suggests the need to accept a degree of overlap. When analysts include some 'official' Soviet organizations within civil society this merely points to the fact that 'no paradigmatic civil society exists in the real world, only concrete individual civil societies, some more mature, or closer to an ideal than others'.[34] As this account of the Russian voluntary sector has demonstrated, civil society was certainly an ideal rather than a reality: it was hard to enjoy a viable existence as a Russian organization entirely independently of the state. A group might *feel* as though it had nothing in common with the state, but nevertheless be forced to seek help from state agencies and become to some extent incorporated within state structures. This is surely an entirely 'normal' phenomenon – reflecting the experience, for example, of many British voluntary organizations who both need government grants and dislike the dependence this implies. Polish civil society in the 1970s, like the much smaller dissident movements in the USSR and Czechoslovakia, was the unusual case. After 1991 in Russia, voluntary organizations began to go through a learning process, coming to terms with the fact that there was not necessarily anything wrong with depending on government grants, as long as the government respected the organization's independence to a reasonable degree.[35] Of course, definitions of reasonableness varied enormously, before as after 1991.

Some organizations were happy to work with the *perestroika*-era authorities. A borough branch of VOI in Bryansk, for example, expressed gratitude to the local authorities, from whom they claimed to have had only help and good advice.[36] Others were more reluctant to accept such guidance, but realised the practical necessity of approaching the authorities. Members of the Radonezh Society, for example, 'always had a definite opinion about the Godless authorities, and believed that they deserved no trust whatsoever. But, at the same time, we take into account the realities of living in a given society'.[37]

Almost all organizations had to establish some kind of contact with the local authorities. Naturally, however, association and cooperation was based on the perception that this would be the most beneficial approach for the organization to adopt, in its own self-interest. A nice example of such decision-making was given by the St Panteleimon Brotherhood. After considerable obstruction, the Brotherhood was finally offered the possibility of registration in March 1990 on condition that it chose as its sponsor the FMZ, Children's Fund or Red Cross. The Ministry of Justice took the line that 'without a political guarantor you won't be registered'. At this point the Brotherhood chose the Red Cross because it was perceived to be the least bureaucratic and least connected to the KGB.[38]

Until October 1990 registration was a process which almost inevitably involved making compromises, and led to 'heated discussions' within organizations.[39] After the appearance of the new law on associations it became easier for organizations to register without making unacceptable concessions such as taking on unwelcome 'sponsoring organizations'. On the other hand, widespread alienation from the communist regime by 1991 meant that 'the prestige of such registration [had become] very low, especially because organizations that [had] not registered [were] able to continue functioning without state interference'.[40]

Sometimes cooperation with the state was hedged with moral qualifications. 'The most important thing is to keep our Christian consciences clean; otherwise the entire meaning of our association would be lost.'[41] In practice, such qualifications could make cooperation very difficult. Novosibirsk *Miloserdie*'s position was that although it was prepared to cooperate with any official or unofficial organization, *Miloserdie*'s very high principles and independence were to be maintained – a considerable proviso. Consequently, *Miloserdie* worked almost wholly within the informal sphere.[42]

Other groups were obstinately informal, eschewing any kind of link with official organizations. In Apatity YMCA, for instance, 'everyone tried to act independently of the authorities'.[43] This particular charity was fortunate in its Norwegian links: in practice only groups which had good connections with foreign charities – the FSI being the outstanding example – or were purely concerned with mutual emotional support could really hope to function independently. In the latter case, it might be argued that the activities remained firmly within the 'personal' sphere and hence could not be considered to constitute part of civil society.

It was characteristic of many organizations to dream of setting up their own medical and economic institutions independently of the state. For example, the 'liquidators' who formed the Siberian branch of the Chernobyl Union hoped to set up their *own* medical centre, i.e. one which would be under the control of their voluntary organization, rather than the state. They planned to set up cooperatives to provide work for disabled members, bypassing the state VTEK.[44]

As a measure of democratization occurred, some groups were able to overcome their alienation from the state. Drug abusers in Leningrad, for example, though initially experiencing 'a vehement desire to avoid any dealings with official organisations or figures in authority', because of the punitive attitude they had always encountered, found that the vehemence of that desire 'softened somewhat over time'.[45]

The way an organization conducted its affairs also demonstrated its degree of independence.[46] Many unofficial organizations asserted their independence by acting in 'non-Soviet' fashion. This ostentatious distancing was a component of 'informal' existence. The *Miloserdie* volunteers, for example, were determined to operate democratically. The Human Soul Fund, which addressed the needs of people with mental illnesses, stated that 'The Fund is a self-managed non-governmental organization, in which the interests of sick people, relatives and doctors are for the first time represented in equal measure. They cooperate in finding solutions to their common problems.'[47] *Memorial* was deliberately decentralized. Similarly, the Leningrad Association of Veterans of the War in Afghanistan, at its founding conference in May 1990, purposely avoided creating centralized structures.[48]

Volunteers contrasted the biblical stress on anonymous good deeds with the shamming, boasting and hypocrisy which pervaded Soviet official life. Even attempting to measure the success of their programmes was anathema to some, since it too reeked of the command economy. Granin remarked that charitable action 'can only be harmed by the introduction of "indicators"'.[49]

Voluntary organizations tried to avoid bureaucratization. 'Our activities are characterized by unanimity and self-management, without constricting legal procedures, and bureaucratic paperwork is hardly conducted.'[50] Many organizations were vague about how many members they had. This was no doubt sometimes the result of inefficiency, but often it resulted from a rejection of the gigantomania and empire-building so typical of official Soviet political culture and of the implication of desire to *control* the membership. Instead, membership was perceived to be an individual, private concern. This attitude was reflected, for example, in Leningrad *Miloserdie*'s refusal to accede to party demands that it introduce membership cards and keep accurate lists.[51] It was commitment to the cause which mattered. 'The main aim of *Memorial* was not membership.' 'Membership dues were not collected, since participation was a moral issue.'[52]

Some organizations avoided appearing to monitor the political affiliation of their members. The Chelyabinsk Association of Soldiers' Mothers deliberately refrained from asking members about their political orientation and party affiliation.[53] Another activist refused to answer my question about the party affiliation of her organization's founders with the rebuke: 'it would be more ethical to ask them personally'.[54]

CHANNELS OF INFLUENCE: LOBBYING AND ITS OUTCOMES

The desirable situation was of course to be simultaneously immune to pressure from the party-state authorities while being able to influence the latter. The successful organization worked on securing channels and mechanisms of influence.

Commonly, in good Soviet style, this meant enlisting the help of powerful individuals to override the objections of minor bureaucrats. Moscow *Miloserdie* achieved registration with the help of Admiral Gaidar; Leningrad *Miloserdie* with the help of Mikhail Gorbachev; children's home pioneer Borodaevskaya in Akademgorodok – the Academy of Sciences' 'company town' – with the aid of the Academy's local head, Koptyug. At least one successful branch of VOI claimed that its achievements were thanks to the patronage of a local factory director. The haphazard nature of such contacts was hardly testimony to a well-functioning civil society or 'law-based state'; rather, it perpetuated the arbitrariness and dependence on figures of authority which marked the Soviet period.

Chapter 3 suggested how even before 1985 disabled activists had exploited and developed their contacts with journalists. Given the emergence of *glasnost*, this now became even more worthwhile. An example of a cause which benefited considerably from media coverage was Lyudmila Rogova's Chelyabinsk kindergarten for children with cerebral palsy. Rogova, who herself had multiple sclerosis, had managed against all the odds to create an outstandingly successful kindergarten in 1988 and then expand and improve it. She did so partly by getting the press on her side. 'The press didn't let me down' was Rogova's understated comment.[55] Articles about the kindergarten appeared in newspapers at all levels, from the national newspapers *Pravda*, *Sovetskaya Rossiya* and *Komsomol'skaya pravda* to local factory house journals.[56] Rogova was presented in the standard heroine mould but despite stereotypes the articles were effective. Other organizations created their own newsletters and newspapers, contributing to the mass of independent publishing activities which characterized the last years of *perestroika*.

Letter writing and visits to official offices also continued to form an important part of the work of the new voluntary organizations. Most new welfare groups tried to get access to special shops, facilities for ordering goods, priority for phone installations, more suitable flats and other services. The decisions were usually made at a local level, depending on resources. For example, in 1989 Novosibirsk was less generous than Omsk.

Of the big funds, the Children's Fund was perhaps the most active lobbyist. In 1988–9 the presidium of the Children's Fund governing body sent the Council of Ministers 'more than twenty suggestions about urgent issues'.[57] The Fund 'got government agencies to adopt a string of urgent measures to help children'. Moreover, the Children's Fund was given a number of Politburo dachas, one of which was turned into a rehabilitation centre for children with cancer. The Fund also managed to get a *nomenklatura* sanatorium in the Crimea made over for the use of inmates of children's homes.[58]

The soldiers' mothers scored a victory when in September 1990 Gorbachev issued a decree on legal protection for servicemen, after a delegation of mothers had met Presidential Council members to press their case.[59] Gorbachev himself met the mothers in November 1990.[60]

Although smaller organizations were often weakly placed to exert pressure on the authorities, they too could exploit the privileges issue, diverting property which the *nomenklatura* was now obliged to vacate to their own organizations. For example, in Tomsk, after a picket in September 1989 by parents of children with cerebral palsy and the children themselves of local government offices, and with help from the Union for Furthering Revolutionary *Perestroika*, a dacha which had been used by the local elite was turned over for their use.[61]

Participation in soviets offered an obvious possible channel of influence. The Organization of Veterans was allocated 75 deputies in the CPD in 1989. The more established charities – the Red Cross and the official peace movement – had ten deputies apiece, while the new Foundations – the Cultural and Children's Funds and the FMZ – had five each. The Sobriety Society had one, indicating its inferior status by 1989 compared with its importance in 1985.[62] VOI, a *Russian* Society, was disappointed in 1989 by the fact that, because it did not exist on a federal level, it was not selected to send deputies directly to the USSR CPD. It unsuccessfully lobbied more fortunate organizations, asking them to sacrifice seats in VOI's favour.[63] Like some women activists, disabled people seem to have been convinced that they could only hope to achieve a real voice in politics if a quota system were maintained, and opened to them. Perhaps this was why, in the 1989 elections, they concentrated on trying to use the quota system, and seem to have put forward only one candidate for a regular constituency. Il'ya Zaslavsky was nominated by Moscow's Oktyabr borough VOI. Several well-known candidates stood down in his favour, disabled people campaigned hard and he was elected, on a radical platform which included the creation of a strong voluntary sector which could compete with state agencies in service provision.[64] Once in parliament, Zaslavsky was in an invidious position, since he was not only regarded as having to solve all disability problems, but was also an active member of the Inter-Regional Group of Deputies and was becoming increasingly convinced that the first step towards solving specific disability problems was to achieve fuller democratization and concentrate on political reform.[65]

Other candidates for the 1989 Congress included disability issues in their programmes. Several other disabled, or formerly disabled, deputies were elected.[66] They raised disability issues in the parliament. For example, the head of VOS complained that up to now he had been able to settle the problems of blind people only through his direct personal link with Ryzhkov, implying that none of the existing official mechanisms was effective in channelling the demands of the blind people's society.[67] As was suggested in earlier chapters, the Supreme Soviet – elected from the Congress – did set up new mechanisms and these produced legislation, although its practical impact was limited by the 'war of laws and parliaments'. Interestingly, the law 'Basic principles of social protection of disabled people in the USSR' introduced quotas of seats for disabled people's organizations in parliaments and councils at all levels. However, the force of this instruction was lessened by the proviso that quotas were to be established only where the arrangement was compatible with existing electoral laws.[68]

Given the importance of republican and local decision-making, the 1990 elections held more promise than those of 1989 for the voluntary organizations. The elections of 1990 seem to have been regarded as offering practical opportunities for many smaller charities and self-help groups, confirming Sedaitis and Butterfield's suggestion that 'the pull to electoral participation became almost irresistable for many mobilized movement groups'.[69]

Small groups could be satisfied with local successes: the Leningrad Large Family organization, for example, successfully sponsored one city and two borough soviet deputies. VOI, the largest of the more or less independent groups, got about 500 deputies elected to soviets at various levels, including the Russian CPD.[70] In Leningrad City Soviet there were four VOI deputies and in Moscow Soviet, three. A special commission for disabled people's affairs was attached to Moscow Soviet. Also very important for VOI was the election of VOI activists at the borough level, where they sat on local social security commissions and in other ways tried to defend the interests of disabled people.[71] However, deputies were frequently perceived as failing their constituents. A disabled activist complained, for example, that Leningrad VOI had elected members to the city soviet but 'they have done nothing for us'.[72] Their disappointment seems to have mirrored that of many environmental and workers' organizations.[73]

The nomination of voluntary organization activists as candidates could achieve publicity, even if they were unsuccessful. For example, although Lyudmila Rogova was not elected to Chelyabinsk city soviet, the media publicized the needs of disabled people and the importance of supporting the voluntary sector. Readers were encouraged to 'vote for charity'.[74]

The moral standing of respected activists was a desirable asset, given the prevailing climate of suspicion of the party-state. Recognizing this, Leningrad party boss Boris Gidaspov tried to exploit the popularity of *Miloserdie*, suggesting at a meeting of the *obkom* that the Society might nominate party candidates for the 1990 elections – an offer which was refused.

Demonstrations by individuals drew public and official attention to the plight of disadvantaged groups. Perhaps most spectacular was the 'tent city' of homeless people on the edge of Red Square, established in July 1990 and broken up only in December.[75] In the provinces, just one activist could cause a stir. In Novosibirsk, for example, VOI's charismatic unofficial leader and founder, Vasil'ev, went on hunger strike in 1989 to campaign for local disabled people's demands and published an appeal in a *samizdat* newspaper.[76] Associations also participated in demonstrations or open-air rallies. A particularly successful case was that of the soldiers' mothers, whose vigil outside the parliamentary deputies' hotel in June 1989 was rewarded by the demobilization of student conscripts. The Dostoevsky Children's Fund was another organization which took part in demonstrations.[77] In late 1989 and in May 1991 Leningrad VOI members demonstrated at the City

Soviet against the non-fulfilment of promises made in a resolution of December 1988.[78] In Vladikavkaz, FMZ employees demonstrated against the war in Ossetia.[79] In Leningrad, the first *Miloserdie* hospital orderlies – appalled by conditions – accused the hospital administration of callousness and planned a public rooftop protest, raising a 'disaster flag'.[80] Although the conflict was smoothed over, the more radical members of *Miloserdie* kept alive the idea of 'disaster flags'. In 1990 they picketed the charity's offices after it had been closed by the authorities. The picket was broken up by riot police.

The activities of the Tomsk parents of children with cerebral palsy and the Chelyabinsk soldiers' mothers have already been mentioned. In these cases, action was conducted jointly with more political informal organizations. There were other examples of cooperation. In Moscow, for example, members of the Committee of Soldiers' Mothers joined with *Memorial*, the Radical Party and anarcho-syndicalists to demonstrate in October 1990 outside the Ministry of Defence in favour of a civilian alternative to military service.[81] In autumn 1989 the Tomsk Popular Movement, a local collection of informal organizations, included a club for deaf people, who arranged a picket of the *obkom* with placards reading 'Listen to deaf people!' and 'We demand social justice!'[82] In Kaliningrad, local informals helped the VOI to 'create an unofficial (almost secret) college of advocates, thanks to whom we can now write our protests, demands and requests in the correct language'.[83] However, sometimes charities and self-help groups felt that they were the victims of attempts at cooption made by more political informal groups. In Novosibirsk, for example, the Afghan veterans resisted such an attempt by *Pamyat*'.[84]

COHESION WITHIN THE SECTOR AND THE GENERATION OF NEW ORGANIZATIONS

A civil society cannot consist only of isolated organizations. In order to function successfully they should enhance their collective power *via-à-vis* the state by successful networking. At the same time, the creation of umbrella organizations facilitates the growth of new groups. Russian organizations were both aware of the need and wary of the dangers of joint action. There were several stages in this process of creating a cohesive voluntary sector.

On the most basic level, new NGOs could extend occasional help to other voluntary organizations, building a sense of cooperation within the community. For example, the Petersburg Our Home Society (for mothers of large families) helped repair clothing for members of VOS.[85] Grassroots organizations ostensibly devoted to defending the interests of a particular social category quite often widened their remit. For example, a Large Family organization in Izanteevka, Moscow *oblast*, aided orphans, disabled people and lone mothers with twins.[86] The society to aid burns victims of the pipeline explosion in 1989 in its turn donated 15,000 rubles to help house fire victims in the Novosibirsk *oblast*.[87]

Some organizations realised the importance of maintaining permanent contact with a variety of local groups. For example the society for people with diabetes in Lomonosov 'maintains constant contact with the St Petersburg and Moscow Societies for People with Diabetes and disabled peoples', large families' and charity societies in Lomonosov.'[88] In Chelyabinsk, Rogova several times sought and received material help from the Chelyabinsk Popular Front. Paradoxically, it was the Children's Fund which – having neglected to provide help itself – recommended her to turn to the Front. Perhaps it felt that informals should stick together.[89] Charities and self-help groups also had connections with other sections of the 'informal' community. Informal healers, for instance, helped sponsor the growth of the voluntary sector, by donating proceeds from their seances to grassroots organizations or giving free parapsychological help.[90] Hence the voluntary sector to some extent nestled within the wider informal sector.

There was also a sense in which Russian NGOs became members of world civil society, although links with Western NGOs were still in their infancy before August 1991. One group which made early international contacts was the Afghan veterans. When they met Vietnam veterans – and in at least one case also veterans of the Falklands War – the *afgantsy* were making a statement about victims of war under all regimes.

Contacts between individual organizations could be facilitated by formal or informal umbrella organizations. *Memorial* in particular seems to have acted as an umbrella for provincial informal associations of all types.[91] *Miloserdie* sometimes played a similar role for charities and self-help groups. In Leningrad *Miloserdie* was a registered organization and hence able to officially sponsor the creation of new NGOs under the pre-1990 legislation. The role of the FSI in spawning new organizations was mentioned above as a conscious attempt to build civil society. The big Funds, particularly the FMZ and the Children's Fund, achieved sufficient local legitimacy in places to perform a similar role: the organizations which clustered under their umbrellas seem to have often felt that they were part of a useful network, not being manipulated by the party authorities. DeBardeleben noted a similar tendency with regard to environmental groups, writing that 'the role of previously existing official conservation societies has... been surprisingly visible.'[92]

A final stage was the creation of organizations by already existing small grassroots organizations to coordinate their efforts and promote networking. Some organizations were wary of creating national structures which might attempt to control member groups. *Miloserdie* considered the creation of a national society and then backed away (see Chapter 5). Women's organizations, meeting at their first conference in Dubna in March 1991, deliberately set up an information network only. However a few such overarching organizations, created from the 'bottom up', emerged before the August coup. One example was the Assocation of Public Societies of Parents with Disabled Children in Leningrad.[93] In March 1991 more than a hundred 'charitable organizations' (including some cooperatives) met at a conference in Moscow under the auspices of the city soviet: the beginning of acollaboration which was to develop and become more institutionalized after the coup.[94]

Fish concludes that in the case of the more political groups, 'the extent of real organizational linkage and integration was very limited'.[95] It seems to have been greater in the case of voluntary organizations, although the process was still very incomplete in August 1991. This was not necessarily a handicap, however, given that most groups were still in their infancy. Sedaitis and Butterfield suggest that 'the decentralized, segmented structure of Soviet social movements is actually best suited to its current need for self-definition and consolidation'.[96]

The related issue of overlap and duplication was one which could also be viewed as both handicap and advantage. On the one hand, civil society was weakened if there were competing, uncooperative organizations, particularly in cases where the CPSU tried to preempt the informal groups by creating its own associations. The traditional, monopolistic outlook was well expressed by the former head of the Soviet Red Cross when he expressed his worries about the creation of the FMZ: was its function not simply to take resources from the Red Cross?[97] The head of Leningrad social security services was similarly sceptical about the claims of competing groups for special favours. 'We have eighteen different categories of special cases for priority housing! The endless attempts to subdivide the little we have only make people feel hostile towards one another.'[98] On the other hand, one could view the multiplicity of similar organizations more positively as a sign of democratization and, even given the shortage of resources overall, a necessity in view of the enormous size of the problems to be tackled. When asked whether *Rabotnitsa*'s Mariya Fund were not competing with *Memorial* – where women were well represented – the *Rabotnitsa* journalist responsible for social affairs suggested that 'the more the merrier' was the most reasonable approach. The Fund was set up after consultation with *Memorial* and was intended to supplement, not compete with *Memorial*'s activities. *Memorial* had about 120 provincial branches, but nevertheless *Rabotnitsa*, with its circulation of over 20 million, was read in locations *Memorial* could not reach.[99]

CHANGING PUBLIC OPINION

Chapters 2–4 suggested that by the early years of *perestroika* there was considerable public scepticism about state services. A July 1989 poll found that only 45 per cent of respondents placed their faith in the state ('social security departments, etc.') to 'most effectively protect the rights of elderly people and pensioners'.[100]

Scepticism about the state contributed to support for a

voluntary sector. However, even by the mid-*perestroika* period such support was still not guaranteed. This was illustrated by the level of public objection to the creation of Leningrad *Miloserdie* in 1988.[101] A disabled war veteran, for example, argued that 'instead of charity... we must force state organizations to work properly.' In 1989, the woman's magazine *Rabotnitsa* provoked 'hundreds' of letters of objection when it set up its fund to help women persecuted under Stalin.[102] 'I read the article... and it made me very upset. The editors call on society to be charitable. But I have a question: why should individuals have to help these people who suffered in the camps, rather than the state?... Why on earth should the country which crippled the lives of these people distance itself from their needs?'[103]

Voluntary organizations had therefore to work to convince the public of their right to exist. In the first instance, this meant raising the status of social groups whose problems had traditionally been hidden from the rest of society, and introducing a sense that CPSU-defined 'merit' was no longer the best criterion for allocating resources. A survey in early 1992 suggested considerable success. It asked 'Which social groups should have first call on the charitable help distributed by funds?' and allowed each respondent to name three groups. The Children's Fund had persuaded the public that children in residential care were the most needy group (59 per cent). Ordinary disabled people (51 per cent) were now a much more popular cause than disabled war veterans (33 per cent). Large families and disabled Afghan veterans came next, with 30 per cent and 28 per cent: again testifying to their own efforts and the force of *glasnost* in effecting a sea change in public opinion.[104]

Success in changing perceptions about who needed help could not itself ensure support for actual voluntary organizations. Nevertheless, self-help groups did command sympathy. A 1989 survey found that VOI was regarded as the most effective of the big voluntary organizations.[105] Now, unlike before 1985, the lobbying of self-help groups in pursuit of their material objectives was increasingly regarded as legitimate. Like the refusal to adhere to CPSU-defined distribution principles, this was also a positive indicator for democratization.

Charitable funds found it harder to gain support, partly because of suspicions of dishonesty, but also because of links to the CPSU. In 1989 apparently only about one in six Russians believed that the large funds did a good job.[106] However, by the end of *perestroika* their rating had improved. One poll found that the most worthwhile funds were considered to be the FMZ (33 per cent) and Children's Fund (25 per cent). Among the urban intelligentsia there was even greater support: 64 per cent and 51 per cent had a 'positive' impression of the FMZ and Children's Fund respectively.[107]

Data from Moscow suggest that there at least the voluntary sector had by 1990 convinced the public of its right to exist – irrespective of attitudes to individual organizations. A survey found that 'opponents of charity form a minority (not exceeding 25 per cent) in all the social groups'.[108] Nationwide, only 12 per cent of educated Russians in early 1992 disagreed with the statement that charity had a vital role to play in tackling social problems, 'given the current weakening of the state'.[109] It was true that to the question 'What practical aims guide the specialized funds in their everyday activity?' 18 per cent favoured the response 'Ensuring a comfortable existence for their employees'. However, the most popular answer (28 per cent) was 'helping to bring up a generation of people able to build a democratic, law-based society'.[110] This was surely promising for democratization.

Finally, one might ask how successfully the charities had achieved their goal of a more caring and tolerant society. There were positive indicators, as suggested above with reference to newly-discovered groups in need. However, in the difficult economic climate it was unsurprising that there were also signs of 'gloomy and repressed malice' against any group which achieved greater access to scarce goods and services – even Chernobyl refugees.[111] By February 1992, 70 per cent of respondents in a Russia-wide survey believed that the majority of their fellow citizens had an 'irritable, malevolent or even hostile attitude to one another.'[112]

Building Political and Civil Society 179

CONCLUSIONS TO CHAPTERS 7 AND 8

In many respects the prospects for Russian civil society in August 1991 seemed bleak. According to Fish, political groups and parties often 'focused less on the development of society than on transformation of the state.'[113] Voluntary organizations too had concerns other than building civil society. Many self-help groups concentrated on survival. For example, by 1991 the Perm Union of Large Families was trying to help its members raise pigs.[114] Charities often focused on distributing Western aid, an activity which did little to strengthen Russian organizations.

Nevertheless, voluntary organizations were engaged in furthering democratization, and not just by the (important) fact of their existence. The preceding section, on public opinion, suggested a number of achievements. To use Fish's term, voluntary organizations did 'develop society', by persuading Russians that self-help groups could legitimately pursue their material interests; that many groups, formerly regarded as 'undeserving' poor, needed public support; and that the voluntary sector had a role to play, alongside the state, in addressing social problems.

This chapter has also shown numerous examples of links between voluntary organizations and other 'informals' and evidence that many charities and self-help groups felt that they were all participating in the same struggle: to push back the power of the party-state. Chapter 7 suggested that the confrontational climate was created in many cases by the authorities themselves. They found it hard to abandon their monopoly on organizing participation in public affairs. They antagonized informals by their clumsy attempts at manipulation. In response, organizations often asserted their independence by deliberately behaving in un-Soviet fashion.

The organizations which survived ascribed their cohesiveness to numerous factors. The sense of urgency and directness of their cause was one. This may help explain their strength, compared to the weakness of political organizations, with their more abstract goals and frequent preoccupation with identity rather than interest articulation.[115] The voluntary organizations were active in pursuing their objectives, utilizing all new political opportunities at their disposal.

By 1991 local and central authorities could rarely ignore the existence of voluntary organizations and their attempts to preempt, coopt, supervize or even destroy the new groups failed sufficiently often for many independently-minded organizations to survive. Of course, the picture varied considerably from town to town, but everywhere the basic outlines were similar. The CPSU had lost its monopoly over organizing participation in public affairs. Who was to blame?

Conservative authorities did not have the political skills to operate successfully in the new environment. They displayed cunning, but their schemes to weaken the voluntary sector were premissed on the assumption that they still possessed the authority to implement decisions. They told *Miloserdie* that it had been supplanted by the FMZ – but *Miloserdie* was not intimidated and simply went on operating. They appointed retired social security chiefs to head local branches of VOI, but disabled people left VOI and set up their own organizations. They tried to split *Memorial* between older and younger members but did not realize that cooperation between generations – a collective attempt at 'repentance', to quote the title of Abuladze's film about the impact of Stalinism – was central to *Memorial*'s *raison d'être*.

Moreover, conservative local officials were under pressure 'from above'. Gorbachev's democratization programme, culminating in the October 1990 law on associations, removed many obstacles to the registration of NGOs and facilitated the creation of a local political society within which charities and self-help groups could operate. In addition, the 1990 elections to some extent resulted in the election of radicals: Leningrad and Moscow presented particularly favourable environments for NGOs.

Alapuro claims that 'Soviet rule disintegrated from above rather than through a sustained challenge from below'.[116] There is clearly much to be said for this argument. However, it is not the whole story. Without the role played by nationalist movements, the USSR might have held together. Without a challenge from self-help groups and charities, the authorities would not have yielded their absolute control over many areas of local welfare and health. The more politicized organizations naturally particularly hastened the process of party decline. *Memorial*, for example, was likely to do more damage in towns where it was self-consciously building local civil society and acting as an umbrella for other opposition groups than where it saw its role as primarily one of charity or self-help. Charities and self-help groups were often more interested in economic victories: a more equitable distribution of jobs and goods. The economic climate was far from favourable for the achievement of such objectives. However, the principle was gained, and this was a moral victory. The sector's most important achievement was probably to force the authorities to stop ignoring social problems, in particular poverty, and recognize the rights of large sections of the Soviet population who had been almost rightless in the past.

9 Conclusions and Epilogue

CONCLUSIONS, 1985–91

State and Society on the Eve of Gorbachev's Accession in 1985

There was no voluntary sector in the USSR before 1985. Officials claimed that charity was a phenomenon which, like feminism or nationalism, could not exist in a socialist state. The state would provide. However, the truth of this claim was increasingly open to question. Before 1985, individuals recognized that the state was unable to meet need in specific cases; among disabled people, there seems to have been widespread understanding that this was part of a more general problem with state welfare provision. Under Gorbachev, *glasnost* made clear to the public at large the extent of this failure and exposed the fact that a growing complex of social problems had been simply ignored by the authorities.

The crisis of the Soviet welfare state stemmed from the priorities of the communist party, which led to both the inefficiencies of the command economy and the creation of a welfare system based on merit and reward. The system provided privileges for the political elite but condemned millions of the politically least important citizens to a life of poverty. When communist officials addressed the Soviet population as 'toilers' (*trudyashchiesya*) they were by implication excluding from citizenship non-working people (other than war veterans). In many cases these were the same social groups who are most disadvantaged in other societies, but there were also victims of Soviet tragedies, such as disabled veterans of the Afghan war or former inmates of Stalin's labour camps.

Party-organized 'voluntary work' performed by citizens – often reluctantly – could not fill the gaps in the welfare state.

A partial exception were the 'voluntary organizations' of blind and deaf people, which provided some self-determination for their members despite their links to the CPSU. Other disabled people, conscious of their inability to participate in public life and deprived in many cases of employment, lobbied officials and the press to create an equivalent organization for themselves, a Society of Disabled People (VOI).

However, those failed by the welfare state did not confine their activities to petitioning the authorities. In some cases, they set up their own self-help groups, unregistered and outside party supervision. A number of independent disabled people's networks and organizations, together with parents' self-help organizations and illegal charity by religious congregations, formed the roots of the post-1985 voluntary sector. The CPSU was already beginning to lose its monopoly before Gorbachev came to power.

The Voluntary Sector under Gorbachev

Perestroika led to greater investment in the welfare state and a more determined approach by state agencies to tackle accumulated social problems, as well as problems posed by post-1985 disasters such as the Chernobyl accident or ethnic conflicts. However, the Soviet welfare state was not easy to reform. Moreover, the fact that the party-state was itself blamed for causing problems – as well as failing to solve them – prompted a search for supplementary forms of welfare provision.

The newly legal private sector of the economy did little directly to bolster state welfare and was regarded with hostility by citizens and officials alike. The creation of a voluntary sector had wider appeal. The voluntary sector would comprise both charities and self-help associations, as well as numerous dual-function or hybrid organizations.

Gorbachev himself responded positively to suggestions that charity become a legitimate feature of Soviet life and welcomed the emergence of charities, official and grassroots. Officials, by sanctioning the creation of new Soviet-wide, party-controlled charities such as the Charity and Health Foundation (FMZ) and Children's Fund, hoped to persuade people to part with the rubles under their mattresses and to use enthusiasm for *perestroika* to revive the official cult of volunteering. Members of the intelligentsia called on Russians to overcome the atomization created by the political system and recover their sense of community responsibility. The *Miloserdie* ('charity') movement was an enthusiastic and successful response to this call, with groups emerging in many Russian cities in 1988–9. Numerous other charities, many connected with the distribution of foreign food parcels, were created in 1990–1.

Disadvantaged social groups quickly took advantage of liberalization to build on the existing network of self-help groups and create many thousands more. Self-help groups were the most common type of pressure group in Russia, uniting many more people than did political or ecological issues. Members often hoped above all to create jobs, but this was not easy to achieve. Mutual emotional support plus energetic lobbying of local authorities for preferential access to services and goods were more successful activities. Often members of self-help groups were not 'toilers' and had previously played no role in public affairs, so their inclusion in public life was in itself significant. Groups of parents, veterans of Afghanistan and Chernobyl and older people were all well represented in the self-help sector. However, groups of disabled people were the most numerous of all. The biggest self-help organization to be founded was VOI, a million-strong society of disabled people which enjoyed both grassroots origins and official support. However, VOI was also weakened by party attempts at control and disagreements between its official and informal wings, as well as by the very diverse types of disability of its members. It frequently splintered under these pressures.

Most voluntary organizations – charities, official and unofficial, as well as self-help groups – had closer links with their local community than with Moscow. This phenomenon reflected the centrifugal forces affecting all Soviet institutions in the second half of *perestroika*. Voluntary organizations, many of which were technically branches of national organizations, often found it hard to identify with their Moscow headquarters and/or prized greatly their own independence of action. This helped blur the distinction between 'official' and 'unofficial' organizations, since the hallmark of an official organization had been its control from Moscow and immunity to influence from the local population. Voluntary organizations sometimes collaborated with other local grassroots organizations, such as independent political groups. Many had contacts with local religious congregations.

Relations between voluntary organizations and the authorities tended to be uncomfortable, though a certain *rapprochement* occurred after 1990. 1990 was the year of the local elections, which brought more reformers onto local councils, and was also the year when shortages became dramatically more acute, which made more and more voluntary groups dependent on the authorities for access to goods on a local level. However, organizations were often very anxious to maintain their autonomy from the authorities. They deliberately broke with Soviet organizational norms, for example in their reluctance to create hierarchies or keep close check on membership numbers. Nevertheless, they were often cohesive organizations, thanks partly to the directness of their cause, and in this they compared favourably with often weaker political organizations, which usually had more abstract goals. The voluntary organizations were active in pursuing their objectives, utilizing all the new political opportunities at their disposal.

If the relationship between the voluntary sector and the authorities was often a conflictual one, the fault probably lay mostly with the authorities themselves. They found it hard to compromise and abandon their monopoly on organizing participation in public affairs. Their attempts to preempt, coopt, supervise or even destroy the new groups displayed cunning but were often ineffective. Moreover, the cards were stacked against conservative local officials, simultaneously under pressure from above and below. The October 1990 law on associations made it easier to establish an NGO and aided the establishment of a local political society within which charities and self-help groups could work. However, without a challenge from self-help groups and charities themselves, the authorities would not have yielded their absolute control over many areas of local welfare and health.

Precarious victories in becoming established and achieving at least some practical objectives were matched by achievements on the part of both journalists and voluntary groups in changing public opinion. Complacency about the Soviet welfare state was shattered and the result was often anger and hostility. More positively, voluntary organizations raised the status of groups such as victims of the Terror and large families and encouraged a more objective assessment of *need*. They helped persuade people that *merit*, as defined by the CPSU, was not the best criterion for determining welfare provision. This was illustrated by the fact that ordinary disabled people came to be regarded as more deserving of support than war veterans.

Russians came to approve of the voluntary sector in general, while remaining suspicious of the motives of anyone engaged in fund-raising. Self-help organizations like VOI commanded more respect than the big charities. Whereas pre-1985, 'voluntary organizations' had not been permitted to pursue their own material advantage, lobbying by self-help groups was now increasingly regarded as being legitimate: a good omen for democratization. The links to the West which the voluntary sector established perhaps also aided the cause of democracy, although at the same time shame at the influx of foreign aid had a nationalist component. Moreover, extensive disillusionment with the state and mistrust of any kind of authority did not promise well for the future of democracy in Russia.

EPILOGUE: THE VOLUNTARY SECTOR SINCE AUGUST 1991

1991 as a Watershed: Differing Perspectives

1991 seems a very obvious watershed in Soviet and Russian *political* history, whether one chooses August, the month of the coup, Yeltsin's victory and the political defeat of Soviet communism, or December and the demise of the USSR. It is tempting, and commonplace, to adopt political watersheds, particularly leadership changes, when describing social processes throughout the whole of Soviet history. After all, the communist party has been extraordinarily influential. The years 1985 and 1991, marking Gorbachev's rise and fall, were adopted as the boundaries of the main part of this book.

Russians who became active in the voluntary sector after 1991 or who had experience of failure in the Gorbachev period sometimes stress the significance of the 1991 watershed. They suggest that comparatively little was achieved before the collapse of communism. 'In 1991 the third sector [in Samara] was still embryonic.'[1] 'From 1985–1991 it was impossible for [disadvantaged social groups] to achieve anything at all. The only exception, in my opinion, was the Committee of Soldiers' Mothers.'[2] 'There can be no question of "human rights associations" or "nationwide organizations" [having existed under Gorbachev].'[3] The evidence presented in this book suggests that such assessments are too negative. The tendency to play down the significance of change under Gorbachev is of course widespread among Russians, with reference to all sorts of areas of activity.

Another commonplace assumption is that need is very much greater today than it was under Gorbachev, or before. By implication, before 1992 charity and self-help were luxuries, whereas now they are urgent necessities. Chapter 2 suggested that such a favourable view of the Soviet 'safety net' is unwarranted. As one charity activist, Konstantin Borovoi, wrote in 1993: 'When I read today about liberal reforms which have "robbed the country and driven old people to search for food in rubbish bins", I wonder about the people who say and write such things. Where were they before, when deprivation and poverty was carefully concealed, when they were only considered to exist "in isolated individual cases"? After all, old people were searching for food in rubbish bins all those seventy years [of Soviet power].'[4]

Clearly both voluntary organizations and social problems have multiplied since 1991. However, while accepting this, it is also important not to exaggerate the differences between the two periods. One should seek continuities as well. Social processes had their own momentum: a momentum which is often hard to chart, but is nevertheless important to recognize. One might draw an analogy between 1991 and 1985. While adopting the year of Gorbachev's accession as a boundary, this book has also argued that 1985 should not be seen as watertight, especially with regard to the disability movement.

Continuity and Change since 1991

1) The Size of the Voluntary Sector
It is impossible to say exactly how many charities and self-help organizations operate in Russia. More than 50,000 officially-registered 'non-profit organizations' existed in 1997. This number excludes religious organizations and consumer cooperatives, but includes many organizations – such as environmental groups or professional associations – which have not been discussed in this book.[5] Isolated local statistics present some evidence about the size of the sector in individual *oblast*s. In Voronezh *oblast*, for example, by May 1994 361 organizations had been registered, and of these '207 were engaged in some form of charitable or community work, defence of civil rights or environmental campaigning'.[6]

2) Types of Charity and Self-Help Group
Local data about Perm, Samara and Voronezh suggests that the 1991 city profile given in Chapter 1 remained to a large extent unchanged. In particular, there were many (largely autonomous) branches of nationwide organizations established before August 1991. Although numerous *charities* have probably appeared and disappeared since 1991, *self-help organizations* continue to preponderate in the voluntary sector and many of the pre-1991 organizations seem to have survived.[7] The majority of causes remained the same. The social problems had mostly been defined before 1991, and these were the years when the various particularly disadvantaged groups had clubbed together: disabled people, parents of large families, veterans of Afghanistan and Chernobyl, and others. Causes had been won in a few places – with, for example, the erection by *Memorial* of local monuments to victims of the Terror – but generally speaking there was every reason for the self-help groups to continue their activities after 1991. Occasionally a new type of group might surface – such as the short-lived Samara 'spinsters" organization[8] – but this was the exception proving the rule.

However, it was also true that after 1991 the emphasis within the voluntary sector shifted somewhat. Certain social problems in particular intensified as a result of the economic reform and breakdown in policing: rising unemployment,

Conclusions and Epilogue

homelessness and crime stimulated the creation of more voluntary organizations working in these areas.[9] The growing confidence of Russian women also resulted in a mushrooming of activities, some now directed at helping women themselves, rather than women attempting to help family members, as had been largely the case in organizations created under Gorbachev.

Organizations created during *perestroika* often evolved to meet new challenges. Soldiers' mothers' committees, for example, protested against the Chechen war. *Miloserdie* in Leningrad – first registered in 1988, and now renamed *Nevskii Angel*, provides an example of successful evolution. The number of volunteers was down – no more than 300 by 1996, but there were 47 paid staff in the same year and the society's work was both more professional and more extensive than it had been in the Gorbachev period. Responding to individual requests by poor and desperate people in St Petersburg remained a priority, with 250,000 to 300,000 clients a year by 1996. It provided permanent home-help services for more than a hundred seriously ill elderly people, stressing that although the services were free of charge they were not amateurish: its volunteers were fully-trained. The charity also engaged in training up to 500 volunteers, social workers and professional voluntary workers annually. As under Gorbachev, it used the local media to promote a cult of volunteering (*dobrovol'chestvo*), but this was now described as 'an element of civil society'. It also attempted to keep a data base on the Petersburg voluntary sector and to promote cooperation between its constituent parts.[10]

Factors Promoting and Hindering Survival and Growth

Voluntary organizations had not been so associated with the old regime that they fell together. As Chapter 8 suggested, many had been hostile to the Soviet regime, while even the most closely connected to the *nomenklatura* system had been asserting a degree of independence, at least in terms of independence from central control and embedding themselves in the local community. These tendencies were further enhanced by the removal of subsidies, with local branches of the Red Cross, for example, becoming self-financing.[11] (The collapse of democratic centralism did not, of course, necessarily indicate that members of the more orthodox organizations – particularly veterans – had abandoned their faith in communism.)

Voluntary organizations had a number of support networks which helped them survive. Foreign connections continued to play a significant role, and foreign NGOs working in Russia multiplied. As under Gorbachev, foreign NGOs such as United Way or the BEARR Trust (established formally in 1992) had a role in developing a sense of coherence within the Russian voluntary sector. Foreign grants, together with commercial activities, seem to have been the main source of income for Moscow and Petersburg non-profit organizations by 1997.[12]

In the provinces, however, it was local government grants which constituted a large part of non-profit organizations' income: an average of 40 per cent, according to one survey.[13] Good relations with local authorities remained crucial, and 1995 survey data suggested that organizations considered forging links with the state to be their most important objective.[14] Important, too, were close links with other local organizations.[15] The traditional role of enterprises in providing benefits for their employees was also continued. Many new 'charities' were simply a cover for factories to continue to try to protect employees.[16]

NGO networks and umbrella organizations were of gathering importance, with new ones being created such as Moscow Charity House (*Dom miloserdiya*), which had close links to the Moscow city authorities. Other cities, such as Yaroslavl and Vladimir, also had 'charity houses'. Another networking organization, founded in 1994, was the Agency of Social Information, which produced weekly newsletters about Russian NGOs and kept a data bank.[17] NGOs working with migrants began to form regional associations such as the Urals Association of Refugees, and in April 1996 local migrants' organizations joined to create a national Forum of Migrant Organizations.[18] On the other hand, networks were not always easy to develop, partly because of the suspicious attitudes prevailing in many organizations.[19] One, for example, refused to give membership details on the grounds that 'we don't supply such information even to the state security services.'[20] Moreover, such networks as did develop were not always of the most desirable kind: opportunities expanded for pseudo-charities with links to business and/or crime.[21]

The establishment of a more adequate legal framework has made it somewhat easier for the voluntary sector to develop, although it took five years for the Russian parliament to pass a law on non-profit organizations and when it was finally passed in 1996 it contained many gaps and ambiguities. Local authorities also have their own by-laws regulating non-profit organizations.[22]

The transition to a market economy has both facilitated and hindered the development of the voluntary sector. The sector has been encouraged to take over some functions performed by the state, for example with some contracting out of social services. However, the immediate effect of economic reform was to impoverish many people, such as state-employed professionals, who might previously have given to charity. In 1997, individual donations constituted only 2–5 per cent of income for non-profit organizations.[23] None the less, donations from businesses, as opposed to individuals, have been an important source of income for provincial voluntary organizations. This seems to have been less true for Moscow and Petersburg.[24] Marketization has made it more feasible for links between small business and self-help to be established successfully, for example, in the women's movement.[25]

Since its birth in the Gorbachev era the Russian voluntary sector has grown into a healthy child. It is difficult today to imagine Russian life *without* a voluntary sector and this is indication too that civil society in Russia is becoming more firmly established. However, the voluntary sector is in many ways not a single entity and the birth and childhood metaphor should perhaps be replaced by a more complex image. Frank Fabel has written that 'self-help initiatives are rather like an escalator, bringing to light things which had been hidden underground.'[26] Anyone who has been in Moscow or Petersburg can visualize the enormously long escalators which are to be found in certain metro stations. The Russian voluntary sector has indeed functioned like an escalator, bringing up into the open problem upon problem, group after group of citizens whose needs had previously been ignored and who had played little or no role in public life. Once above ground they frequently have remained obstinately within public view, participating in the process of *demokratizatsiya* and asserting their right to be treated as citizens even if, as non-'toilers', they have traditionally not been regarded as such. It is true that some activists and organizations appeared only to vanish almost immediately, descending back underground, but the escalator itself continued in motion, bringing more and more new participants to ensure the voluntary sector's survival and growth.

Appendix: the Survey

LIST OF SURVEY RESPONDENTS

Respondent	Location	Short title of organization
Aguzarov	Vladikavkaz	FMZ
Avdeeva	Bryansk	Diabetes Society
Avetisova	Penza	Children's Fund
Babrasheva	Gorno-Altaisk	FMZ
Bitova	Moscow	Centre for Curative Pedagogics
Bolenok	Lobnya	*Memorial*
Burkova	Sverdlovsk	*Korchaginets* Club
Cheremnykh	Kemerovo	Disabled People's Support
Cherepov	Bryansk	FMZ
Chernosvitova	Novo-Zavidovo	*Miloserdie* Fund
Chernyshov [x][1]	Moscow	Children of Russia*[2]
Chukhno	Moscow	Red Cross
Evdokimov	Lomonosov	*Rambov* Diabetes Society
Evseenkova [x]	Vladimir	'Nadezhda' Charity House*
Fridman	Apatity	YM Club
Gladysheva	Moscow	Elizaveta Fedorovna Charity Fund
Gluzinskii	Penza	Union of Veterans of Afghanistan
Gorbon	Vladimir	Family [large families]
Goryacheva	Leningrad	*Dolgoletie* [club for elderly people]
Gureev	Moscow	*Medinvest** [heart problems]
Gusev [x]	Moscow	Kolomenskoe Charity Fund
Guseva	Kirovsk	*Memorial*
Gutin	Bryansk	Not Yet Evening [disabled peoples' club]
Ivakin	Bryansk	VOI borough organization
Kalinichevs	Moscow	Journal *Preodolenie*

193

Respondent	Location	Short title of organization
Karev	Orsk	VOI borough organization
Katel'nitskii	Pskov	VOG
Khlebushkina	Penza	FMZ
Kholchev	Moscow	Football for Disabled People
Kichatov	Kaliningrad	Pushkin Society
Kienya	Moscow	Only Mummy
Klimov	Ufa	[charity at Cyril and Methodius Cathedral]
Krivonozhko	Bryansk	FMZ borough organization
Kovalenko	Moscow	Tereza Charity Society*
Kovaleva	Pskov	FMZ
Kropachev	Krasnodar	*Memorial*
Kuzmich	Omsk	Lyubena [disabled people's association]
Kuznetsova [x]	Samara	*Samaryane** [intelligentsia organization]
Lepeshkina	Leningrad	Incomplete Family Club [renamed Family Centre]
Litvinenko	Leningrad	Second Life [heart transplants]
Lozhkin	Abez	*Memorial*
Lutskevich	Voronezh	Large Family
Maksimov	Moscow	*Invachess* [disabled people's chess society]
Man'ko	Moscow	Maternal Glory [large families]
Marchenko	Moscow	Mother's Right [deceased servicemen]
Masterupolo	Moscow	St. Panteleimon Brotherhood
Matveeva	Staraya Kupavna	*Memorial*
Matyukin [x]	Segezha	*Memorial*
Medvedev	Novgorod	Young Prisoners in Fascist Camps
Mendelevich	Orel	*Memorial*
Molchanova	Leningrad	Large Family
Navrotskii	Ivdel	*Memorial*
Negreev [x]	Moscow	Lifeguards' Society

Appendix: the Survey 195

Respondent	Location	Short title of organization
Nikiforov	Moscow	Radonezh religious cooperative
Paaso	Petrozavodsk	Memorial
Panteleev	Nizhni Novgorod	Assn of Victims of Communist Terror*
Pasynkov	Salavat	Memorial*
Pavlova [x]	Moscow	Human Soul
Petelin	Lipetsk	Memorial
Pogozhev	Leningrad	VOI borough organization
Podshivalov	Moscow	Folk Warriors (Bogatyri)
Rodionov	Leningrad	VOS, musical association
Rogova	Chelyabinsk	Lesenka kindergarten
Savel'ev	Tula	World without Violence
Serafim [x]³	Kaluga	(Orthodox Chuch)
Serbskii [x]	Bratsk	Memorial
Shapp	Sterlitamak	Memorial
Shevchenko	Leningrad	Nevskii Centre for Large Families
Shipulina	Leningrad	Diabetes Society
Sobol' [x]	Moscow	Jewish Veterans' Union (SEIVV)
Sobolev	Sverdlovsk	Federation of Deaf Chessplayers
Soshina	Solovki	Memorial
Tkalya	Pskov	Red Cross
Tokarev	Terbuny	Memorial
Vasil'eva	Ulan-Ude	FMZ
Verkina	Vladimir	[family children's home group]*
Verkina	Vladimir	[family children's home]
Vodyakova	Povorino	[family children's home]
Yakovets	Slyudyanka	Memorial
Yakovleva	Kostroma	FMZ
Yatskova	Vladivostok	Memorial
Yur'eva	Moscow	Pushkin Society
Zhil'tsova [x]	Gorno-Altaisk	Memorial
Zinchenko	Chelyabinsk	Soldiers' Mothers
Zubakov*	Pskov	Northern Pilgrim

Appendix: the Survey

TRANSLATION OF SURVEY QUESTIONS[4]

Name and address of organization
Questions about you:

1. Name [and status in organization][5]
2. When did you begin working for your organization?

Questions about your organization from its founding to August 1991:

1. Who founded the organization? (Name, position, age, party membership, other data)
2. When:
   - was the idea of founding the organization conceived?
   - was the first meeting of volunteers?[6]
   - was an organizing committee set up?
   - was the founding conference held?
   - was the organization registered?
3. What new aspects of the local political and social environment made the organization's creation possible? What used to hinder the creation of this type of organization in your town?
4. At the time the organization was founded, did you know of any similar organizations in the town or of any unsuccessful attempts to create such organizations in the past? If so, which?
5. How did you determine whom to help and how to help them?
6. What were the organization's main objectives? How successfully were they achieved?
7. Did the organization have paid employees? If so, how many? Did activists express worries about the creation of a paid staff?
8.1 How many volunteers worked for the organization at various times? If there was a rise or fall in numbers, why did this occur?
8.2 Please characterize the volunteers by age, sex, social status, etc.
9.1 Did the organization have a membership?

Appendix: the Survey

9.2 If it did, how many members were there at various times?
9.3 How many rubles per annum were collected in dues?
10. Did work for the organization unite the volunteers or was there instead a degree of fragmentation? Why did this happen?
11. Did the local authorities, CPSU and *Komsomol* impinge[7] on the work of the organization before August 1991? Please give specific examples.
12. What was the attitude of the majority of volunteers and members of the organization to the existing power structures? Did you have discussions among yourselves on this issue? (For example, about whether to register the organization or not.)
13. Did the organization possess or was it connected with enterprises or cooperatives? If so, how much income did they generate for the organization?
14.1 Did the organization receive help from private individuals (outside the organization)? If so, from whom? What type of help?
14.2 Did the organization receive help from: VOS; VOG; VOI; Children's Fund; FMZ; Peace Fund; Red Cross; veterans' organizations and councils; other national funds and non-governmental organizations (which)?; other funds or associations protecting the interests of various social groups? If so, how did they help?
14.3 Did the organization receive help from: trade unions; local authorities (council executive committee, social security department, etc.); CPSU; *Komsomol*? If so, how did they help?
14.4 Did the organization receive help from: new political organizations (which?); religious congregations and organizations (which?); the media (which?); cooperatives and enterprises; other organizations and institutions? If so, how did they help?
15. Which organizations did your organization help and how?
16. Did your organization ever participate in political activities (for example, sponsoring candidates in local government elections or taking part in rallies and marches)? If so, please give specific examples.

[1] [x] indicates that letters/supporting material were sent without a questionnaire, except in the case of children's home and CHF respondents who were sent slightly different lists of questions in the form of a letter. However, many of these also completed copies of the standard questionnaire, which I had asked them to pass on to other organizations.
[2] * indicates an organization founded after the coup of August 1991.
[3] Letter stating that there were no Orthodox charities in the bishopric before 1992.
[4] The pilot survey, in December 1992, was slightly less detailed but essentially the same. Most of the questionnaires were sent out in late summer 1993. A few were sent in 1996.
[5] This question was added to the 1996 questionnaires, but most of the earlier respondents made clear their status.
[6] *aktivisty*
[7] The Russian *vmeshivat'sya* can have negative connotations ('to interfere') and it was interesting to see how respondents interpreted this word.

Notes

CHAPTER 1: *DEMOKRATIZATSIYA* AND THE VOLUNTARY SECTOR

1. It is impossible to write about civil society without positioning oneself somewhere on a definitional minefield. My definition is intended to include *some* economic activities – cooperatives of disabled people, for example. Moreover, it focuses not just on the existence of non-state organizations but also on the political implications of that existence (mediating between individual and state) and the normative implications of the word 'civil': implying a connection with citizenship and democracy-building.
2. See Saraksina, p. 19, for definition and absence of definition of the word in Soviet dictionaries and encyclopaedias. Not only *blagotvoritel'nost'* (philanthropy) but even *miloserdie* (charitable feeling, compassion) was sometimes omitted. On the other hand, *miloserdie* could be used in a positive sense before 1985. See I. Fedorova.
3. *Ulitsa Miloserdiya.* Granin.
4. I am grateful to Duncan Leitch for his comments on 'charity'.
5. See Urban, Smith and Fish for particularly useful discussions of the Gorbachev period in this wider context.
6. '*Arshinom obshchim ne izmerit'*', F. Tyutchev, '*Umom Rossiyu ne ponyat'*', *Stikhotvoreniya* (Sverdlovsk, 1980) p. 44.
7. See Bibliography. Of the academic works, Matthews, M., 'Perestroika and the rebirth of charity', in Jones, Connor and Powell (eds), is an excellent account of developments up to 1988. Brody and Boris is more general, as is Reiner. A. White (1993) presents many of the arguments made in this book. Leitch (1997), while focusing on a small case study of Voronezh in the post-communist period, makes many perceptive judgements on the Soviet era. Fabel, F., 'Self-help initiatives: forces of self-healing within Russian society?' in Segbers and de Spiegeleire (eds) is brief and published in 1995, but provides a thoughtful discussion of issues relevant also to the earlier period, based on analysis of four Petersburg organizations. Nina Belyaeva (Interlegal Research Center) has written extensively and more theoretically on civil society and the voluntary sector. IRIS also raises important theoretical points, but focuses mostly on the post-1991 era. Publications by Russian and British charities present a mass of information on the more recent period. They include Young and Legendre (Charities Aid Foundation); the *BEARR* and *Healthprom Newsletters*; *Third Sector* (Moscow: Interlegal); and, in Russian, *Vestnik blagotvoritel'nosti* (Moscow: Moscow Charity House and *Soprichastnost'* Fund) and *Den'gi i blagotvoritel'nost'* (Moscow: CAF and *Soprichastnost'*).

There are a number of directories produced in the post-1991 period. Chizhov (1992), in Russian, is the most detailed. Others are Harvey (ch. 14); Ruffin, McCarter and Upjohn; Vessey (Perm); Ousow (Samara); *Petersburg*; Yntemna (available in Russian and English).

Of specific organizations, *Memorial*, which was of course much in addition to a charity/self-help organization, has attracted the most attention. Smith's is the most thorough and analytical treatment; Adler's is also helpful. A. White (1995) discusses *Memorial*, particularly its provincial aspects, more thoroughly than in this book. Devlin and Fish make useful points on *Memorial* within their wider discussions of independent political organizations. For other charities and self-help groups, see the Bibliography.

8. Most letters were written to Helvi Häkkelä, one of the Voronezh activists described in Chapter 3. Of these letters, the largest number are from Mikhail Karev, one of the most vocal of disabled activists under Gorbachev, who was based in Orsk (Orenburg *oblast*), and Nina Vishnyakova, a severely disabled journalist from Sverdlovsk, whose diary was published posthumously in 1990.
9. Three visits to Russia 1977–82, including the academic year 1981–2 in Voronezh; six visits, totalling seven months, February 1987–August 1992.
10. Zinchenko questionnaire.
11. Schopflin, ch. 7.
12. Hauslohner (1989) p. 44.
13. Arato, A., 'Social movements and civil society in the Soviet Union', in Sedaitis and Butterfield (eds), p. 199; Butterfield, J. and Weigle, M., 'Unofficial social groups and regime response in the Soviet Union', in ibid., p. 175.
14. Smith pp. 17–18.
15. Fish p. 172.
16. Lewin p. 103.
17. Shlapentokh p. 13.
18. Lapidus p. 129.
19. See e.g. Pilkington (1996); Riordan (ed.) (1989); A. White (1989 ('Cultural enlightenment') and 1990); Dobson, R., 'Youth problems in the Soviet Union', in Jones, Connor and Powell (eds). An excellent summary of the literature for and against the existence of informal groups before 1985 is to be found in Leitch (1993), ch. 1.
20. On 'exit', see Lapidus p. 129.
21. *Klub samodeyatel'noi pesni*.
22. *Samodeyatel'nye* pp. 115–9.
23. Urban p. 26.
24. Easton, P., 'The rock music community', in Riordan (ed.) (1989), especially pp. 47 and 79.
25. See A. White (1990).
26. Warner pp. 195–8.
27. See e.g. 'Those who didn't complain'.
28. On Baikal in the 1960s, see e.g. Ziegler pp. 53–7.

29. See Yanitsky, chs. 2 and 3 for a detailed analysis, and also: Harvey p. 213; *Samodeyatel'nye* pp. 114–15.
30. Fish's otherwise excellent book is a notable example.
31. Brown; Chernyaev.
32. *XIX vsesoyuznaya* pp. 74–5, p. 47.
33. Lapidus p. 121.
34. Leitch (1993), unpaginated Synopsis.
35. Gorbachev's comment to his wife on the eve of his election as General Secretary.
36. *Clive Anderson*.
37. See e.g. Urban pp. 63–5.
38. Moses; Fish.
39. Arato, op. cit., p. 208.
40. Leitch (1993) arrives at a similar conclusion p. 16.
41. On the figures, see e.g. Tolz (1989) p. 4 and (1990) ch. 2.
42. A. White ('Cultural enlightenment') p. 243.
43. Pavlovsky and Meyer.
44. Berezovsky et al. (my count and analysis); 134 were nation-wide organizations and a minimum of 261 were based in Moscow or Leningrad.
45. Interlegal (1991).
46. Harvey p. 207.
47. Leitch (1993) p. 27.
48. An *oblast* is the largest administrative unit below republican level.
49. *Vserossiiskoe obshchestvo invalidov*.
50. This figure does not include 1,900 primary organizations in workplaces and homes. Tsentral'noe p. 4.
51. Tsentral'noe pp. 3–4.
52. Leitch (1993, 1996) and Yntemna suggest the same conclusion. Of the 32 questionnaires I received from groups which were not branches of national organizations (including *Memorial*) only five or six were charities. (The existence of a number of hybrids makes it hard to be definitive.)
53. Chizhov p. 15.
54. See e.g. Young p. 15, who refers to the 1992 VTsIOM survey analysed in more detail in Sazonov et al. and Popov and Sazonov.
55. 'Tochka otscheta'; Sazonov et al.
56. Zinchenko questionnaire.
57. Chizhov (my analysis). I excluded foreigners and a few people whose sex is indeterminable from the index. The exact percentages were 65.5 per cent men and 34.5 per cent women.
58. Vessey (my analysis).
59. These conclusions are based on analysis of the 43 organizations (excluding *Memorials*) who completed questions about social composition in my questionnaire. *Memorial* is discussed in A. White (1995).
60. Urban p. 95.
61. Molchanova questionnaire.
62. A. White (1995).
63. Pogozhev questionnaire.

CHAPTER 2: 1985: THE STATE IN CRISIS

1. Soldantenkov p. 5.
2. *Polozhenie* p. 11.
3. There is almost no reference, however, to the role of party policy-making in the standard works on Soviet health care and social security, presumably because evidence is hard to find. Ryan is an honourable exception, although even he provides only one illustration of how 'the Party does indeed play a separate and decisive role in the government of health provision'. Ryan (1978) p. 12.
4. Cook p. 51.
5. Cook p. 52.
6. *Polozhenie* p. 89.
7. *120 let* p. 57.
8. Feltham and Meiroyan p. 18.
9. Matthews (1986) p. 115.
10. Jones, Connor and Powell (eds), Introduction p. 8.
11. Perevedentsev; Powell, D., 'Aging and the elderly', in Jones et al. (eds) pp. 174–5.
12. Matthews (1986) p. 116; Karaseva pp. 35–7; Powell, op. cit., pp. 188–9.
13. *Sovetskaya Rossiya*, 15.7.83, quoted in Hegelson (1989) p. 59.
14. Feschbach and Friendly.
15. Field, M., 'Soviet health problems and the convergence hypothesis', in Jones et al. (eds) p. 83. Powell, in the same volume, has slightly different figures (p. 117).
16. Pavlov; interview information from V. Venediktov, former head of the Soviet Red Cross, 1992; Ryan (1990) p. 146.
17. See, for example, *USSR Health Service* (1970). Aggregate statistics concealed the existence of very different doctor–patient ratios in ordinary and elite medical institutions.
18. Evans.
19. Uzlikova p. 36.
20. Udintsev and Gorbunova p. 31.
21. Chesnokova (1.89).
22. Tsentral'noe p. 3.
23. See Matthews (1989) pp. 113, 119.
24. A. White (1990) p. 77.
25. Raymond, P., 'Disability as dissidence: the Action Group to Defend the Rights of the Disabled in the USSR', in McCagg and Siegelbaum (eds) p. 239.
26. Mikhailova.
27. Letter from R. Shivite to *Ogonek*, no. 15, 1987, 11.
28. 'Oni i my'.
29. Glick p. 23.
30. Kas'yanenko and Godin.
31. Abramkin,'Dangerous' p. 24.
32. Sarkisyan p. 29.
33. Kostikov.
34. Matthews (1978) p. 130.

35. Ibid.; Voslensky.
36. Gorbachev (1987) p. 23.
37. Cook p. 49 gives figures of 5 and 6 per cent respectively for the early 1980s.
38. See Madison (1988) p. 181.
39. On inequality and its justifications within the labour force, see Yanowitch. On academic debate about the legal nature of the right to social security as enshrined in the 1936 and 1977 constitutions, see Madison (1988) p. 185.
40. See e.g. Matthews (1986) p. 119.
41. Quoted in Glick p. 34.
42. See, for example, Pekur (7.87).
43. Chesnokova (4.89).
44. M. Karev, letters to H. Häkkelä, 17.3.80, 5.8.80.
45. On the fate of orphans, see Harwin (1996) pp. 20–3. Harwin suggests that the overall standard of homes was low. However, there were naturally exceptions: for a favourable description of one home, recorded in a personal diary, see Vishnyakova (1990). Moreover, many ordinary families lived in abject poverty in communal barracks, so comparatively speaking even inadequate children's homes might possess some advantages over private dwellings.
46. *Doma prestarelykh i invalidov*. Calculated from Powell, op. cit., p. 185.
47. Andreeva (1978) p. 61; Andreeva (1977) p. 36; Rudakov p. 26.
48. See e.g. Hegelson pp. 61–2 and Powell, op. cit., p. 184.
49. Gubakov et al. p. 2; Samarina; Komarova (1986) p. 5.
50. This was true not only in the press but also in personal conversation between social security officials and clients. For example, one official told a sceptical disabled activist that her attempt to create a self-help group was unnecessary: a single disabled person could always find companionship in a comfortable residential home. By shouting this ideological truism at the woman – seated beside him – he was able to reduce her to tears. He then tried to reinforce his argument by referring to his personal authority, reminding her that he had previously been the local mayor. Presumably he felt that he was on shaky ground. T. Zagvozdina, letter to H. Häkkelä, 6.10.71.
51. 'Odinochestvo' and Zolotova.
52. For example: Altunin; Edel'; Rad'ko; Kleva.
53. Letter from resident of home in Oksoch to H. Häkkelä, 7.1.68.
54. Häkkelä et al.
55. Rudakov pp. 26–7.
56. Likhanov (1987) p. 14 (*not* AW's translation).
57. Ibid. p. 8.
58. *Polozhenie* p. 93.
59. Harwin, 'Child Protection' pp. 69–70.
60. Sutton, A., 'Special education for handicapped pupils', in Riordan (ed.) (1988) p. 90.
61. Ibid. p. 87. An inspection in Tula and the Chelyabinsk *oblast* revealed that this had 'often' occurred.
62. See e.g. Cook p. 51.

63. Andreeva (1971) p. 33.
64. Parfenova.
65. Dunn, S. and Dunn, E., 'Everyday life of the disabled in the USSR', in McCagg and Siegelbaum (eds) p. 288.
66. 'A vremya'.
67. Dyskin et al. The decline was attributed partly to the ageing of people disabled in the Second World War.
68. Udintsev and Gorbunova, p. 33. On rural issues, see Kravchenko. A series of letters from N. Sedova to Häkkelä convey vividly the plight of rural disabled people.
69. For the 24th and 25th congresses, see Andreeva (1971) p. 33 and Gorbunova and Petrova p. 7.
70. Grafova; Gus'kov, 'Komu' p. 11; Udintsev and Gorbunova p. 34; Uzlikova p. 38.
71. This was attributed to the implementation of the Council of Ministers' decree of 14.9.73, no. 674. See Uzlikova p. 38. For a survey of the issues and regulations, see Pankin.
72. Komarova (1981) p. 5.
73. See e.g. Steele.
74. Gorbunova and Petrova p. 7.
75. Udintsev and Gorbunova p. 33. However, disabled war veterans could be left off the official list of employees so that they would not adversely affect the enterprise's average. Hegelson p. 65.
76. Uzlikova p. 37.
77. Grafova.
78. Udintsev and Gorbunova p. 34.
79. Andreeva (1971) p. 31; Uzlikova p. 37. The Russian term was *inspektora po trudoustroistvu*.
80. Parfenova.
81. The Russian is *trudovaya rekomendatsiya*.
82. Chesnokova (1.89).
83. Chesnokova (1.89).
84. Parfenova.
85. Demenkova. See Madison (1988) on complaints within the social security system more generally.
86. Häkkelä, 'Elene Rzhevskoi'.
87. Unsurprisingly, this rule was broken in practice, leading to the exploitation of the disabled people concerned. For example, Mikhail Karev in Orsk was permanently employed in the accounts office at his residential home but his official title was 'cloakroom attendant'. He was dismissed and reemployed every two months and refused the entitlements due to a permanent employee. M. Karev, letter to H. Häkkelä, 17.3.80.
88. 'Vozvrashchenie'.
89. Kleva.
90. Puchkov et al.
91. Kabakov.
92. Ryan (1978) p. 132.
93. 'Gotovy'.

94. Lushnikov.
95. Gorbachev (1987) p. 21.

CHAPTER 3: 1985: SOCIETY IN CRISIS

1. Gorbachev (1987), p. 24.
2. Tat'yana Zaslavskaya was a sociologist who became one of Gorbachev's advisors. Her 1983 'Novosibisk Report', suggesting that worker alienation was a source of Soviet economic underperformance, was an important influence on Gorbachev's thinking.
3. Vlasov: Lindenmeyr; Bokhanov.
4. See *Soviet Constitution* p. 176.
5. Hegelson p. 53.
6. *Vserossiskoe obshchestvo spasaniya na vodakh*.
7. *120 let* p. 15.
8. See, for example, the definitions discussed in a standard textbook, Brenton pp. 7–9.
9. See A. White (1990).
10. Shlapentokh pp. 116–17.
11. Kuebart, F., 'The political socialisation of schoolchildren', in Riordan (ed.) (1989) p. 107.
12. Shlapentokh p. 101.
13. Kuebart, op. cit., p. 117.
14. I. Fedorova.
15. D'yachenko, 'Obrashchayus''.
16. Hegelson p. 52.
17. Friedgut p. 285.
18. Ryan (1978) p. 20.
19. Madison, B., 'Social programs for the disabled in the USSR', in McCagg and Siegelbaum (ed.); Neumyvakin; interviews at VOS, Leningrad, April 1988; Klyushnikov and Matveev; Kulicheva. The Russian names of the societies were *Vserossiiskoe obshchestvo glukhikh* and *Vserossiiskoe obshchestvo slepykh*.
20. Almost all the seminal articles mentioned in the section below, on the press and VOI, drew the analogy of VOS and/or VOG, as did much of the writing of the Gorbachev period.
21. Madison, 'Social programs' pp. 191–2.
22. Grafova; Borutskaya.
23. For two examples in Penza, see Andreeva (1971) pp. 31–2.
24. Petukhov.
25. Madison (1968) pp. 183–4; Konstantinov; Glick p. 2; Kupriyanov ('*Perestroika* has solved'); interviews with Yurii Kiselev; T. Zolottseva, deputy president of VOI; Yurii Misyurev, disabled activist, Moscow, July–August 1992.
26. Häkkelä, second letter to V. Stakhov [1970/1].
27. Madison, 'Social programs' p. 169.
28. Teague p. 78.
29. Sichka; M. Karev, letter to Häkkelä, 5.8.86.

30. S. White (1983) p. 51.
31. On letter writing and the official response, see e.g. ibid. or Teague ch. 5.
32. This issue is explored below, in the section on the press and VOI, and also by Teague pp. 80–2.
33. See e.g. McAndrew.
34. Helvi Häkkelä's personal archive contains a number of examples.
35. Karev to A. White, 18.9.93.
36. Karev to Häkkelä [1975 or 6].
37. They replied that VOI could not be created at the given time because of the difficult economic situation and international tensions. Karev to Häkkelä, 15.5.83.
38. N. Sedova, undated letters to Häkkelä [1960s].
39. e.g. Häkkelä to CPSU Central Committee, 10.8.77.
40. 'Pros'ba'; letter from K. Protsenko to 'Sedova's group', 13.2.80. Another disabled activist then wrote to *Goskomtrud* to complain about Protsenko's reply, but received a similar rebuttal. Yu. Ryabochkin to Karev, 23.6.80.
41. 'Predlozhenie'; handwritten list of some of the signatories to a letter to Presidium of the Supreme Soviet; 'Obrashchenie invalidov'; letter from I. Shmatov, Voronezh *oblsobes*, to Häkkelä, 26.2.80.
42. 'Pros'ba'; 'Obrashchenie invalidov'.
43. e.g. Rudenko (4.84); Ermachenko.
44. Kononenko.
45. Kononenko to Häkkelä, 12,12.74.
46. Gus'kov, 'Komu', p. 9. Gus'kov claimed that during the same period Voronezh *oblsobes* had failed to find work for a single disabled person.
47. Kononenko to Häkkelä, 10.2.75.
48. Häkkelä et al., 'Bol'shoi' lomot'?'
49. T. Gavrilova to Häkkelä, 27.11.81.
50. Häkkelä to White, 17.6.94.
51. Letter no. 1 from Häkkelä to V. Stakhov, [1970].
52. T. Zagvozdina, undated (1974?) letter to Häkkelä.
53. Letter from Voronezh residents to *Komsomol'skaya pravda*, in response to Trius, 'Tol'ko li'.
54. Karev questionnaire.
55. G. Golovatyi to Häkkelä, 26.5.86.
56. For example, N. Morzhina at *Komsomol'skaya pravda* helped the *Korchaginets* Club from very beginning; it was said to have been with her help that they found most of their members. O. Burkova to Yu. Misyurev, 26.10.84.
57. See, for example, letters between 'Alla Borisovna' and Häkkelä, 17.7.76; 17.6.77 (*sic*). Vishnyakova and Kononenko were long-standing friends.
58. Vishnyakova (1968) and (1990); Vishnyakova to Häkkelä, various.
59. In *Sotsial'noe obespechenie*: Häkkelä to White, 17.6.94.
60. Grafova.
61. Vyatkin (1.71) and (12.70).

Notes 207

62. S. Konovalov.
63. Gus'kov, 'Trud'; 'God rozhdeniya'.
64. Vishnyakova to Häkkelä, 14.9.73.
65. Rzhevskaya. For example, the residents at a sanatorium sent their collective response (Puchkov et al.). Qv. Chernoshkur (3.87).
66. See e.g. E. Kuz'min to Häkkelä [1975]. On *Minsobes* and Rzhevskaya, see Kononenko to Häkkelä, 12.12.74.
67. Golovatyi to Häkkelä, 26.5.86.
68. *Razorvannyi krug*. A final chapter of the book (as published in 1994) was written in 1981 and analyses some of the letters Fertman received. On the response, see Neuimina, p. 203. The suggestion about VOI is on p. 152 of the book version. Fertman's case had already been publicised by Vyatkin (12.70).
69. Azarova; 'Sporit' s sud'boi'.
70. Vishnyakova to Häkkelä, 6.4.71. Qv. A. Ivanova to Häkkelä, 9.5.71; D'yachkov (6.88).
71. Zagvozdina to Häkkelä, 6.10.71.
72. Shul'gina.
73. For example, Vishnyakova, to Häkkelä, 6.4.71, considered that Golubev's questionnaire (see below) was 'only meant for home-dwellers' (*domashnie*).
74. Vishnyakova to Häkkelä, 6.4.71.
75. Hankiss.
76. Glick pp. 3–4.
77. Golubev, 'Anketa'; Komitet.
78. Golubev to Häkkelä, 13.9.71.
79. Sedova to Häkkelä [1971?]. For another positive response see Ivanova to Häkkelä, 9.5.71.
80. Zagvozdina to Häkkelä, 6.10.71.
81. Vyatkin (1.71); Zagvozdina, op. cit.
82. Ibid.; Golubev, 'Anketa' (note by H. Häkkelä); Zagvozdina, ibid.
83. Golubev. 'Slovo'; Borutskaya.
84. A. Ivanova, op. cit.
85. Golubev to Häkkelä, 13.9.71; Zagvozdina, op. cit.
86. Ibid.
87. Ibid.; Glick pp. 4–5.
88. Golubev to Häkkelä, 13.9.71, on Samoilenko (Kiev).
89. Zagvozdina, op. cit.
90. Ibid.
91. Gavrilova to Häkkelä, 27.11.81.
92. 'Ustav "Prometeya"'.
93. Ukraine, Belorussia, Kazakhstan: see Gus'kov, 'Komu' p. 12.
94. Zagvozdina, op. cit.
95. Ibid.
96. Vishnyakova to Häkkelä, 15.9.72.
97. Gus'kov, 'Komu', pp. 12–13; Tkachenko; Vakhtina.
98. *Slovo druga*, no. 7, 1983; Shenkman.
99. For Gus'kov's biography and character, see Altunin.
100. See e.g. Gus'kov, 'Komu', pp. 2–3.

101. Rzhevskaya.
102. 'O dopolnitel'nykh'.
103. *Inter alia*, the management tried to cheat and exploit the workshop. See Sichka.
104. Unpublished letter from Gus'kov, Häkkelä and others to *Literaturnaya gazeta*, 17.7.76.
105. Ibid.; Gus'kov (8.87); 'A vremya'; Glick, pp. 43–4.
106. In June 1978 Zagvozdina circulated a request to members to help Gus'kov, followed by a model letter of complaint to the authorities and a list of official addresses.
107. Karev to Häkkelä, 17.3.80. The leading spirit of the group was apparently Tatyana Zavertaeva.
108. 'Zhenya' to Häkkelä, 27.10.84.
109. O. Kameneva to Häkkelä, 7.3.83.
110. Kameneva to Häkkelä, 10.5.82; Gus'kov to Häkkelä, 25.3.85.
111. Kameneva to Häkkelä, 24.10.83.
112. Kameneva to Häkkelä [summer 1982].
113. Kameneva to H. Häkkelä, 24.10.83. The newspaper, unsurprisingly, was *Komsomol'skaya pravda*.
114. Kameneva to Häkkelä, 10.5.82.
115. 'Zhenya', op. cit.
116. *Initsiativnaya gruppa po zashchite prav invalidov*.
117. Glick p. 11.
118. Ibid. pp. 16–17.
119. On the Action Group see Glick; Raymond in McCagg and Siegelbaum, op. cit; Alexeyeva pp. 411–13. Raymond suggests that it more or less ceased to exist after Fefelov was forced to emigrate in 1982, but according to Kiselev (interviewed by AW, Aug. 1992), this is untrue.
120. Glick pp. 19–20.
121. 'Obrashchenie invalidov'.
122. Zagvozdina to Häkkelä, 16.6.82, 14.11.83.
123. Karev questionnaire, 18.9.93.
124. Karev questionnaire.
125. Gus'kov to Häkkelä [April 84].
126. N. Popov.
127. On *Konkordo*, see Grishin and Prisyazhnuk; Grishin. The club organized other activities, such as yoga.
128. The *Klub druzei po perepiske 'Korchaginets'*, later the *Vsesoyuznyi zaochnyi klub 'Korchaginets'*, was named after Pavel Korchagin, hero of Nikolai Ostrovsky's novel *How the Steel was Tempered*.
129. Guskov to Häkkelä, 25.3.85.
130. Saar; Fomin; Babin.
131. Fomin; Zabelin.
132. Pogozhev questionnaire.
133. Shul'gina; Solovei (1986); Pekur and Solovei; 'Bol' ne prokhodit'; Misyurev.
134. Shenkman; Khaustova.
135. Gutin questionnaire.

Notes 209

136. Letter from G. Golovatyi and G. Gus'kov to Gorbachev [1986]; Chernoshkur (1987).
137. Morzhenko; Chizhov p. 96; *Vremya* (Soviet TV, Channel 1), 27.2.91.
138. Molchanova questionnaire.
139. Chizhov p. 125.
140. Interview with Borodaevskaya (1989); Sanatina.
141. Van der Voort.
142. Chizhov p. 133.
143. Nikiforov questionnaire.
144. See e.g. Dobrovol'skaya et al. (1989) p. 285.

CHAPTER 4: *PERESTROIKA* AND THE VOLUNTARY SECTOR

1. Lushnikov, writing about the experience of Leningrad *Miloserdie* Society.
2. D'yachenko, 'Obrashchayus'' p. 7.
3. The anti-alcohol campaign is discussed comprehensively in S. White (1996) and for that reason will not be covered in this chapter.
4. Postanovlenie TsK, SM i VTsSPS '*O pervoocherednykh merakh po uluchsheniyu material'nogo blagosostoyaniya maloobespechennykh pensionerov i semei, usileniyu zaboty ob odinokikh grazhdanakh*'.
5. Matthews (1989) p. 29.
6. *Itogi* p. 21.
7. Jacobs (10.8.90) pp. 3–4. On the pension law, see also Powell in Jones, Connor and Powell (eds), op. cit., pp. 186–7.
8. *Vsesoyuznaya organizatsiya veteranov voiny i truda*. Its charter is in *Trud*, 28.12.86, 2. On its goals – the chief of which was patriotic education – see Izgarshev. See also Matthews, '*Perestroika and the rebirth of charity*', in Jones, Connor and Powell (eds) p. 158. On party membership of deputies, see election results in *Izvestiya*, 5.4.89, 2–12.
9. Karev to Häkkelä, 5.8.86.
10. Hegelson pp. 59–61.
11. Portugeis.
12. Interview with V. and D. Lytkin, Novosibirsk *Miloserdie*, 1989; Matthews, 'Perestroika', op. cit.
13. Bobkov.
14. *Territorial'nye tsentry sotsial'nogo obespecheniya ili kluby dobrykh druzei*. See 'L'goty'.
15. 'Kriterii'.
16. '*O merakh po dal'neishemu uluchsheniyu uslovii zhizni invalidov s detstva*'.
17. Karev, op. cit.
18. Two disabled activists claimed in a letter to Gorbachev that the problem was that those responsible for implementing the decreees were not themselves disabled: see Gus'kov and Golovatyi p. 4.
19. *Polozhenie* p. 94; Harwin (1996) pp. 70–1 on the 1987 resolution.
20. Matthews, op. cit., p. 158.
21. 'Fond i ego "Zabota"'; 'Vzroslym i detyam'; 'Zavodskoi fond miloserdiya'.

210   Notes

22. Savvateeva p. 43.
23. Tsyganov.
24. 'Srochno'.
25. Cook p. 187.
26. Protsenko; Oliver p. 98.
27. 'Profsoyuzy'.
23. See for example Sakharov p. 91.
28. Lakhno.
29. *Vsesoyuznaya assotsiatsiya spasatelei.* See Samokhin; 'Spasateli'.
30. 'Geografiya miloserdiya'.
31. Maksimova.
32. Nadezhdina; 'Komandu otmenili'.
33. Lavrent'eva.
34. 'Davaite, vse vmeste'; 'Pomnim, skorbim'. The Russian name was *Novosibirskoe tovarishchestvo postradavshikh pod Ufoi,* and the society met under the aegis of the local Charity and Health Foundation.
35. 'Budem pomnit".
36. Vitkovskaya.
37. Kozlov, V., 'Social and geographical analysis of the flow and territorial distribution of refugees and migrants in Russia', in Segbers and de Spiegeleire (eds) p. 44.
38. Jacobs (21.9.90).
39. Sarkisyan p. 29.
40. Powell, op. cit., p. 187.
41. Jacobs (10.8.90) p. 3.
42. *Itogi,* p. 19.
43. *Detskii fond imeni V. I. Lenina.*
44. Shcherbakov p. 5.
45. Aguzarov questionnaire.
46. Kienya questionnaire.
47. Tsentral'noe p. 9.
48. See e.g. Bridger et al.
49. Valer'yanov. *Vsesoyuznaya assotsiatsiya spetsialistov po okhrane truda,* founded late May 1990. (There already existed organizations in Leningrad, Kharkov and Primorskii krai.)
50. Interview with Yu. Kiselev, 1992; Ivakin.
51. Harwin, 'USSR' p. 639.
52. Cook suggests the same, p. 89.
53. Jacobs (31.8.90) p. 6.
54. V. Pavlov.
55. 'Kriterii'.
56. 'Davaite delat"; Sviridova; Antonenko; 'Kriterii'. The charity firms were named *Vechernie zori* ('Evening glow').
57. 'Vozlyubi'.
58. *Vechernii Novosibirsk,* 10.7.90, 1 and 13.2.90, 3.
59. Untitled item in *Moskovskaya pravda,* 23.3.90, abstract in *RB* (see Bibliography).
60. See e.g. Goryunov; *Sobesednik* no. 52, 1987.
61. See e.g. Galeotti (1995) pp. 104–7.

62. Chesnokova (1.89).
63. The Baikal-Amur railway, parallel to the Trans-Siberian.
64. Granin.
65. D'yachenko, 'Obrashchayus".
66. Bobkov.
67. Borovoi pp. 19–20.
68. *Vechernii Novosibirsk*, 13.2.90, 2.
69. Astakhov and Burkov p. 90.
70. Borovoi.
71. *Moskovskoe invalidnoe kooperativnoe ob"edinenie*.
72. Tsygankova; Savel'ev.
73. 'Proizvodstvennye'. For an example of a successful VOI enterprise, see Chizhov pp. 77–8. The *Invalidnaya pomoshch'* cooperative in Moscow's Kuibyshev borough was set up jointly by VOI and the social security department. It provided both workplaces and also charitable help for poor disabled people. In 1989–91 the cooperative gave more than 150,000 rubles-worth of financial and other help. By 1992, however, it was in difficulties.
74. Tsentral'noe p. 9.
75. Gurinovich p. 3.
76. 'Support'.
77. Chesnokova (21.11.89); '"Opora"'.
78. See e.g. Stepanova and Kolesnikova on *Ortolyuks* and *Ortotekhnika* in Leningrad; Vasil'kova, 'Khodit', 'General'nym' and Gurinovich on *Invatekhnika* in Moscow.
79. See Cook pp. 134–8 on the chequered history and eventual near prohibition of medical cooperatives.
80. Gurinovich p. 3.
81. e.g. Chizhov; *Blagotvoritel'nye organizatsii Moskvy*.
82. For example, *Invapomoschch'*, see above.
83. Tsygankova.
84. 'My zhdem'; Trehub.
85. Matthews (1992) pp. 61–2.
86. Ibid.
87. *Sovetskii Krasnyi Krest segodnya* contains copies of five articles from the national press on this subject (pp. 147–9, 152).
88. Crow.
89. Yntemna p. iii.
90. See Chapter 5.
91. Yntemna pp. iv–v.
92. Ibid., my analysis.
93. Ibid. p. vii.
94. There are many examples. See e.g. Valyuzhenach.
95. See e.g. Brody and Boris; 'Priorities'.
96. Interview with Mary Yntemna at United Way, July 1992; *United Way Program Update*; Chizhov pp. 184–5.
97. British Emergency Action in Russia and the Republics.
98. BEARR Trust.
99. Tsygankova.

CHAPTER 5: CHARITIES

1. Kalinina. (The organizations listed were: the Council of Party Veterans (Old Bolsheviks' Choir); the Committee of Veterans of War and Labour; the Fund for Aid to Blockade Survivors; the Association of Victims of Illegal Repressions; 'youth organizations of a communist orientation'; and the Children's Fund.)
2. This is the translation adopted by the Foundation. 'Fund' could also be used for *Fond*, while *Miloserdiya* might be translated 'Mercy'.
3. *Soyuz obshchestv Krasnogo Kresta i Krasnogo Polumesyatsa SSSR.*
4. Cherkasov p. 9.
5. Interviews at the Red Cross with L. Cherkasskaya and D. Venediktov (head of the Soviet Red Cross 1986–92); *Sovetskii Krasnyi Krest segodnya*; 'Miloserdie i "Miloserdie"'; Shirinskii; Muzei Sovetskogo Krasnogo Kresta.
6. 'Tochka otscheta' pp. 41–2.
7. Ibid.
8. *Fond mira.*
9. 'Fond mira'.
10. Ibid.
11. Kutateladze.
12. *I lyazhet* p. 1.
13. Venediktov interview; Rakhimov; Venediktov; L. Zhukova.
14. Gorbachev had recently become *Prezident SSSR.*
15. 'Rezolyutsiya Uchreditel'noi konferentsii', in *Sovetskii FMZ... Osnovnye dokumenty* p. 1.
16. 'Miloserdie i sochuvstvie'.
17. Khlebushkina questionnaire.
18. On one clinic in Vladimir, see *Iz opyta* pp. 41–3. On the Edelweiss 'charity cooperative' nursing agency in Tula, see 'Bolee 100'.
19. 'Primite'.
20. *Itogi* p. 55.
21. *Ob itogakh* pp. 16, 19.
22. *Itogi* p. 55; *Iz opyta* pp. 13, 14, 40.
23. *Otchet* p. 3; *Itogi* pp. 2, 69–72.
24. Kutateladze, on the national board; Lytkins interview, on Novosibirsk; Bokova, on Voronezh.
25. *Vo imya dobra* p. 26.
26. Lytkins interview.
27. 'Miloserdie – kategoriya'.
28. Interview with L. Kabanova, FMZ (Moscow), 1992.
29. 'Po-tul'ski'.
30. Vasil'eva questionnaire.
31. 'Dela tekushchie'.
32. Kovaleva questionnaire.
33. Yakovleva questionnaire.
34. *Rukovoditeli.*
35. Kovaleva questionnaire.
36. Questionnaire (anonymity preserved).

37. 'Razdeli chuzhuyu bedu' pp. 9–10; interview with N. D'yachenko, Leningrad *Miloserdie*, 1990; *Itogi* pp. 14–15.
38. *Ob itogakh* p. 25.
39. Ibid. p. 3.
40. *Otchet* p. 2.
41. Men'shikov in *Ob itogakh* p. 29.
42. *Iz opyta* pp. 56–9.
43. 'Rezolyutsiya', op. cit, p. 2.
44. *Itogi* p. 10; *Ob itogakh* p. 7.
45. *Itogi* p. 5, re. commissions; *Vo imya dobra* p. 42.
46. Ibid.
47. *I lyazhet* pp. 15, 27.
48. 'Miloserdie – kategoriya'.
49. *Otchet* p. 4. This figure did not include money held by the auxiliary commissions in their own accounts.
50. *Iz opyta* p. 56.
51. *Itogi* p. 15; *Iz opyta* pp. 56–9.
52. *Vo imya dobra* p. 7.
53. Ibid. p. 28.
54. *Otchet* pp. 24–5, p. 5.
55. *Komsomol'skaya pravda*, 21.2.91, 2.
56. 'Dela tekushchie'; 'Dollary tsenoyu v zhizn".
57. *Vo imya dobra* p. 31.
58. *Otchet* p. 4.
59. Lasovskaya (24.5.90).
60. *Iz opyta* p. 39.
61. *Ob itogakh* pp. 2–3.
62. *Detskii fond imeni V. I. Lenina*.
63. Likhanov (1990) p. 234.
64. Harwin (1996) p. 72.
65. Waters p. 33.
66. *Polozhenie* p. 15.
67. Artsruni.
68. *Literator*, no. 5 (10), 16.2.90, 2 (letter); L'vova.
69. Likhanov (1987), p. 4.
70. For a collection of Likhanov's writings from 1985 see Likhanov (1990). For the 'cuckoo mother' campaign see Waters. On libraries, see 'Vo imya cheloveka'.
71. *Polozhenie* p. 14.
72. Likhanov (1990) p. 234.
73. Mironova.
74. L'vova.
75. Ibid.
76. Undated (early 1992?), typescript 'Doklad', sent with Avetisova questionnaire.
77. L'vova.
78. Avetisova questionnaire.
79. The scandal is described in Waters pp. 132–4.
80. Kalinina.

214 Notes

81. Waters.
82. Venediktov interview.
83. *Sovetskii fond kul'tury.*
84. Gorbachev (1996) p. 276.
85. Kichatov and Yur'eva questionnaires.
86. Warner p. 192. The English title is that used by the FSI. The Russian is *Fond sotsial'nykh izobretenii.*
87. Warner p. 189.
88. *Foundation.*
89. *Fond molodezhnoi initsiativy.*
90. Interview with Alferenko; *Foundation*; interview with staff at the Novosibirsk FYU, July 1989; Warner. The FSI was launched in July 1987. See 'Fond 700344'. On *'Dolg'*, see e.g. *Komsomol'skaya pravda*, 24.1.88; 13.8.88; 17.8.88.
91. 'Ustav FSI'.
92. *Foundation.*
93. *Bogatyri.*
94. Podshivalov questionnaire; *Realizatsiya programm za 1991 god.*
95. *Mir bez nasiliya.*
96. Savelev questionnaire.
97. Chizhov p. 48.
98. Ibid. pp. 48-9; *Krasnyi Krest segodnya* p. 62.
99. *Fond Marii.*
100. 'Nado uspet"; 'Dopisannaya stroka'.
101. Ibid.
102. *Pravo materi.*
103. Marchenko questionnaire.
104. *Miloserdie* means 'charity', 'mercy' or 'kindness'. In view of the term's complexity, and to avoid confusion with the names of other charities (*blagotvoritel'nye organizatsii*), it seems sensible to use the Russian word.
105. Chumakov.
106. Verbitsky interview.
107. Bokova.
108. Urban pp. 96-7.
109. On the origins of *Miloserdie*, see e.g. N. D'yachenko, 'Shkola' and 'Obrashchayus"; Bogoslovskaya (1987).
110. 'S otkrytym'.
111. From his speech at the founding conference of 'Leningrad', 5.4.88, in *Dom*, no. 1, Oct. 1988, 9.
112. D'yachenko, 'Obrashchayus"', p. 7.
113. Information on *Miloserdie* from interviews with V. Lebedev and N. D'yachenko (Leningrad *Miloserdie* Society) and D. Neklyudov (Christian Democrats/*Dolg*), April 1990; *Samodeyatel'nye* pp. 53-4 ('Chelovek'); *Obshchestvo miloserdiya*; Leningrad Charity Society.
114. D'yachenko, 'Obrashchayus"' p. 8.
115. In 1991 it was renamed the *Soprichastnost'* ('Empathy') Fund.
116. Interview with A. Verbitsky, July 1992. See Matthews, 'Perestroika', op. cit.; or Pantuev for a more sceptical view of *Sobesednik*.

Notes 215

117. Mulina, 'Zhdite'; Mulina, 'Delovye'; V. Zhukova. See Bokova regarding Voronezh, and A. White (1989) regarding Novosibirsk.
118. Bokova; Verbitsky interview; Mulina ('Delovye'); Mulina and Fatecheva; Lushnikov; Verbitsky and D'yachenko interviews.
119. Bokova.
120. Lytkins interview.
121. V. Litvinov (1991).
122. Bokova.
123. D'yachenko, 'Po vashim pros'bam'; Birchenough.
124. Kremina.
125. *Mir i chelovek.*
126. Chizhov p. 47.
127. *Polozhenie* pp. 92–3.
128. Harwin (1992). I am grateful to J. Harwin for her comments to me on the homes. Most of what follows is based on interview information from Z. Borodaevskaya (Novosibirsk, 1989) and L. Yashunina (Children's Fund, Moscow), July 1992 and from my questionnaires.
129. *Pravda*, TASS communiqué, 28.12.88, p. 3; Yashunina interview.
130. Sanatina, and editorial comment to Sanatina's article, with interviews of borough officials.
131. Vodyakova questionnaire.
132. Borodaevskaya interview; Verkina, Vodyakova and Solov'yeva questionnaires/letters.
133. *Polozhenie* p. 93.
134. Harwin (1996) p. 101.
135. Vitkovskaya; Jacobs (21.9.90).
136. *Komitet po okazaniyu ekonomicheskoi, sotsial'noi, kul'turnoi i yuridicheskoi pomoshchi bezhentsam.*
137. *Komitet russkikh bezhentsev.*
138. *Obshchestvennyi komitet po delam bezhentsev i vnutrennikh migrantov 'Grazhdanskoe sodeistvie'.*
139. Chizhov pp. 75–6, 112.
140. Hegelson p. 67.
141. *Miloserdie – dobrota* p. 21.
142. Vessey pp. 31–2.
143. Tarasevich; Shvedova.
144. See e.g. Ryzhkov; *Ogonek*, no. 39 (Sept.) 1989, letter from Moscow Society for the Protection of Animals (*Moskovskoe gorodskoe obshchestvo zashchity zhivotnykh*) p. 4; entries in *Rossiiskaya blagotvoritel'nost'* pp. 24, 32, 124 on a Zoos Fund, a Canine Centre and the Rossiyanin Fund for Protection of Animals.
145. Oliver. Oliver's story stops before the emergence of church-run organizations. These are partly discussed by van de Voort and Troyanovsky. J. Anderson has a helpful section (pp. 174–6), which explores briefly some of the key issues.
146. Oliver pp. 106–7.
147. Van der Voort p. 82–3.
148. Putrenko.
149. Van der Voort p. 82.

150. Krylov and Likholitov.
151. Antic, p. 1.
152. 'Razdelyayut' (and follow-up article, Krasnopol'skaya); Matthews, 'Perestroika', in Jones et al., op. cit., p. 166.
153. Troyanovsky p. 58; Oliver p. 107.
154. Van der Voort p. 85.
155. *Soyuz Pravoslavnykh Bratstv*. See van der Voort pp. 82–3.
156. Ibid.
157. *Dmitrievskoe sestrichestvo* or *Svyato-Dimitrievskaya obshchina sester miloserdiya*. See Eroshok.
158. *Obshchestvo 'Radonezh'*.
159. Nikiforov questionnaire; Chizhov p. 132.
160. *Bratstvo Svyatogo velikomuchenika tselitelya Panteleimona*.
161. Masterupolo questionnaire; Chizhov p. 56; Troyanovsky p. 58.
162. *Bratstvo Ksenii Blazhennoi*.
163. Interview with seminarist member of the Brotherhood of Kseniya the Blessed, Leningrad, April 1990. Chizhov has information on three further brotherhoods, all in Moscow (Prince Vladimir, Bishop Tikhon and Bishop Aleksei), pp. 37, 41, 56.
164. 'Iz vystupleniya patriarkha'.
165. Chizhov.
166. Ibid. p. 110.
167. Oliver p. 104.
168. Lytkins interview.
169. Chizhov p. 18.
170. *Assotsiatsiya 'Sem'ya mira'*.
171. Chizhov p. 32.
172. Troyanovsky pp. 54–5.
173. Chizhov p. 146.
174. Ibid. pp. 69, 116. (*Banim-banot, Tsedek, Agavas Isroel', Rakhamim*).
175. D'yachenko interview.
176. Chizhov pp. 69, 116
177. One exception was the 'Night Hostel' charity (*Nochlezhka*), established in Leningrad in 1989. See e.g. Fabel, F., 'Self-help initiatives: forces of self-healing within Russian society?' in Segbers and de Spiegeleire (eds) pp. 93–4.

CHAPTER 6: SELF-HELP ORGANIZATIONS

1. Vasil'ev.
2. *Tsentr lechebnoi pedagogiki*.
3. Chizhov p. 177–8; Bitova questionnaire.
4. *Dusha cheloveka*.
5. Chizhov p. 42.
6. *Vtoraya zhizn'*.
7. Litvinenko questionnaire.
8. Unless otherwise stated, the following information is drawn from *Memorial* activists' questionnaires. See the Appendix.

9. See A. White (1995).
10. Questionnaires; the Memorial address list and Berezovskii et al. provide many examples.
11. Zhzhenova pp. 12, 15, 17.
12. Chizhov pp. 65–6, entry 'Sostradanie'.
13. *Soyuz byvshikh maloletnikh uznikov fashistskikh kontslagerei.*
14. Medvedev questionnaire; Litvinov (1993).
15. G. Yakovlev.
16. Medvedev questionnaire; Litvinov (1993); Malevskii.
17. *Assotsiatsiya sovetskikh evreev-veteranov voiny, partizan, uznikov kontslagerei, getto i ikh detei.*
18. Chizhov p. 32.
19. *Zhiteli Blokadnogo Leningrada.*
20. Chizhov pp. 69–70.
21. Komarova (1986) p. 6.
22. *Komitet Fonda 'Miloserdie'.*
23. Chernosvitova questionnaire; Chizhov pp. 76–7.
24. For a more detailed account, see A. White (1997).
25. Tolz (21.9.90) p. 30.
26. Kirbasova pp. 230–1; *Moskovskie novosti*, no. 8, 1990, 8–9.
27. Melnikova et al.
28. See A. White (1997); Shreeves (21.9.90) pp. 6–7; Tolz (21.9.90) p. 30.
29. See Galeotti (1992), ch. 7; Lipovskaia.
30. *Narodnyi komitet za osvobozhdenie sovetskikh voennosluzhashchikh 'Nadezhda'.*
31. Aleksandrov; 'Solntse svobody'; 'Vernut' rodine'; Galeotti (1995) pp. 94–6.
32. Z. Borodaevskaya, quoted in Sanatina.
33. Tsyganova.
34. *Sovetskii fond 'Mnogodetnaya sem'ya'.*
35. 'Ustav Sovetskogo fonda' and Leonidova.
36. P'yanykh.
37. Chizhov mentions a number of organizations who listed 'raising the prestige of large families' as one of their constitutional goals. See also Kapustin on the Moscow society's main goals.
38. *Nash dom.*
39. *Tol'ko mama.*
40. Kienya questionnaire.
41. *Mapulechki Moskvy.*
42. Chizhov p. 97.
43. Vessey p. 55.
44. W. Rule, 'Introduction: Equal players or back to the kitchen?', in Rule and Noonan p. 3.
45. Chizhov p. 105.
46. Petukhov interview, July 1989.
47. Chizhov pp. 30–1. *Assotsiatsiya roditelei detei-invalidov po zreniyu.*
48. *Gorodskaya assotsiatsiya obshchestvennykh organizatsii roditelei detei-invalidov.*
49. Chizhov pp. 125–6. *Organizatisya roditelei detei-invalidov Frunzenskogo raiona.*

50. *Obshchestvo semei s det'mi-invalidami ADIS*.
51. *Obshchestvo sotsial'noi reabilitatsii 'Spasenie sem'i'*.
52. On *Gumanist, ADIS* and *'Spasenie sem'i'*, see Chizhov pp. 102, 122–4.
53. For some examples of groups for children with physical disabilities, *ARDIZ, Allergik, Assotsiatsiya glukhikh 'Rossiya', Kontakt, Rodnichok, Ozerki*, see ibid., pp. 30–1, 34–5, 36, 64–5, 73, 89.
53. Such a group existed, for example, in the Cheremushkino borough of Moscow. See Chizhov p. 114.
54. Chizhov p. 167.
55. Similar societies were founded in other republics. Estonia's was established first, in 1987.
56. 'A vremya'; Pekur (1987). The Kemerovo club was established with support from the local social security department and *Komsomol*. See Cheremnykh.
57. *Chto takoe*, manuscript version only.
58. Shul'gina.
59. D'yachkov mentions sector head L. Dorofeeva.
60. Gus'kov to Häkkelä, 25.3.85.
61. Malysheva (1987).
62. Vasil'ev.
63. O. Burkova, in 'Sozdanie'.
64. *Chto takoe* (Serpukhov).
65. See, for example, Chernoshkur (1987).
66. This was the main reason given officially for the creation of VOI. See Trubilin.
67. Misyurev p. 1. The resolution's implementation left much to be desired. See Ovchinnikova.
68. V. Volkov et al. p. 6; watered-down version of same in 'Bol' ne prokhodit'.
69. On the Federation, see Malysheva (1988).
70. Letter to AW, 18.8.93.
71. Malysheva (1987); Steele; Panov; Berezina.
72. 'Obresti'.
73. Kolmakov.
74. Interviews with Zolottseva, Kiselev and Misyurev.
75. 'Galya' (inmate of residential home), letter to Häkkelä, 13.4.88.
76. Zolottseva interview; see below.
77. Trubilin.
78. *Ustav VOI* p. 7.
79. VOI's official founders included the Ministries of Social Security and Health, VTsSPS, the *Komsomol*, VOS and VOG. Conference materials were published in *Sotsial'noe obespechenie*, no. 11, 1988.
80. Interview with V. Malakhov, Novosibirsk VOI, July 1989.
81. Malakhov interview; Vasil'ev; interview with Petukhov and observation of him at work, 1989.
82. 'Ot imeni'.
83. 'Miloserdie dolzhno';'Prioritet'; 'Mnogo del'; 'Zakon nashei'.
84. 'Ob osnovnykh nachalakh'.
85. 'Zakon ob invalidakh'.

Notes 219

86. 'Nekotorye itogi'.
87. 'Ne podavat''.
88. 'K Verkhovnym sovetam'.
89. Tsentral'noe, p. 12.
90. Tsentral'noe.
91. 'Interv'yu iz "polupodvala"'.
92. For example in the Fokino borough, Bryansk (Ivakin questionnaire) or in Orsk (Karev questionnaire).
93. The letter is in *Nadezhda*, no. 1, 1990, p. 3.
94. Kolmakov; Ryzhova.
95. This paragraph, and what follows, is based on numerous accounts in VOI periodicals *Kontakt*, *Vestnik MGOI* and *Nadezhda*.
96. Karev to Häkkelä, 5.6.90.
97. *Assotsiatsiya molodezhnykh invalidnykh organizatsii*.
98. 'U molodykh'.
99. Chizhov p. 25.
100. Chizhov pp. 26–7; Kupriyanov, 'Perevorot'.
101. *Obshchestvo diabetov*.
102. *Miloserdie – dobrota* pp. 5–7.
103. Avdeeva, Evdokimov and Shipulina questionnaires; interview with G. Gerasimova (Moscow), 1992.
104. *Blagotvoritel'naya assotsiatsiya glukhikh 'Rossiya'*. Chizhov pp. 35–6.
105. *Rossiiskaya shakhmatnaya federatsiya glukhikh*. Sobolev questionnaire.
106. Katel'nitskii questionnaire.
107. Pursglove.
108. See Galeotti (1995) chs 5 (pp. 93–4) and 6.
109. On an alienated group, see A. White (1989). See V. Konovalov, who suggests that a 'Vietnam syndrome' was common. Galeotti, however, believes that the majority of *afgantsy* were able to integrate back into Soviet society and preferred to do so rather than to identify with the veterans' movement. Galeotti (1995), pp. 103–4.
110. *Soyuz veteranov Afganistana*.
111. Gluzinskii questionnaire.
112. See A. White, 'Social movements'.
113. See e.g. V. Konovalov.
114. The figure is from Usichenko, the quotation from 'Telemarafon Chernobyl''.
115. Lasovskaya (28.5.90); 'Dolgoe ekho'.
116. Lasovskaya, op. cit.
117. *Soyuz 'Chernobyl''*.
118. 'Dolgoe ekho'.
119. Yntemna.

CHAPTER 7: THE COMMUNIST RESPONSE

1. Chumakov.
2. Kalinichevs and Marchenko questionnaires.
3. Baleva (1.89.)

4. Kupriyanov, 'Perevorot'.
5. Kutateladze.
6. Kupriyanov, 'Perevorot'.
7. D'yachenko, 'Obrashchayus''.
8. Man'ko questionnaire.
9. 'Kriterii'.
10. See *Sotsial'naya zashchita*, no. 1, 1990 p. 68; Venediktov interview.
11. Sekretariat.
12. Fish p. 124.
13. Ibid.
14. Kutateladze.
15. Baleva (1.89).
16. Bokova.
17. Kropachev questionnaire.
18. Baleva (1.89.)
19. Chizhov pp. 123–4. For the Soviet categorization of mental disability, see Sutton, A., 'Special education for handicapped pupils' (pp. 75–6) or A. Suddaby, A., 'Children with learning difficulties' (pp.141–2) in Riordan (ed.) (1988).
20. D'yachenko, 'Ispytanie'.
21. D'yachenko, 'Obrahchayus'; 'Ispytanie'.
22. Grigorii Syrkov, in 'Nado uspet''.
23. Butterfield and Weigle.
24. Urban p. 102.
25. Butterfield and Weigle p. 187.
26. Brovkin pp. 248–9.
27. Lytkins interview.
28. Tolz (1989), p. 6; Verbitsky interview.
29. Maksimov questionnaire.
30. Belyaeva (1994) p. 3.
31. Maksimov questionnaire.
32. Yur'eva questionnaire.
33. Questionnaire evidence.
34. Karev to Häkkelä, 5.6.90.
35. Avdeeva and Shipulina questionnaires.
36. Petelin questionnaire.
37. Antic.
38. Feltham and Meiroyan pp. 26–7.
39. Ibid., p. 27.
40. Bitova questionnaire.
41. Shipulina questionnaire.
42. Mironova pp. 3–4.
43. Kuznetsova letter.
44. Gurinovich p. 3.
45. Paaso questionnaire.
46. E. Fedorova (1991).
47. Bokova.
48. Ligachev p. 110; Gill p. 88.
49. Poret.

Notes 221

50. Man'ko, Molchanova, Lutskevich questionnaires.
51. Shipulina questionnaire.
52. D'yachenko, 'Ispytanie'.
53. Bokova. Of course, British journalists do not always obtain access to residential homes.
54. Man'ko questionnaire.
55. Lozovaya.
56. Kholchev questionnaire.
57. Katel'nitskii questionnaire.
58. Ibid.
59. Pogozhev questionnaire.
60. Bokova.
61. 'V Moskovskom'.
62. *Dom*, 2, November 1988, p. 6.
63. Bokova.
64. Sekretariat.
65. 'Otkrytoe pis'mo chlenov', p. 4.
66. Interviews with M. Milonova, G. Spegal'skaya, I. Petrenko and A. Tokarev, Moscow *Memorial*, July–Aug. 1992; 'Otkrytoe pis'mo chlenov'; Iofe and Proshina; Zaikin. In Leningrad the analogous organisation was originally named *Spravedlivost'*.
67. 'Ushchemlenie'; 'Popravim'.
68. They made the longstanding communist and disabled rights campaigner Misyurev feel distinctly unwelcome because of his party affiliation. Misyurev interview.
69. Lytkins and A. Zhelobov (*Memorial*) interviews, Novosibirsk, July 1989.
70. Sekretariat.
71. Chernoshkur (8.88).
72. On the composition by age of VOI officials, see Tsentral'noe.
73. The local authorities in Orsk, for example, tried to edge out Mikhail Karev, a long-standing and vocal activist, from the leadership of the local VOI. See Karev, 'Nuzhny'.
74. Malyshchenko. She was described as being 'of the Romanov cohort', a reference to Grigorii Romanov, formerly party leader in Leningrad.
75. Malyshchenko; D'yachenko interview; D'yachenko, 'Leningradtsy'.
76. Medvedev questionnaire.
77. Lutskevich, Zinchenko and Pogozhev questionnaires.
78. Karev questionnaire.
79. D'yachenko, 'Obrashchayus'; Lilenko.
80. *Sovetskaya Sibir'*, 12.7.89, p. 1; Glukhov.
81. Savel'ev questionnaire.
82. D'yachenko interview.
83. Navrotskii, Petelin, Kropachev and Tokarev questionnaires. See White (1995).
84. Ibid.
85. Katel'nitskii questionnaire.

CHAPTER 8: BUILDING POLITICAL AND CIVIL SOCIETY

1. Kupriyanov (6.89).
2. *Foundation.*
3. Belyaeva (undated) p. 9.
4. T. H. Rigby, quotation in Alapuro, p. 212.
5. *Vserossiiskii fond sotsial'no-pravovoi zashchity i reabilitatsii invalidov.*
6. Chizhov p. 61.
7. Karev questionnaire.
8. *Obshchestvennyi tsentr 'Sodeistvie'.*
9. Chizhov p. 113.
10. *Blagotvoritel'nyi fond zashchity zhertv sudebnykh oshibok vo imya Nikolaya Chudotvortsa.*
11. Chizhov p. 46.
12. See A. White (1995) for examples within *Memorial.*
13. Zinchenko questionnaire.
14. Marchenko questionnaire.
15. See Buckley.
16. Karev, Marchenko, Gutin and Medvedev questionnaires.
17. See e.g. Samsonov; 'L'goty'.
18. *Kontakt*, no. 7, October 1989.
19. Yur'eva.
20. Evdokimov questionnaire.
21. Litvinenko questionnaire.
22. Lushnikov.
23. Evdokimov questionnaire.
24. Lepeshkina questionnaire.
25. Zalevskaya.
26. Fish p. 67.
27. Pogozhev questionnaire.
28. Chizhov p. 53: *Blagotvoritel'nyi fond 'Yad ezra'.*
29. Ibid. p. 57: *Assosiatsiya grazhdan, nuzhdayushchikhsya v popechenii 'Vera'.*
30. See Fish p. 67, for discussion of the link between broad goals and fissiparous tendencies in more political groups.
31. *Dobrovol'nyi soyuz sodeistviya transportu, ekologii, kul'ture i resheniu sotsial'nykh problem 'TransEKSPO'.*
32. Chizhov p. 68.
33. Nina Belyaeva criticizes such definitions in Belyaeva (undated) pp. 11–12.
34. Salvador Giner, paraphrased in Fish, p. 53.
35. Verbitsky and Yntemna interviews.
36. Ivakin questionnaire.
37. Nikiforov questionnaire.
38. Masterupolo questionnaire.
39. Shevchenko questionnaire.
40. Belyaeva (1991) p. 90.
41. Nikiforov questionnaire.
42. Lytkins interview.
43. Fridman questionnaire.

44. Lasovskaya (28.5.90).
45. Feltham and Meiroyan p. 29.
46. See Fish, p. 117, on the similar stance of political organizations.
47. Chizhov p. 44.
48. *Leningradskaya assotsiatsiya veteranov voiny v Afganistane.* Galeotti (1995) p. 113.
49. D'yachenko, 'Obrashchayus'' p. 7.
50. Nikiforov questionnaire.
51. D'yachenko interview.
52. Yakovets and Lozhkin questionnaires.
53. Zinchenko questionnaire.
54. Molchanova questionnaire.
55. Rogova questionnaire.
56. See e.g. E. Fedorova (both articles); Shinkorenko.
57. *Polozhenie* p. 110.
58. Ibid. pp. 108–9.
59. Tolz (21.9.90) p. 36.
60. Galeotti (1995) p. 98.
61. *Vechernii Novosibirsk*, 16.1 and 18.1.90; 12.2 and 19.2.90; SibIA *Press-Byulleten'*, 25, 4 and 26, 3.
62. *Izvestiya*, 5.4.89, 2–12. Those chosen for membership of the Supreme Soviet were: 11 veterans, two deputies from peace organizations; one deputy from each of the Funds and one from the Red Cross. See Mann et al.
63. Malysheva (1989).
64. Kabakov; *Vestnik MGOI*, no. 1, April 1989, p. 2; Malysheva (1989); Zaslavsky; 'Miloserdie dolzhno byt' effektivnym'; 'Ot imeni.'
65. 'Nashi znakomstva'; 'Same Difference'; Steele (on Zaslavsky as head of the Oktyabr borough); Verbitsky interview.
66. They included V. Dikul', circus weightlifter, pioneering physiotherapist and president of the All-Union Federation of Sport for Disabled People; R. Odzhiev, a disabled Afghan veteran; and A. Neumyvakin, head of the Society of Blind People (a delegate from the FMZ). On Odzhiev, see Kushkov.
67. Neumyvakin.
68. 'Ob osnovnykh nachalakh'.
69. Butterficld and Sedaitis, 'The emergence of social movements in the Soviet Union', in Sedaitis and Butterfield (eds) p. 7.
70. Tsentral'noe p. 9.
71. Pantyukhina.
72. Pogozhev questionnaire.
73. Ziegler, C., 'Environmental politics and policy under perestroika', in Sedaitis and Butterfield (eds) p. 128; Sedaitis, op. cit., p. 19.
74. Kryuchkova.
75. 'Palatki'; Katinskaya.
76. Lytkins interview; interviews with A. Petukhov, V. Malakhov and other activists of VOI, also in Novosibirsk, July 1989; Vasil'ev's appeal, in SibIA *Press-Byulleten'*, no. 36, 1989; Pani; Zykov.
77. Chizhov p. 154: *Detskii fond im. Dostoevskogo.*

78. Murzhenko; 'Piket'.
79. Aguzarov questionnaire.
80. D'yachenko, 'Ispytanie'; Lytkins interview; Baleva (1.89).
81. 'Mothers'.
82. The *Press-Byulleten'* of the Siberian Information Agency, no. 36, 1989, 5, 11.
83. Letter from G. Kramarenko, *Kontakt*, no. 2, 1990, 3.
84. Glukhov.
85. Chizhov p. 118.
86. Ksenin.
87. Lasovskaya (24.5.90).
88. Chizhov p. 68.
89. Matveev.
90. *K sovesti*, no. 3, 1990, 3.
91. See A. White (1995).
92. DeBardeleben pp. 74–5.
93. Chizhov pp. 123, 125. *Gorodskaya assotsiatsiya obshchestvennykh ob"edinenii roditelei detei-invalidov.*
94. *Blagotvoritel'nye organizatsii Moskvy.*
95. Fish p. 70.
96. Butterfield and Sedaitis, op. cit., p. 9.
97. Venediktov interview.
98. A. Avseevich, quoted in Chesnokova (11.89).
99. Interview at *Rabotnitsa* editorial office with I. Zhuravskaya, April 1990.
100. VTsIOM, vyp. 1 (Sept. 1989) p. 11.
101. Solovei (1988).
102. Zhuravskaya interview.
103. Tarasov.
104. Sazonov et al.
105. *Tochka otscheta* p. 41.
106. Ibid.
107. Popov and Sazonov.
108. The survey of 585 Muscovites was by the journal *XX Century and Peace*. Byzov et al. p. 22.
109. Sazonov et al.
110. Ibid.; Popov and Sazonov.
111. Fateyev.
112. Wyman p. 147, citing a Vox Populi survey.
113. Fish p. 55.
114. Poret.
115. See Urban pp. 26–7 on 'identity politics'.
116. Alapuro p. 198.

CHAPTER 9: CONCLUSIONS AND EPILOGUE

1. Kuznetsova letter.
2. Gureev letter and accompanying questionnaire.

Notes

3. Matyukhin letter in lieu of questionnaire.
4. Borovoi pp. 27–8.
5. Legendre p. 13.
6. Leitch (1996) p. 6.
7. Vessey; *Spravochnik*; Leitch p. 11; Harvey p. 205, agrees that 'the survival rate of voluntary organisations appears to be high'.
8. Kuznetsova letter. Kuznetsova had access to the Ministry of Justice's list of registered organizations for the *oblast*.
9. See e.g. Harvey pp. 201–3.
10. *Nevskii Angel*.
11. Young p. 10.
12. Legendre pp. 17–18.
13. Ibid.
14. IRIS p. 27.
15. For a discussion of the (dis)advantages of NGOs' predominantly local orientation, see IRIS 39–40.
16. Vessey, for example, suggests that there were many examples of such charities in Perm *oblast*.
17. Topolevs.
18. Pilkington (1998) pp. 80–1.
19. IRIS p. 30.
20. Panteleev questionnaire.
21. See IRIS p. 35
22. IRIS; Legendre pp. 22–3.
23. Ibid. p. 20.
24. Ibid. pp. 17–18; IRIS p. 17.
25. See Bridger et al. for examples.
26. Fabel, op. cit., p. 99.

BIBLIOGRAPHY

1. Questionnaires are listed in the appendix and references to unpublished letters are in the notes to individual chapters.
2. Published by the Charities Aid Foundation in Moscow.
3. Serial: abstracts of newspaper articles, published by *Soprichastnost'* Fund and the CAF. All references are to Volume 1, *Rossiiskaya blagotvoritel'nost' v 1987–1992 godakh (istoriya v materialakh pressy)*.
4. The house journal of the Ministry of Social Security.
5. Published by *Gumanizm i miloserdie*, a charity associated with the Ministry of Social Security.
6. *Smena* is the name of both a journal and a Leningrad newspaper. All references in this bibliography are to the journal, except Malyshchenko and Shul'gina.
7. Published by the Leningrad branch of VOI.
8. Weekly supplement of *KP*, published in Moscow, not to be confused with the typescript bulletin of the *Korchaginets* Club bearing the same name. All references except Tkachenko are to the Moscow *Sobesednik*.

9. Published by the Moscow branch of VOI.
10. Published in Leningrad by the *Fond invalidov i semei voinov, pogibshikh v respublike Afghanistan.*
11. Published by VOI nationally.
12. Typescript journal of Moscow *Miloserdie.*
13. Weekly newspaper of the Children's Fund.
14. See note 6.
15. Typescript bulletin of the *Korchaginets* Club.
16. Typescript bulletin of the *Korchaginets* Club.
17. See note 6.
18. See note 8.
19. See note 8.
20. See note 8.

Bibliography

SOURCES IN ENGLISH

Abramkin, V., 'Dangerous old women', *XX Century and Peace*, no. 6, 1990, 20–5.
Adler, N., *Victims of Soviet Terror: the Story of the Memorial Movement* (Westport: Praeger, 1993).
Alexeyeva, L., *Soviet Dissent: Contemporary Movements for National, Religious and Human Rights* (Middletown, Conn.: Wesleyan University Press, 1985).
Alapuro, R., 'Civil society in Russia?', in Iivonen, Jyrki (ed.), *The Future of the Nation State in Europe* (Aldershot: Elgar, 1993).
Clive Anderson Talks Back (Discussion between Anderson and Gorbachev) (London: BBC2), 3.11.96.
Anderson, J., *Religion, State and Politics in the Soviet Union and Successor States* (Cambridge: Cambridge University Press, 1994).
Antic, O., 'The charity program and the role of the churches', *Radio Liberty Research*, no. 516, 1988.
Astakhov, P. and Burkov, I., 'Charity for the rich', *Business in the USSR*, no. 90, 90–2.
BEARR Trust (no pp., no date [February 1992?]).
BEARR Trust Newsletter, various issues.
Belyaeva, N., 'Comparative analysis of citizens' associations' activity in Russia, Ukraine, Kazakhstan, Uzbekistan', paper for NCVO International Charity Conference, London, September 1994.
Belyaeva, N., 'From perestroika to democracy?', in Roberts, B. and Belyaeva, N. (eds.), *After Perestroika: Democracy in the Soviet Union* (Washington, DC: Center for Strategic and International Studies, 1991).
Belyaeva, N., 'Rule of law for civil society – or vice versa? Law as a mechanism of interaction between the state and society in the Russian Federation – an insider's view' (typescript).
Birchenough, T., 'The Struggle to Continue', *Moscow Guardian*, 18.6.92.
Brenton, M., *The Voluntary Sector in British Social Services* (London: Longman, 1985).
Bridger, S., Kay, R. and Pinnick, K., *No More Heroines: Russia, Women and the Market* (London: Routledge, 1996).
Brody, D. and Boris, E., 'Philanthropy and charity in the Soviet Union' (draft), later published in McCarthy, K. D., Hodgkinson, V. and Sumariwalla, R. (eds), *The Non-Profit Sector in the Global Community* (San Francisco: Jossey Bass, 1992).
Brovkin, V., 'Revolution from below: informal political associations in Russia 1988–9', *Soviet Studies*, vol. 42, no. 2 (1990).
Brown, A., *The Gorbachev Factor* (Oxford: Oxford University Press, 1996).
Buckley, M., *Redefining Russian Society and Polity* (Westview, Boulder, Co., and Oxford, 1993).

Byzov, L, Guzanova, A and Ladenkov, N, 'Charity, today and tomorrow', *XX Century and Peace*, no. 10, 1990, 20–7.
Cherkasov, A., 'From the history of the human rights movement in Russia', *Third Sector* (Interlegal, Moscow), no. 1, 1994, 9–10.
Cook, L., *The Soviet Social Contract and Why it Failed* (Cambridge, Mass.: Harvard University Press, 1993).
Crow, S., 'Moscow looks hard at its foreign aid program', *Report on the USSR* (Radio Liberty Research, Munich), 10.8.90, 8–9.
DeBardeleben, J., 'The new politics in the USSR: the case of the environment', in Massey Stewart, J. (ed.), *The Soviet Environment: Problems, Policies and Politics* (Cambridge: Cambridge University Press, 1992).
Devlin, J., *The Rise of the Russian Democrats: the Causes and Consequences of the Elite Revolution* (Aldershot: Elgar, 1995).
Evans, A., Jr., 'The decline of developed socialism: some trends in recent Soviet ideology', *Soviet Studies*, vol. 38 (1986), 1–23.
Fateyev, K. 'Heartless charity', *XX Century and Peace*, no. 12, 1989, 25–8.
Feltham, A. and Meiroyan, A., *Drug Abuse in the Soviet Union* (University of Essex Russian and Soviet Studies Centre, Discussion Paper Series, no. 11, September 1991).
Feshbach, M. and Friendly, A. Jr., *Ecocide in the USSR: Health and Nature Under Siege* (London: Aurum, 1992).
Fish, M. S., *Democracy from Scratch: Opposition and Regime in the New Russian Revolution* (Princeton: Princeton University Press, 1994).
The Foundation for Social Innovations [Moscow, 1991/2].
Friedgut, T., *Political Participation in the USSR* (Princeton: Princeton University Press, 1979).
Galeotti, M., *Afghanistan: the Soviet Union's Last War* (London: Cass, 1995).
Galeotti, M., 'The impact of the Afghan War on Soviet and Russian politics and society 1979–1991' (Ph.D. dissertation, London School of Economics, 1992).
Gill, G., *The Collapse of a Single-Party System: the Disintegration of the Communist Party of the Soviet Union* (Cambridge: Cambridge University Press, 1994).
Glick, Mark, 'Disability in the USSR – a dissident view: a case study of the Action Group to Defend the Rights of the Disabled in the USSR' (M.Sc. dissertation, London School of Economics, 1980).
Gorbachev, M., *Perestroika* (London: Collins, 1987).
Gorbachev, M., *Memoirs* (London: Doubleday, 1996).
Hankiss, E., *East European Alternatives* (Oxford: Clarendon Press, 1990).
Harvey, B. (with Stubbs, L.), *Networking in Eastern and Central Europe: a Guide to Voluntary and Community Organisations* (London: Community Development Foundation/Directory of Social Change, 1995).
Harwin, J., 'Child protection legislation as an instrument of Soviet childcare policy and practice', *International Journal of Law and the Family*, no. 3, 1989, 58–71.
Harwin, J., *Children of the Russian State: 1917–95* (Aldershot: Avebury, 1996).
Harwin, J., 'Union of Soviet Socialist Republics: Childcare in the Soviet Union – Law, Policy and Practice', *Journal of Family Law*, vol. 28, no. 3 (1989–90), 627–42.

Bibliography 229

Hauslohner, P., 'Politics before Gorbachev: De-Stalinization and the roots of reform', in S. Bialer (ed.), *Politics, Society and Nationality inside Gorbachev's Russia* (Boulder: Westview, 1989).
Hauslohner, P., 'Gorbachev's Social Contract', in Hewett, E. and Winston, V. (eds), *Milestones in Glasnost and Perestroyka* (Washington DC: Brookings Institution, 1991).
Hegelson, A., 'USSR – the implications of *glasnost* and *perestroika*', in B. Munday (ed.), *The Crisis in Welfare: an International Perspective* (Hemel Hempstead: Harvester Wheatsheaf/St. Martins, 1989).
Holland, B. and McKevitt, T., 'Maternity care in the Soviet Union', in Holland, B. (ed.), *Soviet Sisterhood* (London: Fourth Estate, 1985).
Interlegal Research Center, *Classification of Public Associations registered with the RSFSR Ministry of Justice (26.06.91–2.11.91)* (Moscow [1991/2]).
IRIS (Center for Institutional Reform and the Informal Sector), *Russian Civil Society: Report for the World Bank* (College Park: University of Maryland, 1996).
Jacobs, M., 'Minister of health talks about reform', *Report on the USSR* (Radio Liberty Research, Munich), 31.8.90, 6–7.
Jacobs, M., 'Soviet pensioners finally get a boost', *Report on the USSR* (Radio Liberty Research, Munich), 10.8.90, 2–5.
Jacobs, M., 'USSR faces mounting refugee problem', *Report on the USSR* (Radio Liberty Research, Munich), 21.9.90, 14–18.
Jones, A, Connor, W. and Powell, D. E. (eds), *Soviet Social Problems* (Boulder: Westview, 1991).
Keane, J. (ed.), *Civil Society and the State* (London: Verso, 1988).
Khodekhina, I., 'Volunteering in Russia', in Smith, J., *Volunteering in Europe: Opportunities and Challenges for the 90s* (Berkhamstead: The Volunteer Centre UK, Voluntary Action Research, Second Series, Paper No. 4), 141–3.
Konovalov, V., 'Afghan veterans in Siberia', *Report on the USSR* (Radio Liberty Research, Munich), 26.5.89, 16–18.
Kupriyanov, A., 'Perestroika has solved everything – and nothing', *Disability Now*, August 1990, 7.
Kushkov, Yu., 'New political faces: cooperator', *Moscow News*, 28.5.89, 9.
Lapidus, G., 'State and society: toward the emergence of civil society in the Soviet Union', in Bialer, S. (ed.), *Politics, Society and Nationality inside Gorbachev's Russia* (Boulder: Westview, 1989).
Legendre, Paul, *The Non-Profit Sector in Russia* (London: Charities Aid Foundation, 1997).
Leitch, D., 'Independent Social Organisations in the City of Voronezh, Central Russia, November 1992' (M.Sc. dissertation, University of Birmingham, 1993).
Leitch, D., 'Society in motion: Russia's emerging voluntary sector', *Nonprofit Management and Leadership*, vol. 7, no. 4 (1997).
Leningrad Charity Society, *Information Bulletin*, no. 1 (March 1990).
Lewin, M., *The Gorbachev Phenomenon* (London: Century Hutchinson, 1988).
Ligachev, Y., *Inside Gorbachev's Kremlin* (New York: Pantheon, 1993).
Likhanov, A., *We are All Responsible for our Children* (Moscow, 1987).

Lindenmeyr, A., *Poverty is not a Vice: Charity, Society and the State in Imperial Russia* (Princeton: Princeton University Press, 1996).
Lipovskaia, O., 'New women's organisations', in M. Buckley (ed.), *Perestroika and Soviet Women* (Cambridge: Cambridge University Press, 1992).
Madison, B., *Social Welfare in the Soviet Union* (Stanford: Stanford University Press, 1968).
Madison, B., 'The Soviet social security system: its legal structure and fair hearings process', in Potichnyi, P. (ed.), *The Soviet Union: Party and Society* (Cambridge: Cambridge University Press, 1988).
Mann, D., Monyak, R. and Teague, E., *The Supreme Soviet: a Biographical Directory* (Washington DC: Centre for Strategic and International Studies/Radio Liberty, 1989).
Matthews, M., 'The end of privilege?', in Riordan, J. (ed.), *Soviet Social Reality in the Mirror of Glasnost* (London: Macmillan, 1992).
Matthews, M., *Patterns of Deprivation in the Soviet Union under Brezhnev and Gorbachev* (Stanford: Hoover Institution Press, 1989).
Matthews, M., *Poverty in the Soviet Union* (Cambridge: Cambridge University Press, 1986).
Matthews, M., *Privilege in the Soviet Union* (London: Allen and Unwin, 1978).
Mayer, M., 'A different kind of internationalism', *XX Century and Peace*, no. 2, 1991, 34–8.
McAndrew, M., 'Soviet women's magazines', in Holland, B. (ed.), *Soviet Sisterhood* (London: Fourth Estate, 1985).
McCagg, W. and Siegelbaum, L. (eds), *The Disabled in the Soviet Union* (Pittsburgh: University of Pittsburgh, 1989).
Melnikova, V., Kuznetsova, L. and Kartasheva, G., 'We'll not let our sons be killed', *Moscow News* (Moscow), no. 22, 10–17.6.90, 5, also published as 'Stop this bullying of our soldier sons' in *Moscow News* (London), no. 1, 1–7.6.90, 7.
Moses, J., 'Soviet provincial politics in an era of transition and revolution, 1989–91', *Soviet Studies*, vol. 44, no. 3 (1992).
'Mothers call for draft boycott', *Moscow News* (London), no. 20, 12–18.10.90, 2.
Oliver, S., 'Charity and the churches' in Riordan, J. (ed.), *Soviet Social Reality in the Mirror of Glasnost* (London: Macmillan, 1992).
Pavlovsky, G. and Meyer, M., 'Who? Where? How many?', *Moscow News*, no. 7, 1990, 9.
Peredeventsev, V., 'Growing proportion of aged persons', *Moscow News*, no. 4, 1988, 12.
Petersburg in the Early '90s: Crazy, Cold, Cruel (St Petersburg: Charitable Foundation 'Nochlezhka', 1994).
Pilkington, H., *Russia's Youth and its Culture: a Nation's Constructors and Constructed* (London: Routledge, 1994).
Pilkington, H., *Migration, Displacement and Identity in Post-Soviet Russia* (London: Routledge, 1998).
Popov, N., *The Russian People Speak: Democracy at the Crossroads* (Syracuse, NY: Syracuse University Press, 1995).

'Priorities: Statement by members of the Cultural Initiative Fund Board', *XX Century and Peace*, no. 12, 1989, 29–30.
Pursglove, M., 'The Anglo-Russian School for the Deaf', *Britain-Russia*, no. 92, 9.92, 9–10.
Reiner, T., 'Not-for-Profit Organisations in the Soviet Union: Turning on Some Lights', *Non-Profit and Voluntary Sector Quarterly*, vol. 20, no. 1, Spring 1991, 81–94.
Riordan, J. (ed.), *Soviet Education: the Gifted and the Handicapped* (London: Routledge, 1988).
Riordan, J. (ed.), *Soviet Youth Culture* (Bloomington and Indianapolis: University of Indiana, 1989).
Ruffin, M. H., McCarter, J. and Upjohn, R., *The Post-Soviet Handbook: a Guide to Grassroots Organizations and Internet Resources in the Newly Independent States* (Seattle: Center for Civil Society International, 1996).
Rule, W. and Noonan, N. C. (eds), *Russian Women in Politics and Society* (Westport: Greenwood, 1996).
Ryan, M., *Doctors and the State in the Soviet Union* (New York: St. Martin's, 1990).
Ryan, M., *The Organisation of Soviet Medical Care* (Oxford: Blackwell, 1978).
Sakharov, A., *Moscow and Beyond* (New York: Vintage Books, 1990).
'Same Difference', 5.2.90 (London: Channel 4 TV).
Scanlan, J., 'Reforms and civil society in the USSR', *Problems of Communism*, no. 2, 1988, 41–6.
Schopflin, G., *Politics in Eastern Europe* (Oxford: Blackwell, 1993).
Sedaitis, J. B. and Butterfield, J., *Perestroika from Below: Social Movements in the Soviet Union* (Boulder: Westview, 1991).
Segbers, K. and De Spiegeleire, S. (eds), *Post-Soviet Puzzles: Mapping the Political Economy of the Former Soviet Union: Volume IV: The Emancipation of Society as a Reaction to Systemic Change: Survival, Adaptation to New Rules and Ethnopolitical Conflicts* (Baden-Baden: Nomos Verlagsgesellschaft, 1995).
Shlapentokh, V, *Public and Private Life of the Soviet People: Changing Values in Post-Stalin Russia* (Oxford: Oxford University Press, 1989).
Shreeves, R., 'Mothers against the draft: women's activism in the USSR', *Report on the USSR* (Radio Liberty Research, Munich), vol. 2, no. 38, 21.9.90, 3–8.
Smith, K., *Remembering Stalin's Victims: Popular Memory and the End of the USSR* (Ithaca, NY: Cornell University Press, 1996).
The Soviet Constitution: a Dictionary (Moscow, 1986).
Steele, J., 'Soviet disabled struggle for political recognition', *The Guardian*, 7.2.91, 12.
Tarasevich, I., 'Our fault and our sorrow', *Moscow News*, no. 4, 1988, 2.
Teague, E., *Solidarity and the Soviet Worker* (London: Croom Helm, 1988).
Thomas, S., 'FSU enterprises keep on providing social services', *Transition* (Washington DC: World Bank), vol. 8, no. 1, 2.97, 4.
'Those who didn't complain' (interview with V. Zelendinova), *XX Century and Peace*, no. 11, 1989, 25–7.
Tolz, V., 'Informal Groups and Soviet Politics', *Report on the USSR: Radio Liberty Research Bulletin*, vol. 1, no. 47, 1989.

Tolz, V., *The USSR's Emerging Multiparty System* (New York: Praeger, 1990).
Tolz, V., 'The USSR this week', *Report on the USSR* (Radio Liberty Research, Munich), vol. 2, no. 38, 21.9.90, 28–44.
Topolev, E. and A, 'Russia's Agency of Social Information', *Civil Society … East and West* (Seattle), vol. 4, no. 2 (3–4.96).
Trehub, A., 'The Congress of People's Deputies on poverty', *Radio Liberty Research Bulletin*, 16.6.89, 5–8.
Troyanovsky, I., *Religion in the Soviet Republics: a Guide to Christianity, Judaism, Islam, Buddhism and Other Religions* (San Francisco: Harper, 1991).
United Way Program Update, May 1992 (Moscow).
Urban, M. with Igrunov, V. and Mitrokhin, S., *The Rebirth of Politics in Russia* (Cambridge: Cambridge University Press, 1997).
USSR Health Service (Moscow, 1970).
Vessey, A., *Directory of Voluntary Organisations in the Perm Region, Russia* (Oxford: Oxfordshire–Perm Voluntary Action Link, 1994).
Vitkovskaya, G., 'Forced migrants', *Moscow News* no. 11, 1992, 11.
Voslensky, M., *Nomenklatura: Anatomy of the Soviet Ruling Class* (London: Bodley Head, 1984).
Warner, G., *The Invisible Threads: Independent Soviets Working for Global Awareness and Social Transformation* (Washington, DC: Seven Locks Press, 1991).
Waters, E., 'Cuckoo-mothers and "apparatchiks": glasnost and children's homes', in M. Buckley (ed.), *Perestroika and Soviet Women* (Cambridge: Cambridge University Press, 1992).
White, A., 'New mothers' campaigning organizations in Russia', in Bull, A., Diamond, H. and Marsh, R. (eds), *European Feminisms: Theory and Practice* (Macmillan, 1999).
White, A., 'Charity, Self-Help and Politics in Russia, 1985–1991', *Europe–Asia Studies*, vol. 45, no. 5, 1993.
White, A., 'Cultural Enlightenment in the USSR, Hungary and Poland 1953–1987: Ideology and Leisure Policy', Ph.D. dissertation, London School of Economics, 1989.
White, A., *De-Stalinization and the House of Culture: Declining State Control over Leisure in the USSR, Poland and Hungary, 1953–89* (London: Routledge, 1990).
White, A., 'The Memorial Society in the Russian Provinces', *Europe–Asia Studies*, vol. 47, no. 8, 1995.
White, A., 'Optimists and Oblomovs in Gorbachev's House of Culture', *Soviet Union/Union Sovietique*, vol. 14, no. 2 (1987), 181–95.
White, A., 'Social movements: Unofficial associations and social welfare in Novosibirsk', *Detente*, no. 16 (1989) 26–30.
White, S., 'Political communications in the USSR: letters to party, state and press', *Political Studies*, vol. 31 (1983), 43–60.
White, S., *Russia Goes Dry: Alcohol, State and Society* (Cambridge: Cambridge University Press, 1996).
Wyman, Matthew, *Public Opinion in Postcommunist Russia* (London: Macmillan, 1997).
Yanowitch, M., *Social and Economic Inequality in the Soviet Union* (London: Martin Robertson, 1977).

Young, L., *Charities in Russia* (Tonbridge: Charities Aid Foundation, 1993).
Ziegler, C., *Environmental Policy in the USSR* (Amherst: University of Massachusetts, 1987).

SOURCES IN RUSSIAN[1]

Russian words have been transliterated and are in English alphabetical order; numerals are listed according to their spelling as Russian words (e.g. 120 under *sto*).Notes appear at the end of the 'Notes' section previous.

Periodicals and Serials: Abbreviations

AiF	*Argumenty i fakty*
DB	*Den'gi i blagotvoritel'nost'*[2]
KP	*Komsomol'skaya pravda*
LG	*Literaturnaya gazeta*
LP	*Leningradskaya pravda*
MG	*Meditsinskaya gazeta*
MK	*Moskovskii komsomolets*
MN	*Moskovskie novosti*
MP	*Moskovskaya pravda*
NV	*Novoe vremya*
RB	*Rossiiskaya blagotvoritel'nost'*[3]
SO	*Sotsial'noe obespechenie*[4]
SR	*Sovetskaya Rossiya*
SZ	*Sotsial'naya zashchita*[5]
VL	*Vechernii Leningrad*
VN	*Vechernii Novosibirsk*

Sources

'A vremya ukhodit', *Smena*,[6] no. 22, 1987.
Aleksandrov, E., 'My ne teryaem nadezhdy', *SR*, 29.6.89.
Altunin, V., 'Vechnoe dvizhenie', *Molodoi kommunar* (Voronezh), 29.7.71, 2–3.
Andreeva, N., 'Otkryvayutsya novye vozmozhnosti', *SO*, no. 9, 1971, 30–3
Andreeva, N., 'Pribavit' zhizn' k godam...', *SO*, no. 2, 1977, 35–8.
Andreeva, N., 'Nekrasivaya istoriya', *SO*, no. 3, 1978, 61.
Antonenko, L., 'Dorogie moi stariki', *KP*, 3.10.89.
Artsruni, S., 'Telemarafon miloserdiya', *Pravda*, 9.1.90, 1.
Azarova, G., 'Trudom napolnit' zhizn', *Smena*, no. 2, 1985.
Babin, A., 'Oni sredi nas', *Klub*, no. 2, 1989, 15, 17.
Baleva, R., 'Glavnoe priobretenie', *Sovetskaya Estonia*, 3.9.89.
Baleva, R., 'Vsem mirom', *Sovetskaya Estoniya*, 8.1.89, p. 3.
Berezina, E., 'Sotsial'naya pomoshch': lyudi, sud'by, zakon', *MK*, 19.1.88.
Berezovskii, V., Krotov, N. and Chervyakov, V., *Rossiya: partii, assotsiatsii, soyuzy, kluby* (Moscow, 1991).
Blagotvoritel'nye organizatsii Moskvy (Moscow: Koordinatsionnyi Komitet

blagotvoritel'nykh organizatsii, 1991).
Bobkov, V., 'Nuzhna sluzhba miloserdiya', *Vechernyaya Ufa*, 2.12.87, 3.
Bogoslovskaya, E., 'God miloserdiya', *LP*, 1.5.89, 3.
Bogoslovskaya, E., 'Parol' – miloserdie', *LP*, 9.12.87.
Bokhanov, A., 'Zabytyi fenomen', *SZ*, no. 1, 7.90.
Bokova, E., 'Miloserdiya proshu. Ispoved' neformala,' *LG*, 14.6.89, 13.
'Bolee 100 chelovek otkliknulis' na prizyv...', *Pravda*, 20.10.89.
'Bol' ne prokhodit', *KP*, 29.7.87, 4 (letters).
Borovoi, K., *Tsena svobody* (Moscow, 1993).
Borutskaya, I., 'Vera, volya, trud', *Zdorov'e*, no. 2, 1970, 22–3.
'Budem pomnit'...', *VN*, 9.6.90, 7.
Cheremnykh, L., 'Ne opuskaite ruk!', *Komsomolets Kuzbassa*, 5.1.89, 3.
Chernoshkur, L., 'Ch'ya eto bol'?', *KP*, 6.3.87, 2.
Chernoskhur, L., 'Nadezhda voshla v nash dom', *KP*, 16.8.88.
Chernyaev, A., *Shest' let s Gorbachevym* (Moscow, 1993).
Chesnokova, T., '"Opora" – za aktivnuyu zhizn"', *VL*, 21.11.89.
Chesnokova, T., 'Pochemu plachut u dverei VTEK?', *VL*, 2.1.89.
Chesnokova, T., 'Pomoch' cheloveku', *VL*, 10.11.89.
Chesnokova, T., 'VTEK: segodnya i zavtra', *VL*, 3.4.89.
Chizhov, Yu., *Spravochnik 'United Way': Blagotvoritel'nye organizatsii Rossii* (Moscow, 1992).
Chto takoe Klub 'Korchaginets'? (typescript).
Chto takoe Klub 'Korchaginets'? (Serpukhov, 1987).
Chumakov, A., 'I u miloserdiya est' problemy', *VL* , 7.9.89.
'Davaite delat' dobrye dela', *Izvestiya*, 17.3.89, 6.
'Davaite, vse vmeste', *VN*, 15.3.90, 1.
'Dela tekushchie, dela nasushchnye', *Miloserdie*, no. 11 (19), 3.91, 3.
Demenkova, E., 'VTEK vsegda "prava"', *Stroitel'naya gazeta*, 29.10.87.
Dobrovol'skaya, T., Masteropulo, A., and Poddubnyi, M., 'O perspektivakh vozrozhdeniya khristianskoi blagotvoritel'nosti v Rossii' in *Na puti k svobode sovesti* (Moscow, 1989).
'Dolgoe ekho Chernobylya' (interview with L. Kaurdakov), *Moment istiny* (Novosibirsk), no. 10, 1989, 3.
'Dollary tsenoyu v zhizn"', *Miloserdie*, no. 11 (19), 3.91, 2.
'Dom miloserdiya "Nadezhda", g. Vladimir (Typescript appeal to donors).
'Dopisannaya stroka', *Rabotnitsa*, no. 5, 1990, 27.
XIX vsesoyuznaya partiinaya konferentsiya Kommunisticheskoi partii Sovetskogo Soyuza, Stenograficheskii otchet (Moscow, 1988).
D'yachenko, N., 'Ispytanie miloserdiem', *Izvestiya*, 1.10.88, 3.
D'yachenko, N., 'Leningradtsy b'yut trevogu', *Doverie*, no. 10, 1990, 4–5.
D'yachenko, N., 'Obrashchayus' za pomoshch'yu k miloserdiyu', *Sem'ya i shkola*, no. 9, 1988, 7–9.
D'yachenko, N., 'Po vashim pros'bam', *Kontakt*,[7] no. 5 (August), 1989, 7–8.
D'yachenko, N., 'Shkola sostradaniya', *KP*, 18.11.87, 4.
D'yachkov, S., 'I vse-taki ya nadeyus"', *KP*, 4.6.88, 1.
Dyskin, A., Sharapanovskii, A. and Starodvorskii, I., 'Vozmozhnostei eshche nemalo', *SO*, no. 5, 1978, 39–40.
Edel', E., 'Tikhaya obitel'', *Krokodil*, no. 21, 1978, 4–5.
Ermachenko, 'Dobrota po prinuzhdeniyu', *Molodoi kommunar* (Voronezh),

Bibliography 235

15.12.81, 3.
Eroshok, Z., 'Angely na razvalinakh', *KP*, 7.2.92, 2.
Fedorova, E., 'Spasitel'naya "lesenka"', *SR*, 4.9.91.
Fedorova, E., 'Vverkh po "Lesenke"', *SR*, 27.10.90.
Fedorova, I., 'Tarif na miloserdie', *Molodoi kommunar* (Voronezh), 30.4.81, p. 3.
Fertman, B., *Razorvannyi krug*, (Perm, 1994) [originally published, abridged, in *Zvezda*, no. 12, 1979].
Fomin, S., 'Finish na Ratushnoi ploshchadi', *Sovetskii Krasnyi Krest*, no. 8, 1987, 22–3.
'Fond i ego "Zabota"', *VN*, 29.3.90, 1.
'Fond mira v mire fondov' (interview with V. Maslin), *Miloserdie*, no. 7 (15), 2.91, 3.
'Fond 700344 sotsial'nykh izobretenii', *KP*, 22.7.87, 2.
'Geografiya miloserdiya', *Pravda*, 6.6.89, 1.
'General'nym direktorom...stal Viktor Lizunkov' [untitled announcement], *NV*, no. 37, 1989.
Glukhov, Yu., 'Priem vedet narodnyi deputat N. A. Demakov', *Sovetskaya Sibir'*, 12.7.89, p. 1.
'God rozhdeniya – 1988', *SO*, no. 11, 1988, 2–3.
Golubev, V., 'Anketa oprosa' (typescript), 1970.
Golubev, V., 'Slovo k lyudyam nelegkoi sud'by', *Zdorov'e*, no. 2, 1970, 22.
Gorbunova, N. and Petrova,V., 'Trudoustroistvo invalidov: plyusy i minusy', *SO*, no. 8, 1980, 7–9.
Goryunov, M., 'Komsomol, zachem tebe den'gi?', *Sobesednik*, no. 31, 1987.[8]
'Gotovy li my k miloserdiyu?' (interview with V. Kaznacheev), *Ogonek*, no. 46, 1989, 20–2.
Grafova, L., 'Ne prosto sochuvstvie', *KP*, 24.5.69.
Granin, D, 'O miloserdii', *LG*, 18.3.87, 13.
Grishin, N., 'Klubu dali imya "Soglasie"', *Sovetskaya Estonia*, 11.2.89.
Grishin, N. and Prisyazhnuk, I., 'Obshchestvo "Konkordo" ishchet druzei', *NV*, no. 35, 1989.
Gubakov, G., Novoksionov, P. and Plutnik, A.,'Nuzhna zabota deistviem', *Izvestiya*, 6.2.82, 2.
Gurinovich, V., 'Shag navstrechu', *Smena*, no. 23, 1988, 2–3.
Gusev, G., 'Besprintsipnost'', *Kommuna* (Voronezh), 28.8.71, 1.
Gus'kov, G., 'Komu nuzhny nashi ruki?' (typescript, also published in *SO*, no. 5, 1973).
Gus'kov, G., 'Rezerv rabochikh ruk', *Krymskii komsomolets*, 15.8.87, 3.
Gus'kov, G., 'Trud dlya nas – blago', *SO*, no. 9, 1972, 27–9.
Gus'kov, G. and Golovatyi, G., letter to M. Gorbachev (undated typescript, late 1985/early 1986).
Häkkelä, H., 'Elene Moiseevne Rzhevskoi – nabroski dlya orientatsii', typescript, February 1974.
Häkkelä, H. et al., 'Bol'shoi' lomot'?' (Undated typescript by inhabitants of Voronezh residential home).
I lyazhet na dushu dobro, vyp. 4, Moscow (FMZ), 1991.
Interlegal Research Center, *Predvaritel'naya klassifikatsiya obshchestvennykh organizatsii, ustavy kotorykh zaregistrirovany Ministerstvom yustitsii RSFSR na 26.06.91* [Moscow, 1991].

'Interv'yu iz "polupodvala"' (interview with S. Andreev), *Vestnik MGOI*, 1.91, 1.⁹
Iofe, V. and Proshina, E., 'Slukhi o raskole "Memoriala" neskol'ko preuvelicheny', *VL*, 23.10.90.
Itogi i uroki Goda miloserdiya (Materialy IV Plenuma pravleniya Sovetskogo fonda miloserdiya i zdorov'ya, 16-17 yanvarya 1990 g.) (Moscow, 1990).
Ivakin, E., 'Gor'kie ispovedi, ili komu nuzhna takaya lozh'?', *Bryanskii rabochii*, 1.12.87, 3.
Iz opyta raboty respublikanskikh fondov, kraevykh, oblastnykh, gorodskikh otdelenii, vyp. 5, Moscow (FMZ), 1991.
'Iz vystupleniya patriarkha Moskovskogo i Vseya Rusi, Aleksiya II', *Miloserdie*, no. 11(19), 3.91, 3.
Izgarshev, V., 'Zayavila o sebe', *Pravda*, 7.2.87.
K sovesti, no. 3, 1990.¹⁰
K Verkhovnym sovetam SSSR i RSFSR...', *Nadezhda*,¹¹ no. 5, 3.91, 2.
Kabakov, A., 'Odin ot 7.000.000', *MN*, 29.1.89, 9.
Kalinina, E., (Leningrad *obkom* commission for analysis and prognosis of, and relations with socio-political organisations and movements), 'Zapiska o merakh konkretnoi pomoshchi Leningradskogo oblastnogo komiteta partii obshchestvennym organizatsiyam, podderzhivayushchim KPSS (Proekt)' (undated typescript, probably 1990).
Kapustin, S., 'Soyuz mnogodetnykh, *Pravda*, 8.10.89.
Karaseva, N., 'Nepolnyi rabochii den': problemy vnedreniya', *SO*, no. 7, 1980, 35–7.
Karev, M., 'Nuzhny garantii ravnykh vozmozhnostei', *Kontakt*, no. 9, 1990, 1.
Kas'yanenko, M., and Godin, L., 'Starty za oblakami', *SO*, no. 5, 1983, 61.
Katinskaya, N., 'Izgoi "neob"yatnoi Rodiny"', *Otverzhennye* (undated 'independent newspaper', early 1991).
Khaustova, L., 'Iz zhizni Optimista', *Sovetskaya molodezh'* (Riga), 26.9.87.
'Khodit' nachali zanovo', *Izvestiya*, 19.4.89.
Kirbasova, M., 'My zashchishchaem prava synovei', *Armiya i obshchestvo*, (Moscow, 1990), 229–35.
Kleva, A., 'Gorech"', *Izvestiya*, 30.11.83, 3.
Klyushnikov, E. and Matveyev, L., *Leningradskoe pravlenie VOS* (Moscow, 1986).
Kolesnikova, I., 'Po schetam miloserdiya', *Nedelya*, no. 26, 1989.
Kolmakov, E., 'Razmyshleniya pered s"ezdom', *Nadezhda*, no. 31, 1991, 2.
'Komandu otmenili... No...', *Trud*, 5.7.89.
Komarova, D., 'Odinnadtsataya pyatiletka: nashi zadachi i perspektivy', *SO*, no. 6, 1981, 3–7.
Komarova, D., 'Sotsial'naya programma partii i nashi zadachi', *SO*, no. 8, 1986.
Komitet po provedeniyu oprosa invalidov, 'Obrashchenie' (typescript) 1971.
Kom'kalova, V., 'Miloserdie po takse?', *KP*, 9.2.88.
Kononenko, V., 'Chuzhaya beda', *Rabotnitsa*, no. 11, 1974, 20–1.
Konovalov, S., 'Trudno li vymyt' pol?', *Molodoi kommunar* (Voronezh), 21.2.84, 2.

Konstantinov, V., 'Gosudarstvo v roli vora', *Nadezhda*, no. 1, 1990.
Kostikov, V., 'Blesk i nishcheta nomenklatury', *Ogonek*, no. 1, 1989.
Krasnopol'skaya, N., 'Opeka', *MP*, 19.7.88, abstract in *RB*, 54.
Kravchenko, E., 'S bedoyu ne naedine', *Molodoi kommunar* (Voronezh), 6.2.82, 3.
Kremina, E., 'Vozrozhdenie traditsii', *VL*, 14.4.90.
'Kriterii miloserdiya' (interview with V. Kaznacheev), *Pravda*, 21.5.90, 5.
Krutogorov, Yu., 'Odinokaya starost'?', *SO* no. 9, 1983, 33–6.
Krylov, A. and Likholitov, V., 'Miloserdie', *Ogonek*, no. 38, 1988, also published in *Ogonek-88. Luchshie publikatsii goda* (Moscow, 1989).
Kryuchkova, S., 'Golosuite za miloserdie', *Vestnik 'Poleta'* (Chelyabinsk), 2.2.90.
Ksenin, L., 'Nikto ne ushel bez pokupki', *Sem'ya*, no. 4, 1992, abstract in *RB*, 122.
Kulicheva, N., *Organizatsiya kul'turno-prosvetitel'noi raboty v klubakh i domakh kul'tury VOS* (Moscow, 1985).
Kupriyanov, A., 'Perevorot: vzglyad iz invalidnoi kolyaski', *Nadezhda*, no. 31, 1991, 4.
Kutateladze, O, 'Prikhod i raskhod miloserdiya', *KP*, 13.10.88.
Lakhno, I., 'Po adresu bedy', *Pravda*, 7.07.89.
Lasovskaya, I., 'Kak v serdtse nashem otzovetsya', *VN*, 24.5.90, 4.
Lasovskaya, I., 'Ekho Chernobylya', *VN*, 28.5.90, 4.
Lasovskaya, I., 'My razuchilis' ponimat'?', *VN*, 4.8.90, 5.
Lavrent'eva, N., 'Kto khozyain?', *SR*, 21.10.89.
'Leningrad – ne prosto vstrecha?', *Dom*,[12] no. 3, December 1988, 6.
Leonidova, A., 'Ya gorzhus' svoimi det'mi', *Mnogodetnaya sem'ya*, no. 1 (2.11.89).
'L'goty ili milostynya?' (interview with S. Ivchenkov), *MP*, 7.6.89.
Likhanov, A., *Nedetskie zaboty Detskogo fonda* (Moscow, 1990).
Lilenko, M., 'Daleko ot miloserdiya', *VL*, 4.4.88.
Litvinov, V., 'Na p'edestale svyatosti', *Sud'ba* (Ulan-Ude), no. 1, 5.93, 1.
Litvinov, V., 'Novosti, opyt, problemy', *Nadezhda*, no. 29, 1991, 2.
Logina, N., 'Podgotovka k vneocherednoi II konferentsii LGOI', *Kontakt*, no. 4 (7.89), 3–4.
Lozovaya, E., 'Odinokie serdtsa, odinokie dushi', *SO*, no. 11, 1991, 60.
Lushnikov, A., 'Formula miloserdiya', *KP*, 3.5.89, 1.
L'vova, G., 'Lyudi, kotorykh znayut vse', *Sem'ya*, no. 10, 1990, 3.[13]
Maksimova, E., 'Do groma', *Izvestiya*, 16.6.89.
Malevskii, T., 'Spravka iz kontslagerya, ili chem obernulis' khlopoty v Suzemke', *Sud'ba* (Ulan-Ude), no. 1, 5.93, 3.
Malyshchenko, S., 'Obshchestvo miloserdiya ili kormushka dlya byurokratov?', *Smena*, 4.4.90.[14]
Malysheva, A., 'Beda – ne vina', *KP*, 17.12.87, 2.
Malysheva, A., 'Est' start!', *KP*, 1.3.88.
Malysheva, A., 'Odin za vsekh', *KP*, 4.3.89.
'Mariya: den' za dnem', *Rabotnitsa*, no. 9, 1990, 30.
Matveev, S., 'Kto chem mozhet..., pomogite', *Chelyabinskii trubnik*, 7.2.90, 3.
Miloserdie – dobrota na dele (iz opyta dvizheniya miloserdiya), vyp. 2 (Moscow: FMZ), 1990.

'Miloserdie dolzhno byt' effektivnym' (interview with I. Zaslavsky), *Izvestiya*, 24.8.89, 2.
'Miloserdie i "miloserdie"', *VL*, 7.1.88.
'Miloserdie i sochuvstvie', *AiF*, no. 10, 1989.
'Miloserdie – kategoriya ekonomicheskaya' (interview with S. Fedorov), *Miloserdie*, no. 1 (1990).
'Milostyny ne prosim' (interview with A. Deryugin), *AiF*, no. 14, 1990, 5.
Mironova, S., 'Cherez bol' – k radosti', *Chelyabinskii rabochii*, 30.9-1.10.89, 3–4.
Misyurev, Yu., 'Iz Informatsionnogo byulletenya TsS', *Zerkalo*, no. 8, May 1987, 2.[15]
'Mnogo del u komiteta' (interview with I. Vasil'ev), *Nadezhda*, no. 31, 1991, 3.
Morzhenko, T., 'Razdory v novom dome', *Miloserdie*, no. 11 (19), 3.91, 10.
Mulina, M., 'Delovye al'truisty', *KP*, 27.8.88, 1.
Mulina, M., 'Zhdite, my pridem', *KP*, 5.4.88, 2.
Mulina, M. and Fatecheva, N., 'V pokhod za ideyami!', *Sobesednik*, no. 26, 1988.
Murzhenko, K., 'Reshenie no. 1091: vypolnyaetsya li ono?', *Leningradskii literator*, 8.12.89, 4.
Muzei Sovetskogo Krasnogo Kresta [Moscow, 1979?].
'My zhdem peremen', *Vestnik MGOI*, August 1989, 1.
Nadezhdina, N., 'Skomandovali...', *Trud*, 18.6.89.
'Nado uspet'', *Rabotnitsa*, no. 7, 1989, 14–15.
'Nashi znakomstva', *Dom*, no. 5, April 1989, 10.
'Ne podavat', pomogat'!' (interview with V. Zinov'ev), *Nadezhda*, no. 31, 1991, 3.
'Nekotorye itogi 1990 g. i osnovnye napravleniya raboty VOI v 1991 g.', *Kontakt*, no. 1, 1991, 1.
Neuimina, N., 'Spasibo, lyudi', *Zvezda*, 1980, 201–3.
Neumyvakin, A., speech to the USSR Congress of People's Deputies, 1.6.89, in *Pravda*, 3.6.89, 6.
Nevskii Angel, Sankt-Peterburg: Proekty 1996 goda.
'O dopolnitel'nykh merakh po trudoustroistvu i professional'nomu obucheniyu invalidov', *Izvestiya*, 15.1.77.
Ob itogakh deyatel'nosti Sovetskogo fonda miloserdiya i zdorov'ya za god (so dnya osnovaniya). Informatsiya k zasedaniyu prezidiuma pravleniya SFMZ, 15.9.89 (Moscow: FMZ, 1989).
'Ob osnovnykh nachalakh sotsial'noi zashchishchennosti invalidov v SSSR', *Izvestiya*, 15.12.90, 2.
'Obrashchenie invalidov... Leonidu Il'ichu Brezhnevu' (typescript petition) [1979/80].
'Obresti dostoinstvo', *KP*, 6.4.88.
Obshchestvennoe mnenie v tsifrakh (Moscow: VTsIOM), various issues.
Obshchestvo miloserdiya 'Leningrad' (Leningrad, 1989).
'Odinochestvo', *Ogonek*, no. 39, 1981.
'Oni i my' (interview with S. D'yachkov), *Ogonek*, no. 42, 1988, 14–16.
'"Opora" zhdet pomoshchi', *KP*, 13.10.89.
'Ot imeni naroda' (interview with I. Zaslavsky), *MG*, 9.7.89, 3.

Bibliography 239

Otchet o rabote pravleniya SFMiZ...sentyabr' 88g.-noyabr 1990 g. (Moscow: FMZ).
'Otkrytoe pis'mo chlenov Obshchestva lits, postradavshykh ot repressii' (Moscow, autumn 1989, typescript).
'Otkrytoe pis'mo S"ezdu narodnykh deputatov', *Vestnik MGOI*, May 1989, 1.
Ovchinnikova, I., 'Vse deti nashi', *Izvestiya*, 5.1.87.
Pani, A., 'Golodovka – metod ili sledstvie?', *Fakel*, no. 2, 1989.[16]
'Palatki u Kremlya', *MK*, 3.8.90, abstract in *RB*, 83.
Pankin, M., 'Novoe polozhenie ob usloviyakh truda nadomnikov', *SO*, no. 4, 1982, 51–4.
Panov, V., 'Kak pereiti dorogu?', *Stroitel'naya gazeta*, 11.11.87, 4.
Pantuev, K., 'Delovye al'truisty Mariny Muliny', *Dom*, 2, November 1988, 8.
Pantyukhina, O., 'Rabota i plany perovchan', *Vestnik MGOI*, no. 5, 1990, 2.
Parfenova, O., 'Kvadratnyi treugol'nik', *Trud*, 29.6.89.
Pavlov, V., 'Blagotvoritel'nost' na dele', *Nedelya*, no. 39, 1989.
Pekur, V., 'Boites' ravnodushiya', *Trud*, 11.7.87, 2.
Pekur, V. and Solovei, P., 'K polnokrovnoi zhizni i trudu' (letters), *Trud*, 25.1.87.
Petukhov, A., 'Dat' rabotu invalidam', *SO*, no. 11, 1988, 10.
'Piket u Mariinskogo', *Kontakt*, June 1991, 2.
Polozhenie detei v SSSR (Moscow: Children's Fund, 1990).
'Pomnim, skorbim,' *VN*, 22.5.90, 1.
Popov, N., 'Levsha vse-taki prav', *Megapolis-Express*, 15.7.92, 28.
Popov, N. and Sazonov, V., 'Ob"ekt otsenki – fondy', *Delovoi mir*, 5.6.92, 14.
'Popravim delo bez "bortsa"', *MP*, 14.2.88 (letters).
Poret, A., 'Mamashiny neschast'ya, *Kuranty*, 10.8.91.
Portugeis, M., letter under heading 'Obshchestvo "Miloserdie": byt' ili ne byt'?', *VL*, 12.12.87.
'Postanovlenie Soveta Ministrov RSFSR "O merakh po uluchsheniyu sotsial'nogo obsluzhivaniya invalidov v RSFSR"', *Vestnik MGOI*, no. 6, 1990.
'Po-tul'ski', *Miloserdie* (Moscow), no. 1, 1990.
'Pravo na zdorov'e,' *VN*, 7.6.90, 4.
'Predlozhenie Verkhovnomu Sovetu SSSR o sozdanii edinogo Vsesoyuznogo obshchestva invalidov...na baze...VOS i VOG' (typescript petition) [1979/80].
'Primite russko-yazychnykh bezhentsev!', *VN*, 3.4.90, 1.
'Printsipy deyatel'nosti Moskovskogo obshchestva miloserdiya (Proekt)', *Dom*, no. 1, October 1988, 2.
'Prioritet – miloserdiyu' (interview with N. Bosenko), *Izvestiya*, 28.7.89.
'Professiya – roditeli', *SZ*, no. 1 (1990), 19.
'Profsoyuzy – detyam Chernobylya', *VN*, 13.6.90, 2.
'Proizvodstvennye struktury VOI po sostoyaniyu na 01.07.91' (Tables distributed at the Society's congress in October-November 1991).
'Pros'ba Verkhovnomu Sovetu SSSR ot invalidov strany', 1.11.79 (typescript petition).
Protsenko, A., 'Den'gi dlya Chernobylya. Ikh sobirala vsya strana. Kak imi

rasporyadilis'?', *Izvestiya*, 28.9.89.
Puchkov, I. and twenty-one other disabled people, manuscript letter to the editors of *Literaturnaya gazeta*, 26.8.74.
Putrenko, T., 'Budem miloserdny!' *LG*, 4.5.88, 13.
P'yanykh, G., '"Mnogodetnaya sem'ya" mozhet lishit'sya kormil'tsa', *Kommersant* 18.3.91, abstract in *RB*, 23.
Rad'ko, N., 'Vremya pokoya', *LG*, 17.9.80.
Rakhimov, R., 'Nuzhen Fond miloserdiya', *Sovetksii Krasnyi Krest*, no. 10, 1987.
'Razdeli chuzhuyu bedu', *MG*, 7.5.89, reproduced in *Sovetkskii Krasnyi Krest segodnya*, 9–12.
'Razdelyayut nashu bol'", *MP*, 5.4.88, abstract in *RB*, 54.
Realizatsiya programm za 1991 god (Moscow: ASP 'Bogatyri'/FSI, 1992).
Rokhatsevich, E., 'Voskresnyi detskii sad Lyudmily Rogovoi', *Zavodskoi signal* (Chelyabinsk), 8.8.89, 2.
Rudakov, P., 'Proekty nado sovershenstvovat'", *SO*, no. 10, 1984, 26–7.
Rukovoditeli Fondov miloserdiya i zdorov'ya soyuznykh, avtonomnykh respublik i kraevykh, oblastnykh, gorodskikh otdelenii (Moscow, 1991).
Ryzhkov, V., 'On slonikhe shlet poklon...', *Pravda*, 30.12.90.
Ryzhova, A., 'Vchera, segodnya, zavtra', *Vestnik MGOI*, no. 5, 1991, 1.
Rzhevskaya, E., , 'Vozvrashchenie', *LG*, 14.8.74.
'S otkrytym serdtsem', *Izvestiya*, 4.12.87.
Saar, S., 'Uchastniki avtoralli – invalidy', *SO* no. 5, 1983, 38.
Samarina, A., 'Sovershenstvovanie raboty domov-internatov', *SO*, no. 1, 1981, 13–15.
Samodeyatel'nye obshchestvennye organizatsii, part 1 (Moscow Popular Front, 1988).
Samokhin, A., 'Spasatel' v bede ne ostavit', *Izvestiya*, 8.11.89.
Samsonov, G., 'Est' li obshchestvo invalidov v Leningrade?', *Kontakt*, no. 5, August 1989.
Sanatina, Yu., 'Zhelaem Vam muzhestva', *Molodost' Sibiri*, 10.6.89, 10.
Saraksina, L., 'Reabilitatsiya dobra', *Vek XX i mir*, no. 4, 1989, 18–21.
Sarkisyan, D., 'Bez doma', *SZ*, no. 1, 7.90, 29–30.
Savel'ev, V., 'Ne khotim byt' obuzoi', *Vechernyaya Moskva*, 12.9.89.
Savvateeva, T., 'Miloserdie dolzhno stat' normoi', *SO*, no. 1, 1991, 42–3.
Sazonov, V., Popov, N. and Volkova, R., 'Blagovoritel'nost' – eto khorosho, no luchshe, esli zanimat'sya eyu budut drugie', *Delovoi mir*, 15.5.92, 15.
Sekretariat TsK KPSS, Postanovlenie 'Ob ob"edinenii "Memorial"', 11 November 1988.
Shcherbakov, V., 'Povorot k cheloveku', *SZ*, no. 1, 7.90, 2–5, 64–5.
Shenkman, S., 'Trudno byt' optimistom', *Fizkul'tura i sport*, no. 8, 1987, 23–5.
Shirinskii, P., 'Chtoby ne bylo odinochestva', *Krasnyi Krest segodnya*, no. 11, 1987.
Shul'gina, E, 'Bol' ne chuzhaya', *Smena*, 15.5.87.[17]
Shvedova, Yu., 'Beregite brat'ev men'shikh', *Trud*, 24.7.88.
Sichka, I., 'Proekt Gus'kova', *Sovetskii patriot*, no. 36, September 1990.
Soldantenkov, I., 'Po puti, nachertannomu partiei', *SO*, no. 9, 1977, 5–9.

Bibliography

'Solntse svobody', *MK*, 14.6.89.
Solomenko, E., 'V psikhushkakh – normal'nye deti', *Izvestiya*, 5.10.91, 4.
Solovei, P., 'Vremya dlya miloserdiya', *VL*, 5.2.88.
Solovei, P., 'Vstan' i idi', *VL*, 21.4.86.
'Sostav Prezidiuma Tsentral'nogo pravleniya Vserossiiskogo obshchestva invalidov', *SO*, no. 11, 1988, 19.
Sovetskii fond miloserdiya i zdorov'ya. Soviet Charity and Health Foundation (Moscow, 1989).
Sovetskii fond miloserdiya i zdorov'ya. Osnovnye dokumenty (Moscow, 1989).
Sovetskii Krasnyi Krest segodnya (Moscow [1991]).
'Sozdanie oblastnykh obshchestv invalidov', *Fakel*, no. 2, 1989.
'Spasateli. Professiya ili obraz zhizni nemnogikh nastoyashchikh muzhchin?', *Miloserdie*, no. 11 (19), 3.91, 9.
'Speshite delat' dobro!' (interview with V. Men'shikov), *MG*, 8.2.89.
'Sporit' s sud'boi', *Smena*, no. 10, 1985.
Spravochnik nekommercheskikh organizatsii, Samarskaya oblast' (London: BEARR Trust, 1996).
'Srochnaya trebuetsya valyuta', *VN*, 16.6.90, 5.
Stakhov, V., 'O lyudyakh trudnoi sud'by', *Zvezda*, no. 2, 1970, 218–22.
Stepanova, I., 'Devochka s medvezhonkom', *VL*, 13.12.88.
120 let Vserossiiskomu obshchestvu spasaniya na vodakh (Moscow, 1991).
Sviridova, N., 'Oglyanut'sya, uvidet', pomoch'', *MK*, 13.5.89.
Tarasov, I., 'A u menya vopros', *Rabotnitsa*, no. 1, 1990, 27.
'Telemarafon Chernobyl'', *VN*, 25.4.90, 1.
Tkachenko, A., 'Chto takoe Tovarishchestvo vzaimopomoshchi "Prometei"?', *Sobesednik*, no. 3, September 1986, 1–2.[18]
'Tochka otscheta', *Informatsionnyi byulleten'* no. 2, 1991, 36–51 (Moscow: Red Cross).
Trius, I., 'Tol'ko li nadomniki', *KP*, 27.1.66.
Trubilin, N., 'Pravo byt' nuzhnym', *SR*, 30.3.88, 2.
Tsentral'noe pravlenie VOI, 'Otchetnyi doklad Vneocherednomu s"ezdu VOI' [October 1991].
Tsyganov, I., 'Million s auktsiona', *Sem' s plyusom*, no. 43, 1991, abstract in *RB*, 121.
Tsygankova, E., 'Komu on nuzhen, eto MIKO?', *Nadezhda*, no. 14, 1991.
Tsyganova, L., 'Mnogodetnaya sem'ya – blago li?', *VN*, 19.3.90, 3.
Tupikin, V., et al., 'Miloserdie po subbotam?', *Sobesednik*, no. 33, 1987.[19]
'U molodykh est' svoi trudnosti' (interview with Yu. Bausov), *Nadezhda*, no. 10, 1991, 3.
Udintsev, E., and Gorbunova, N., 'Zadacha gosudarstvennoi vazhnosti', *SO* no. 3, 1980, 31–4.
'Ushchemlenie sovesti: pis'mo s kommentariem o tom, kak spekuliruyut na zashchite prav invalidov', *MP*, 9.12.87.
Ustav Fonda sotsial'nykh izobretenii (1991).
'Ustav Novosibirskogo Gorodskogo Ob"edineniya "Miloserdie"' (1989).
'Ustav "Prometeya"' [1970].
'Ustav Sovetskogo fonda "Mnogodetnaya sem'ya"', *Mnogodetnaya sem'ya*, no. 1, 2.11.89.
Ustav Vserossiiskogo obshchestvo invalidov (Moscow, 1988).

Uzlikova, T., 'Vse eto radi lyudei', *SO*, no. 11, 1978, 36–8.
'V Moskovskom gorkome partii', *MK*, 18.8.88.
'V zhivykh ostalos' dvesti dvenadtsat'', *VN*, 18.4.90, 2.
Vainshtein, L., 'Sil'naya "slabaya zhenshchina"', *Trud*, 2.6.90.
Vakhtina, L., 'Pochemu sozdano obshchestvo?', *Vestnik MGOI*, no. 4, 1990, 1.
Valer'yanov, E., 'VASOT. Chto eto takoe?', *VN*, 4.8.90, p. 3.
Valyuzhenach, G., 'Ne oskudela b ruka dayushshego', *AiF*, no. 52, 1990.
van der Voort, Feodor 'Praktika i bogoslovie blagotvoritel'nosti v Russkoi Pravoslavnoi tserkvi', *Put' Pravoslaviya*, no. 2, 1993, 67–88.
Vasil'ev, G., 'Nam mnogoe po plechu', *Sobesednik*, no. 40, September 1987, 10.[20]
Vasil'kova, E., 'Naperekor sud'be', *Sotsialisticheskaya industriya*, 10.1.89.
Venediktov, D., 'Opirat'sya na massy', *MG*, 1.4.87.
'Vernut' rodine ee synovei' (interview with N. Kozyrev), *Izvestiya*, 17.6.89.
Vestnik blagotvoritel'nosti (Moscow: Moscow Charity House/*Soprichastnost'* Fund), various issues.
Vishnyakova, N., *Dnevnik Niny Vishnyakovoi* (Sverdlovsk, 1990).
Vishnyakova, N., 'Pis'ma drugu', *Neman*, no. 3, 1968, 150–72.
Vlasov, P., *Obitel' miloserdiya* (Moscow, 1991).
'Vmesto s vami', *Rabotnitsa*, no. 3, 1991.
'Vo imya cheloveka budushchego' (interview with A. Likhanov), *Bibliotekar'*, no. 9, 1988 reproduced in *Detskii fond deistvuet*, pp. 83–6.
Vo imya dobra i miloserdiya, vyp. 3 (Moscow: FMZ, 1991).
Volkov, V., et al., 'V redaktsiyu gazety 'Komsomol'skaya pravda', *Zerkalo*, no. 8, May 1987, 5–6.
'Vozlyubi blizhnego svoego', *SO*, no. 1, 1991, 40.
Vozvrashchenie k zhizni' (interview with K. Kabanov), *LG*, 12.3.75, 13.
VTsIOM, *Obshchestvennoe mnenie v tsifrakh*, various issues.
Vyatkin, A., 'Mesto sredi vas', *KP*, 14.1.71 (abridged version of 'Tsena', below).
Vyatkin, A., 'Tsena nepodvizhnosti', *Kurortnaya gazeta*, Yalta, 25.12.70, continued as 'Est' takoi gorod', 29.12.70, 2.
'Vzroslym i detyam', *VN*, 16.4.90, 1.
Yakovlev, G., 'L'goty "detyam voiny"', *Pravda*, 24.10.89.
Yanitskii, O., *Ekologicheskoe dvizhenie v Rossii. Kriticheskii analiz.* Moscow: Russian Academy of Sciences, Institute of Sociology, 1996).
Yashina, T., 'Ya – protiv', *Trud*, 3.3.88, 4.
Yntemna, M., United Way International Moscow Liaison, *Opyt raspredeleniya inostrannoi gumanitarnoi pomoshchi blagotvoritel'nymi organizatsiyami Moskvy* (Moscow, March 1992).
Yur'eva, R., 'Svet vzaimnoi dobroty', *Nadezhda*, no. 14, 1991, 7.
Zabavskikh, E., 'Besplatnyi obed – za chei schet?', *LG*, 10.1.90, 12.
Zabelin, L., 'I podaril klub nadezhdu', *VL*, 21.3.88.
Zaikin, V., 'V neoplatnom dolgu', *Izvestiya*, 18.10.89.
'Zakon nashei zhizni' (interview with A. Osadchikh), *Preodolenie*, 1991, 28–9.
'Zakon ob invalidakh v respublikakh Rossii', *Nadezhda*, no. 31, 1991, 2.
Zalevskaya, E., 'Im nas ne ponyat'', *Kontakt*, no. 6, 1991, 2.

Zaslavsky, I., 'Invalidov predstavlyayu ya odin', *NV*, no. 15, 1989, 25.
'Zavodskoi fond miloserdiya', *VN*, 15.2.90, 1.
Zhukova, L., 'Nuzhnoe delo', *MG*, 1.4.87.
Zhukova, V., 'U semidesyati nyanek', *Sobesednik*, no. 21, 1988.[21]
Zhzhenova, M., 'Materialy k teme "Istoriya Leningradskogo otdeleniya Obshchestva 'Memorial''' (typescript).
Zolotova, Z., 'Stariki v dome', *Ogonek*, no. 18, 1982, 26.
Zykov, N., 'Za chertoi miloserdiya', *Sovetskaya Sibir'*, 16.4.89.

Index

1991 as watershed, 186-7

Abramkin, Valerii, 159
Abuladze, Tengiz, 180
accidents, industrial, 23, 26, 35
Action Group to Defend Rights of Disabled People, 58-60, 153
adolescents, *see* young people and students
adoption, 108-9
Adventists, 95, 115
Afghan veterans, 14, 65, 76, 77, 80, 100, 128, 136-7, 167, 173, 174, 177
  mothers, widows, 70, 123-4
  prisoners of war, 123-4
Afghan Veterans' Union, 137
  ageing of Soviet population, 22-3
  Agency of Social Information, 190
aid, foreign/humanitarian, 15, 67, 71, 74, 83-5, 94, 102, 110, 115, 126, 133, 179, 184
AIDS, 90, 102
Akademgorodok (Novosibirsk), 63, 168
Alapuro, R., 180
Alaska, 100
alcohol abuse, 21, 24-5, 111, 116
Aleksii, Patriarch, 114
Alexander Nevsky Monastery, 114
Alferenko, Gennadii, 8, 99-101
altruism, 42, 109, 163, 167
Amateur Song Club, 8
America(n), *see* USA
amputees, 137
Anarchists, 160
Anarcho-Syndicalists, 173
Anderson, John, 232n.145
animals, 111
'antagonism, complete' (official, towards NGOs), 146, 156

Anti-AIDS, 102
anti-alcohol campaign, 25, 67
anti-fascist work, 121
anti-semitism, 115
Anti-SPID, 102
Apatity, 166
Apparel', 134
Armenian earthquake, 1988, 71, 88
army, *see* soldiers
arteli (workshops), *see* Promkooperatsiya
association, (non)freedom of
  pre-1985: 1, 6-9, 100
  from 1990: 13, 15, 147, 166
Assotsiatsiya molodezhnykh invalidnykh organizatsii, 134
Assotsiatsiya obshchestvennykh organizatsii roditelei detei-invalidov, Leningrad, 126, 175
Assotsiatsiya sovetskikh evreev-veteranov 121
Astrakhan, 94
astrologers, 101
atomization, 132, 161
August 1991 coup, 141, 186
autistic children, 126
avoidance (official, of NGOs), 150-1

Baikal, 8
Balashikha, 71
Baltic republics, 19-20, 21, 56, 60, 61, 69, 91
Baptists, 106, 114-15
Bashkir rail disaster, 1989, 72, 174
Bausov, Yurii, 134
BEARR Trust, 84, 190
Befrienders' International, 110
beggars, 15, 26, 45, 63
Belgorod, 106
believers, *see* churches, volunteers
Belomorsk, 107

Index

Belorussian Ministry of Social Security, 62
benefits (*posobiya*), 26, 68, 124
  see also pensions, *Minsobes*, welfare state
black market, 70
Blind Children, Association of Parents, 126
blind people, 171
  see also VOS (Society of Blind People)
Blockade of Leningrad survivors, 104, 121
blood donors, 87
boarding education, 30–1
Bogatyri, 101
Bokova, Elizaveta, 145, 150, 151, 152
Bonner, Elena, 59, 110
Borodaevskaya, Zoya, 63, 168
Borodin Quartet, 102
Borovoi, Konstantin, 79, 187
Braithwaite, Jill, 84
Brezhnev, Leonid, 6, 20, 22, 24, 28–31, 40, 48, 59, 77–8, 127, 159
Bristol, 115
brotherhoods, Orthodox, 113–14, 165–6, 233n.163
Brown, Archie, 9
Bryansk city/*oblast*, 62, 75, 90, 148, 160, 165
Burkova, O'lga, 60–1, 128
business activities of NGOs, *see* cooperatives, voluntary organizations
business, support for charity, 191
  see also cooperatives
Butterfield, Jim 146, 150, 171, 175
byvshikh maloletnikh uznikov fashistskikh kontslagerei, Soyuz, 121, 155, 160

campaigns, official
  anti-alcohol, 25
  Miloserdie ('Charity'), 76
  Zabota ('Care'), 69
camps, concentration/labour, *see* prisoners

cancer, children with, 126, 169–70
Car Enthusiasts' Association, 61
'Care' Campaign, 69
Caringness and Charity, 143–4
'catchall' charities, 108, 164
censorship, 25, 50
Center for Curative Pedagogics, 118–9
Central Asia, 20, 97
Central Committee, *see* CPSU
cerebral palsy, 62, 149, 169, 173
Charitable Organizations of Russia, 14, 114, 217n.7
charity, 2, 10, 14, 16, 42, 44, 62–5, 75–81, ch. 5, 106, 122, 138, 172, 177–8, 190
  before 1917, 42, 107
  1917–1985: 2, 25, 29–30, 42, 63, 182–3
  beneficiaries, 15, 90, 177
  donations, 15, 70, 71, 79, 86–7, 94, 103, 114, 124, 191
  v. power/money, 163, 167
  v. self-help, 2, 118, 130, 138
  see also aid, funds, voluntary organizations, *individual organizations and categories of beneficiary*
Charity and Health Foundation, *see* FMZ
charity houses, 190
Charity Know How, 84
Charity societies, *see Miloserdie*
Charity Street, St Petersburg, 2
Chazov, Evgenii, 24, 76
Chechnya, 189
Chelovek, 104
Chelyabinsk, 97, 149, 155, 159, 169, 172, 173, 174
Chelyabinsk Popular Front, 174
chemists, 101
Chernobyl
  accident/public response, 23, 71, 90, 114, 136–7, 178
  victims' groups, 14, 71, 101, 136–8, 158, 167
Chernobyl Liquidators' Union ('Chernobyl Union'), 101, 137–8, 158, 167

Chernyaev, Anatolii, 9
Cheshire, Leonard, and Cheshire Homes, 84
chess societies, 135, 148
Chess Federation of Deaf People, 135
child care, 30, 34, 115, 149, 169
children
  abuse, 26, 120
  Christian charities, 113, 114, 115
  mortality, 97
  poverty, 73–4
  socialization, 43, 103
  see also Children's Fund, children's homes, disability, fathers, large families, lone parents, mothers, parents, volunteers, young people
Children with Epilepsy, Fund, 126
Children's Fund, Dostoevsky, 172
Children's Fund, Lenin, 10, 14, 72, 87, 88, 95–8, 104, 108–9, 110, 113, 169–70, 177, 178, 183
  and other NGOs 121, 122, 155, 166, 175
children's homes
  Christian, 113
  'of family type', 97, 108–9
  state orphanages, 20, 27, 30–1, 33–4, 40, 61, 63, 82, 88, 96–7, 107, 109, 115, 177, 220n.45
Christian belief, 162, 166
Christian Democrats, 104, 155
Christians, see Church
Chumak, Alan, 94
Church and churches
  charity, 42, 63, 71, 111–5, 183
  and secular NGOs, 93, 94, 103, 114, 126
  see also Adventists, Baptists, Lutherans, Orthodox Church
Church of St Nicholas the Miracle Worker, Leningrad, 63
citizen(ship)
  definition, 26
  diplomacy, 100, 101
Civil Cooperation, 110
civil society, 1, 13, 41–2, 50, 76–7, 101, ch. 8, 189, 191, 216n.1
  world, 174
clothes, second-hand, 90
collective farms, 47, 70
  see also rural Russia
collectivist values, 47, 70
Committee for Economic, Cultural and Legal Help to Refugees, 110
Committee of Russian Refugees, 110
Committee of Soviet Women, 154
committees of soldiers' mothers, see soldiers' mothers
Communist Party of the Soviet Union, see CPSU
community care, 69
compensation, from state, 120, 138, 146
complacency, official, 24–8, 151
complaints to officials, 46–8
compromises (NGOs with CPSU), 141
comrades' courts, 121
Concordo, 60
conflicts of interest in Soviet society, 25, 42
conflictual models (state v. society), 11, 114, 140–6, 179, 185
  see also CPSU
Congress of People's Deputies, Russia, 171
Congress of People's Deputies, USSR, 38, 68, 69, 79, 82, 92, 95, 131, 142, 147, 170–1
  Inter-Regional Deputies' Group, 160, 171
conservation, 8–9, 175
conscripts, see soldiers
Constitution (1977), 32, 42–3, 47, 144, 147
convergence theory, 22
Cook, Linda, 70
cooperation (official, with NGOs), 148–9, 152, 165–6
Cooperation Centre, 159
cooperatives, 35, 45, 66, 79–81, 101
coopt(at)ion (official, of NGOs),

146, 153–5, 165–6
Council of Ministers, USSR, 35, 43, 169
Council of Veterans of War, Soviet, 45–6
coup, August 1991, 141, 186
CPD, *see* Congress of People's Deputies
CPSU (Communist Party of the Soviet Union), 1, 6, 40, 42–3, 54, 55, 68, 177, 179–81, 181, 186
　Central Committee, 46, 47, 48, 50, 53, 100, 127, 128, 144, 147, 150, 152
　conflict with NGOs, 11, 55, 127, 129, ch. 7, 179–80
　control of NGOs, 57, 70, 76, 91, 98, 100, 104–5, 129, ch. 7
　membership, among volunteers, 101, 161, 168
　Nineteenth Conference (June–July 1988), 9–10, 142
　Politburo, 104–5
　Twenty-Fifth Congress,(1976) 25
　Twenty-Seventh Congress, (1986) 68
　see also Leningrad: CPSU, Moscow: CPSU
CPSU-supportive NGOs, 42, 45, 68–9, 72, 81, 86–99, 121, 178
crime/dishonesty, 79, 83, 124, 134, 178, 189, 191
Crimea, 50, 59
Criminal Code, 159
Cultural Fund, Soviet, 99, 170
Cultural Initiative Fund, 84
culture, houses and palaces, 8, 76, 147
Curative Pedagogics, 118–19
Czechoslovakia, 48, 50, 165

data banks, 189, 190
day-care centres, 32, 69
deaf people, 27, 135–6, 173
　see also VOG (Society of Deaf People)
Deaf People, Russian Charitable Association of, 135

DeBardeleben, Joan, 175
decay of Soviet-type systems, 6
decentralizing trends, 1988–91, 91, 98, 104–5, 131, 134, 138, 142, 161, 164, 167, 184–5
decrees/resolutions, official (of the CPSU Central Committee, Council of Ministers, *Goskomstrud, Komsomol* and/or Central Trade Unions)
　Chernobyl 'liquidators' (1990), 138
　children in care (1985, 1987), 69
　children's homes of family type (1988, 1989), 108
　people disabled from childhood (1986), 69
　disabled people's social services (1990), 132
　employment and residential care (1976), 57
　Memorial (1988), 144
　pensions (1985), 68
　prisoners in Nazi camps (1989), 121
decrees, presidential
　legal protection of servicemen, 170
decrees, Russian Supreme Soviet presidium
　cruelty to animals, 111
democracy in NGOs, 13, 52, 56, 105, 142, 163–4, 167
democratic centralism, collapse, *see* decentralizing trends
Democratic Union, 154, 160
'democrats', 147–8
demonstrations, 160, 172–3
denunciations, 153
Deryugin, A., 130, 133, 154
'deviant' social behaviour, 25
Detskii fond, *see* Children's Fund
diabetes, people with, 14, 17, 92, 134–5, 149, 151, 163, 174
Dikul', Valentin, 240n.66
disabled people, 9, 16, 17, 22, 25–7, 79, 81, 87, 107, 111, 137, 163, 174
　1921–56: 44–6

disabled people – *continued*
1956–85: 46–62
access (buildings, transport), 27, 92, 131
Baltic republics, 56, 60, 61
beneficiaries of charity, 87, 90, 104, 130, 174, 177
children, 14, 62, 80–1, 90, 97, 118, 125–6, 134, 145, 161–2
disablement from childhood, 26, 69
complaints/petitions to officials, 46–8, 58
definitions, 35, 131
degrees of disability, 35–6, 52, 135–6, 154
deputies, 38, 131, 170–2
dissent, 56–60, 153
divisions, 126, 130–1, 133–6, 154, 160–1, 164
(un)employment, 34–8, 45, 48, 53–4, 56, 68, 74, 79–80, 119, 126, 167
(non)integration into wider society, 25, 45, 53, 119
letter-writing networks and clubs, 51–3, 54–6, 57–8, 60–1
media, 49–51, 128, 148, 153, 169
official attitudes, 29–30, 44, 68, 129–31
pensions/benefits/poverty, 68, 73–4, 131
political prisoners, 59
self-determination, 56, 61, 127, 130
sport/games, 16, 61–2, 128–9, 135, 148, 151
women, 55, 57–8, 60
young people, 134
see also Chernobyl, *Minsobes*, residential care, veterans, VOI, *other organizations*
Disabled People's Football Association, 151
Disabled People's Physical Culture, Soviet Federation, 129
Disabled Sport, RSFSR Federation, 129

disasters, man-made and natural, 70–2, 87–8, 136
dissidents, 8, 58–60, 113, 153, 159, 165
dobrovol'chestvo, 189
doctors, 25, 94, 110, 113, 118–19, 135, 149, 167
Dolg, 100
doma miloserdiya, 190
donations, *see* charity
Dostoevsky, Fedor, 100
Dostoevsky Children's Fund, 172
Draugiste/Draugo Jodis, 56
drownings, 20
drug/substance abuse, 20, 25, 90, 111, 114, 149, 167
Druzhba, 56
Dubna conference, 1991 175
Dusha cheloveka, 119, 167
'Duty' programme, 100
D'yachenko, Natal'ya, 145–6

earthquake, Armenian, 71, 88
Eastern Europe, 21
'ecocide', 23
ecology, *see* environment
economic crisis, 1990–91: 111, 125, 132–3, 163, 164, 179
economic reform, 35, 66, 73–4, 86, 188, 191
education, 131, 167–8
see also USSR Ministry of Education
elderly people, *see* older people
elections, 155, 160, 161, 170–2, 180
electoral laws, 132, 170–1
Elektrosignal, Novosibirsk, 70
Elektrostal, 151
elite privileges, *see nomenklatura* privileges
emigration, 115
emotional support, 119, 120, 125, 126, 166
enterprises, state, 35–6, 70, 86, 94–5, 97, 113, 132, 154, 169, 190
environment, 8–9, 13, 13, 23, 72, 101, 172, 175

epilepsy, 126
Eskimos, 100
Esperantists, 60
Estonia, 56, 91
ethnic conflict, 72–3, 88, 109–10
Eurovangelism, 115
exclusion, social, 21–2, 25–7, 29–40, 177
executive committees, local soviet, 148
'exit' from Soviet system, 7, 26, 41, 43, 100

Fabel, Frank, 191
factory charities, 70
  see also enterprises
Falklands War veterans, 174
families, *see* children, large families, parents
family children's homes, *see* 'children's homes of family type'
fathers, 125
Fedorov, Svyatoslav, 89, 91, 92, 93, 102
Fedorova, Volya, 155
Fefelov, Valerii, 58–9, 60, 75
Feniks, 61, 104
Fertman, Boris, 51, 224n.68
fire victims, 107, 174
first aid, 87
Fish, M. Steven, 7, 11, 144, 175, 179
FMZ (Charity and Health Foundation), 14, 72, 89–95, 99, 110, 112, 113, 130, 170, 173, 183
  and *Miloserdie*, 103, 106, 152, 162, 164, 175, 176, 178, 180
  and other NGOs, 120, 122, 141–2, 144, 150, 166, 175
'Folk Warriors', 101
Fond Marii, 102, 176, 177
Fond miloserdiya i zdorov'ya, *see* FMZ
Fond sotsial'nykh izobretenii, *see* FSI
food, *see* meals, shortages
Football Association, Disabled People's, 151
Former Young Prisoners in Fascist Concentration Camps, Union, 121, 155, 160
Forum of Migrant Organizations, 190
fostering, 33, 63, 108–9
Foundation for Social Innovations, 99–101, 158, 166, 175
Foundations for Youth Initiatives, 100, 128
French television, 75
Friedgut, Theodore, 44
Friendship (Lithuania), 56
FSI (Foundation for Social Innovations), 99–101, 158, 166, 175
fundraising, *see* charity: donations; voluntary organizations: business activities
'Funds' (collective title for Children's Fund, FMZ, Peace Fund, Red Cross), 13, 72, 87–99, 110, 116, 178
Funds for Youth Initiatives, 100, 128

Gaidar, Admiral, 168
Galich, Aleksandr, 8
generational issues, 162
  see also volunteers: age
Georgia, 88, 115
Germany, humanitarian aid, 94, 110
ghetto inmates, 121
Gidaspov, Boris, 103, 172
Gladyshev, S., 105
glasnost, 20, 32, 36, 41, 50, 66, 75, 77, 82, 88, 96, 99, 103, 107, 119–20, 123, 124, 128, 146, 147, 156, 163, 169, 177, 186
  see also media
Golovatyi, Gennadii, 59, 60
Golubev, Vasilii, 53–4, 55, 58, 59, 224n.73
Gorbachev, Mikhail, 6, 9–11, 17, 20, 24–5, 28, 39, 40, 41, 66, 77, 78, 85, 89, 95, 99, 100, 105, 111, 123, 127, 133, 144, 147, 152, 160, 168, 170, 183, 186, 187, 226n.18

Gorbacheva, Raisa 99
Gorky/Nizhnii Novgorod, 57, 127, 133
Gorno-Altaisk, 120
Goskomtrud, 23–4, 69, 73, 127, 143
Grafova, Lidiya, 110
grandparents, 23
Granin, Daniil, 66, 78–9, 89, 92, 104–6, 111, 112, 119, 143, 145, 155, 167
Grazhdanskoe sodeistvie, 110
guardian families (*opekunskie sem'i*), see children's homes 'of family type'
Gumanizm i miloserdie, 143–4
Gus'kov, Gennadii, 50, 56–7, 59, 60

Häkkelä, Helvi, 59, 217n.8
Harwin, Judith, 220n.45, 232n.128
halls of residence, student, 27
Hammer, Armand, 84
Harvey, Brian, 12, 13
Hauslohner, Paul, 6
headteachers, 119
healers, unconventional, 94, 174
health inspectors, 74
health care,
  non-profit, 87, 90, 114, 115, 120, 126, 167
  commercial, 80, 90
  state, 20, 23, 24, 28, 67, 70, 89
  see also FMZ, doctors, hospitals, nurses, USSR Ministry of Health
Hegelson, Ann, 44
helplines, 110
Helsinki Watch Group, 58, 59, 159
heroine mothers, 124
historical research (charitable service), 120
Holy Synod, Commission for Moral Education and Charity, 112
home employment, 35, 122, 125
home-helps, 69, 87–8, 89, 91, 93, 104, 106, 114, 189
homelessness/housing, 27, 31–3, 73, 109, 110, 116, 119, 124, 137, 172, 189

homes, family: attitudes, 30–4
homes, residential, see residential care
Hope Committee, 123–4
hospices, 84
hospitals/sanatoria, 70, 72, 82, 90, 106, 112, 113, 114, 115, 149, 170, 173
hostels, student, 27
houses of charity, 190
houses of culture, 8, 76, 147
'human factor', 41, 66, 76, 104
Human Soul Fund, 113, 167
humanitarian aid, see aid, foreign
hunger strikes, 172
'hybrid' organizations (charity/self–help), 2, 118–20

idealism, 116
ideology, 28–9, 36, 37, 39, 41, 75, 131, 144, 151
industrial accidents, 23, 26, 35
inflation, 70, 73
informal groups, 12, 16, 101, 103–7, 111–16, 119, 129
  and CPSU, chs. 7–8
  self-help, ch. 6
  see also official/un-Soviet features
influence, channels, 168–72
Inhabitants of Blockaded Leningrad, 121
Initsiativnaya gruppa po zashchite prav invalidov, 58–60, 153
intelligentsia, 16–17, 77–8, 93, 100, 102, 104, 109, 112, 113, 119, 178, 184
interests, conflicts of, in Soviet society, 25, 42
International Committee for the Rescue of Russian Prisoners of War in Afghanistan (USA), 123–4
International Disabled Olympic Games, 27
International Foundation for Survival and Development of Humanity, 84
Inter-Regional Deputies' Group, 160, 171

Index 251

Invachess, 148
Invasport, 61
Iskra, 57–8, 59, 60, 128
Israel, 115
Ivanovo, 53, 59, 106
Ivchenko, S., 158
Izanteevka, 174
Izvestiya, 75, 104, 112

Jewish organizations, 115–16, 121
Jewish War Veterans, Partisans, Concentration Camp and Ghetto Inmates and their Children, Association of Soviet, 121
journalists, *see* media
justice, miscarriages, 159

Kaliningrad city/*oblast*, 135, 173
Kameneva, Ol'ga, 57–8
Karelia, 120, 131
Karev, Mikhail, 47, 50, 59, 60, 217n.8, 221n.87, 238n.73
Kasparov, Garry, 102
Kazan, 106
Kaznacheev, Viktor, 39, 69, 75, 76, 129, 142, 143
Kemerovo, 127
KGB, 51, 120, 124, 152, 166
Kharkov, 71
khozraschet, 80
Khrushchev, Nikita, 20, 22, 26, 28, 31, 50, 54
Khusainov, Faizulla, 58
kindergartens and nurseries, 30, 34, 149, 169
Kinderdörfer, 108
Kiselev, Yurii, 53, 58–60, 153
Knowledge Society, 93
KOESKYU (Committee for Economic, Cultural and Legal Help to Refugees), 110
kolkhozy, 47, 70
see also rural Russia
Kolomna, 106
Komarova, Domna, 62, 127, 129
Komitet russkikh bezhentsev, 110
Komitet sovetskikh zhenshchin, 154
Komsomol, 42, 44, 48, 51, 77, 96, 99–100, 103, 104, 105, 127–8, 136, 148, 150, 151, 154
Komsomol'skaya pravda, 49, 50, 99, 105, 128, 129, 169
Konkordo Esperanto society, 60
Kononenko, Veronika, 48
kontrol', *see* CPSU, control of NGOs
Koptyug, A., 168
Korchaginets Club, 58, 60–1, 127–8
Kostroma, 92
Krasnodar, 73, 145
Krasnoyarsk, 94
Kropachev, Sergei, 145
Kseniya, Blessed, Brotherhood of, 114
Kuebart, Friedrich, 43
Kuibyshev/Samara, 106, 149, 187, 188
Kupriyanov, A., 158
Kutateladze, Oleg, 144–5

labour shortage, 68
labour therapy, 37
Lapidus, Gail, 7, 10
'large' families, 13, 14, 62, 73, 113, 124–5, 149, 150–1, 156, 174
Large Families, Association of Russian, 124
Large Families' Union, Perm, 150, 179
Large Family Association, Voronezh, 155
Large Family Fund (*Mnogodetnaya sem'ya*), 124
Large Family Organization, Leningrad, 171
Latvia, 60, 61, 91
laws (regional), 191
laws (Russian)
electoral, 132, 170–1
non-profit organizations (1996), 191
rehabilitation of 'enemies of the people' (1991), 120
laws (USSR)
association (1932), 42, (1990) 13, 15, 147, 166, 185
disabled people (1990), 131, 171
freedom of conscience (1990),

laws (USSR) – *continued*
  112
  'individual labour activity'
    (1986), 79
  Marriage Code (1968), 31
  pensions (1990), 68, 74, 131, 134
law-based state, 178
lawyers, 110, 138, 173
learning difficulties, children with,
  33–4, 126, 145, 118–19
Lefthanded Person, 60
legal help, independent, 110, 119,
  125, 138, 159, 173
legitimacy crisis of Soviet regime
  by 1985, 28, 40, 41, 43
  by 1990, 78, 142–3
leisure pursuits, 8, 43, 110, 126,
  132
Leitch, Duncan, 10, 217n.19
Lenin, Vladimir, 124
Lenin borough, Moscow 149
Leningrad/Petersburg, 14, 44, 51,
  59, 61, 62, 63, 78, 80, 90, 98,
  103–6, 112–14, 115, 121, 123,
  126, 135, 143, 149, 151, 156,
  160, 167, 176, 178, 189, 190,
  191
  CPSU, 87, 148, 149, 154, 168,
    172
  soviets, 96, 141, 148, 151, 171–2,
    172–3
  VOI (Society of Disabled People)
    see LGOI
Leningrad Association of Public
  Organizations of Parents with
  Disabled Children, 126, 175
Leningrad Association of Veterans
  of War in Afghanistan, 167
'Leningrad' Charity Society
  (*Miloserdie*)/*Nevskii Angel*,
  103–7, 141, 145, 151, 154,
  156, 168, 172, 173, 175, 177,
  189
Levsha, 60
Lewin, Moshe 7
letter writing
  disabled people's networks,
    51–3, 54–6, 57–8, 60–1
  to officials/press, 46–51, 53, 68,
    78, 129, 133, 152, 169
LGOI (*Leningradskaya gorodskaya
  organizatsiya Obshchestva
  invalidov*), 127, 151, 155,
  160–1, 163–4, 171–2, 172–3
libel (official, of volunteers), 156
life expectancy, 20
Lifeguards' Society, 42
Ligachev, Yegor, 150
Likhachev, Dmitrii, 99, 111
Likhanov, Al'bert, 33, 51, 96, 111
liquidators, *see* Chernobyl
Lipetsk, 120, 148
Literaturnaya gazeta, 49, 50, 78, 110
Lithuania, 56
Litvinov, Vladimir, 121
local authorities, *see* soviets
Loginov, Gennadii, 60
Lomonosov (town), 163, 174
lone fathers, 125
lone mothers/parents, 14, 62, 74,
  125, 174
Lugansk, 70
Lushnikov, Aleksei, 104–5
Lutherans, 106
Lyubutka, 145

Makashev, Al'bert, 155
*maloletnie uzniki fashistskikh
  kontslagerei*, 121, 155, 160
Mapulechki Moskvy, 125
Marchenko, Veronika, 103
Mariya Fund, 102, 176, 177
Materiinskaia slava (Maternal
  Glory), Leningrad, 62
meals, free, 76, 79, 90, 91, 107,
  113, 115
media, 103, 104, 126, 136–7, 145,
  156, 160, 169, 172
  charity activists, 102, 110, 119
  CPSU control, 148
  and disabled campaigners,
    49–51, 128, 148, 153, 169
  local v. national, 50, 156
  *see also glasnost, individual
    newspaper titles*
medical charities/self-help groups,
  118–9
medicine, *see* health care

Memorial, 13, 14, 16, 105, 110, 119–20, 144, 145, 148, 150, 152–4, 156, 158, 159, 160, 162, 167, 168, 173, 174–5, 176, 180, 188, 217n.7
men's organizations, 16, 125, 136
Men'shikov, Vadim, 89, 91, 92, 94
mental illness, 119, 167
'Mercy' Society, *see Miloserdie*
methodology, 4–5
MGOI (*Moskovskaya gorodskaya organizatsiya Obshchestva invalidov*) 127, 129, 153, 172
middle ground in *perestroika* politics, 141, 145, 158
migrants, 190
 see also refugees
MIKO, 79–81, 84
military service, *see* soldiers
military training of children, 43, 137
militia, *see* police
Miloserdie ('Charity') campaign, 76
Miloserdie societies, 14, 103–7, 112, 115, 116, 118, 141–2, 143, 145–6, 147, 150, 151, 152, 153, 154, 156, 166, 167, 168, 172, 173, 175, 177, 180, 184
miners, 101
Ministers of Social Security, 24, 61
 see also Kaznacheev, Komarova
Ministries
 see Belorussian, Russian/USSR Ministries of Health, etc. ;
Minsobes Minsobes (Russian Ministry of Social Security), 23, 27, 32, 36, 37, 41, 48–54, 61, 76, 79, 97, 134, 180
 attitudes to clients, 29, 48, 58, 68, 176
 and disability movement, 50, 52, 54–6, 127–31
 and other NGOs, 89, 104–5, 143–6, 150, 151, 154, 158, 160–1, 162
Mir bez nasiliya, 101, 156
Mir i chelovek, 108
miscarriages of justice, 159
misunderstanding (officials v. NGOs), 150

Mnogodetnaya sem'ya, 73
Mobility International, 84, 134
Moldavian Red Cross, 87
Molodezhnyi servis, 77
monasteries, 88, 114
moral dimension of *perestroika*, 10, 40, 77, 82, 89, 96, 99, 107, 119–20, 123, 125, 128, 142, 178
Morzhina, N., 223n.56
Moscow, 14, 46, 53, 58, 59, 62, 72, 74, 80, 83, 110, 112, 115, 121, 128–9, 133, 138, 149, 151, 152, 153, 159, 170, 173, 178, 190, 191
 CPSU, 53, 76, 147, 152
 Miloserdie, 103, 105–6, 107, 118, 147, 152, 168
 oblast, 71, 125, 148, 151, 174
 soviets, 69, 81, 83, 84, 129, 148, 149, 172, 175
 VOI (Society of Disabled People), *see* MGOI
 see also provinces, MIKO
Moscow Disabled People's Cooperative Association (MIKO), 79–81, 84
Moses, Joel, 10
Moskovskaya pravda, 153
mothers, 16, 62–3, 80, 109, 118, 122–6, 136, 163
 see also Afghan veterans, disabled children, lone mothers, parents, soldiers' mothers
Mother's Right, 102–3, 160
'multi-child' families, *see* large families
multiple sclerosis, 169
Mummy-Daddies (*mapulechki*), 125
museum employees, 119
music education/therapy, 126
Mytishchi, 125

Nadezhda committee, 123–4
Nagornyi Karabakh, 110
Narodno-Trudovoi Soyuz (NTS), 75
Nash dom, 174
nation(alism), Russian, 77, 186
nature protection teams, 8–9

Nazi concentration camp survivors, 121, 155, 160
need, perceptions, 29, 177, 179, 186, 187
networking of NGOs, 106, 127, 173–6, 189, 190–1
Neumyvakin, A., 240n.66
'neutralization' (official, of NGOs), 149
Nevskii Angel, 189
 see also Leningrad Charity Society
New Economic Policy (NEP), 77–8
New Soviet Person, 25
NGOs, see voluntary organizations
Nicholas the Miracle Worker Fund, 159
Night Shelter, 233n.177
Nizhnii Novgorod/Gorky, 57, 127, 133
NIMBYs, 109
Nochlezhka 233n.177
nomenklatura 122, 189
 appointment principle (not) applied to new NGOs, 13, 91, 95, 101, 102, 104–5, 116, 124, 129–30, 142, 154–5
 privileges, 28–30, 67, 74, 82–3, 131, 141, 146, 169–70
non-working citizens, 17, 26–7, 182
North Ossetia, 73, 162, 173
Norway, 166
Novgorod, 121, 155, 160
Novosibirsk city/*oblast*, 8, 63, 65, 70, 72, 76, 82, 91, 94–5, 100, 106, 108, 115, 126, 127, 128, 130–1, 137, 147, 153, 156, 166, 168, 169, 172, 173, 174
Novo-Zavidovo Charity Fund, 122
'nuclearization' of families, 23
Numerov, N., 152–3
nurses, 87, 90, 114

Obshchestvo spasaniya na vodakh, 42
Obshchestvo trezvosti, 14, 170
occupational disease, 26, 35
Odzhiev, Rizoali, 240n.66

official/un-Soviet features of NGOs, 86, 105–6, 116, 122, 142–3, 160, 166, 167, 168, 184–5
Ogonek (Moscow), 102
Ogonek (*samizdat*), 55
Oktyabr borough, Moscow, 148, 149, 170
Okudzhava, Bulat, 8
older people, 23, 68–9, 79, 87, 89, 107, 110, 114, 116, 122, 176, 187, 189
 see also residential care
Olympic Games, 27, 47
Only Mummy, 125
Omsk, 57, 169
Opora, 80
Optimist, 61
Optina Pustyn, 88
Organization of Veterans of War and Labour, 14, 68–9, 122, 130, 154, 170, 226n.8
orphans, 33, 96, 174
 see also children's homes
Orsk, 148, 155, 159, 160
Orthodox Brotherhoods, Union, 113
Orthodox Church, 63, 91, 93, 94, 111–14
Ortsport, 61
Ossetia, North, 73, 162, 173
Ossetia, South, 162
Our Home, 174

Pamyat', 173
parents, 9, 16, 17, 62–3, 82, 96, 109, 122–6, 149
 see also disability, fathers, lone parents, mothers, soldiers' mothers
parishes, see Orthodox Church
'parliamentary charity elite', 92
partisans, 121
part-time work, 35, 122, 125
party, see CPSU
patients, 118–20, 167
Peace Fund/official peace movement, 61, 68, 71, 72, 88–9, 95, 99, 110, 113
peace marches, 101

Index

Pedagogical Search (*Pedagogicheskii poisk*), 63
pen clubs, *see* letter writing
pensions and pensioners, 22–4, 38, 62, 68–9, 73–4, 79, 87, 90, 92, 93, 104, 116, 121–2, 127, 176
Penza, 90, 97, 137
Perm, 111, 125, 150, 179, 188, 242n.16
Perm Union of Large Families, 150, 179
Person/Man Association (*Chelovek*), 104
'personal' sphere of society, 164, 167
petitions, 47–8, 58
Petersburg, *see* Leningrad
Petrovsky, Boris, 89
Petrozavodsk, 150
Petukhov, A., 130–1, 133
pharmacies, charitable, 114
philanthropy, *see* charity
Phoenix Club, 61, 104
pickets, 170, 173
Pimen, Patriarch, 112, 114
Pioneers, 44
pluralism, 142, 144
Poland, 161, 164–5
police, 27, 54, 149, 151, 173
political culture, *see* ideology
politicization of NGOs, 159–61
Politburo, 69, 104–5, 169
Political Red Cross, 87
polls, *see* public opinion
pollution, *see* environment
Popov, Gavriil, 102, 148, 159
POWs (Afghanistan), 123–4
poverty, 25, 73–4, 82, 124, 125, 131, 147, 187, 189, 191
Pravda, 49, 51, 108, 143, 169
Pravo materi, 102–3, 160
preemption (official, of NGOs), 5, 146, 152–3, 176
prescription charges, 74, 120, 121
Presidential Council, 170
(ex-)prisoners
  of Nazis, 121, 155, 160
  Stalin period, 102, 119–21, 146

1960s–1980s, 27, 59, 92, 114, 120
prisoners of war, Afghanistan, 123–4
privilege
  nomenklatura, 28–30, 67, 74, 82–3, 131, 141, 146, 169–70
  war veterans, 29
Producers' Cooperative Union of Disabled People, 54, 60, 131
Prometei (Prometheus) Association, 51–9
Promkooperatsiya invalidov, 54, 60, 131
propaganda of success, 24–8
prostheses, 26, 79, 80, 137
provinces, comparison with Moscow/Leningrad, 2, 14, 59, 90, 100, 103, 106, 119, 129, 147, 184–5, 190, 191, 242n.15
  see also decentralizing trends
provinces and dissent, 59
pseudo-charities 191
Pskov, 91, 135, 151, 157
psychiatrists and psychologists, 110
'public aid associations', 42
public opinion
  pre-1985, 49–50
  post-1985, 74–5, 96, 120, 125, 176–7, 186
  see also glasnost, media
public organizations (*obshchestvennye organizatsii*), 42
Pushkin Society, 99, 148

quota systems, 132, 170–1

Rabotnitsa, 48, 102, 146, 176, 177
Radical Party, 173
radio, 78, 113, 153
Radio Liberty, 153
Radonezh Society, 63, 113, 165
Rasputin, Valentin, 111
Rebirth, Leningrad, 114, 149
'rebound' theory, 7
Red Cross, 13, 14, 71, 72, 83, 87–8, 91, 99, 104, 110, 123, 150, 156, 166, 170, 176, 189
Red Square, 172

refugees, 70, 72–3, 90, 109–10, 162, 172, 178, 190
see also homelessness
registration of organizations, 12, 105, 107, 113, 114, 129, 152, 154, 156, 166, 175
see also Russian Ministry of Justice
rehabilitation centres, 57, 62, 169
religion, see Churches, Adventists, Baptists, Jewish organizations, Lutherans, Orthodox Church
religious education, 113
Repentance, 180
'repressions', see Stalinism
rescue teams, 71
Rescue Teams, Soviet Association of, 71
residential care, 30–4, 69, 76, 113
'homes for disabled and older people', 31–2, 34, 37, 40, 90, 128, 133, 148, 151, 159, 221n.87
residential-production complexes, 56–7
see also children's homes
resolutions, see decrees
retribution 146
Revolutionary Perestroika, Union for, 170
rights, human 159, 161, 181, 187
riot police, 173
'rock community', 8
Rockefeller Foundation, 84
Rogova, Lyudmila, 149, 169, 172, 174
Romania, 83
Rossiya Association of Deaf People, 135
Rovno, 106
Rubinov, Anatolii, 110
Russian Ministries of Education, Health, see USSR/Russian Ministry of…
Russian Ministry of Justice register of organizations, 12, 101, 156, 166
Russian Ministry of Social Security, see Minsobes

Russian nation(alism), 77, 186
Russian Societies of Blind, Deaf, Disabled People, see VOS, VOG, VOI
Russian Supreme Soviet, 111
Ryan, Michael, 38–9, 219n.3
Rybinsk, 94
Ryzhkov, Nikolai, 150, 171

St Panteleimon Brotherhood, 113–14, 166
St Petersburg, see Leningrad
Sakhalin, 76
Sakharov, Andrei, 59, 102
Samara/Kuibyshev, 106, 149, 187, 188
Samaritans, 110
samizdat
disabled people's, 55, 56, 57, 61
political, 172
religious, 63, 113
Saratov, 59, 96
Save the Family, 126
schools, 104, 113
Schöpflin, George, 6
'Second Cold War', 60
Second Life, 119
Sedaitis, Judith, 171, 175
Sedova, Nina, 47
self-help, 2, 13, 14, 46–65, 81–2, 107, 115, ch. 6, 183–4, 191–2
self-help v. charity, 2, 118, 130, 138
Sem'ya, 96
Sem'ya mira, 115
Serpukhov, 128
service-providing organizations, 2, 107
see also charities
Shakhmatnaya assotsiatsiya glukhikh, 135
shame at charity, 25, 75
sheltered housing, 32
Shlapentokh, Vladimir, 7, 43
shortages, 70, 74, 111, 120, 133, 169, 185
Siberian Information Agency, 156, 172
sign language, 136

single parents
 see lone parents
sisterhoods, Orthodox, 113
slander (official, of volunteers), 156
Slovo druga, 56
Smena (Moscow), 51, 96
Smith, Kathleen, 7
Sobesednik (Moscow), 105, 231n.116
Sobriety Society, 14, 170
social contract, 30
Social Democrats, 160
social exclusion, 21–2, 25–7, 29–40, 177
social injustice, 28–30
 see also privilege
social organizations, *see* public organizations
social problems
 before 1985, ch. 2
 after 1985, 181
 see also glasnost
social security/services 19, 67–9, 76, 129
Social Security Ministry, *see* Minsobes, Belorussian Ministry
Societies of Blind, Deaf, Disabled People, *see* VOS, VOG, VOI respectively
Socio-Legal Defence and Rehabilitation of Disabled People, Fund, 159
Sociological Association, Soviet, 110
sociologists, 7, 101, 110
Sodeistvie, 159
soldiers, 17, 103, 123–4, 173
soldiers' mothers/parents, 5, 14, 103, 123–4, 144, 155, 159, 170, 172, 173, 187, 189
solidarity and Solidarity, 161
Solzhenitsyn, Aleksandr, 53
Soprichastnost' Fund, 231n.115
 see also Moscow: *Miloserdie*
Soros, George, 84
Sotsial'noe obespechenie (journal), 50
Sovetskaya Rossiya, 72, 169
Soviet Social Problems, 22
soviets, local 74, 79, 91–3, 98, 108–10, 121, 122, 132, 140–57, 163, 165, 180–1, 190
Soviet, Supreme (Russia), 82, 111
Soviet, Supreme (USSR), 46, 47, 48, 68, 82, 114, 129, 131, 171
 committee on veterans and disabled people, 131
Soyuz byvshikh maloletnikh uznikov fashistskikh kontslagerei, 121, 155, 160
Spark penclub, 57–8, 59, 60, 128
'splintered' authorities, policy implications, 147–9
'splintered' NGOs, 74, 134, 161–4, 173–6
spasatelei, Assotsiyatsiya obshchestv, 71
Spasenie sem'i, 126
'spinsters', 188
sports/games, 16, 61–2, 128–9, 135, 148, 151
Spravedlivost', 238n.66
state interventionism, post-1985, 67–70
Stalin(ism) and victims, 102, 119–20, 124, 144, 153, 177, 180
Starovoitova, Galina, 110
State Committee for Labour and Social Issues, *see* Goskomtrud
Stavropol, 73
strikes, 70
students, 8–9, 27, 172,
 see also young people and students
subbotniki, 43–4
suicides, 110–11
Sumgait, 110
support, emotional, 119, 120, 125, 126, 166
Supreme Soviet, *see* Soviet, Supreme
surgery, 119
survey for *Democratization in Russia*, 5, Appendix
Sverdlovsk/Yekaterinburg, 49, 60, 77, 128, 135
Svetlyi, 135
Synod Commission for Moral Education and Charity, 112

Tatar Republic, 59
teachers, 97, 104, 109, 113, 118, 119
telephone helplines, 110–11
Temperance Society, 14, 170
Tent City, 172
Teresa, Mother, 115
Terpsichore, 8, 100
Terror, see Stalin
Tkachenko, Anatolii, 60
Togliatti, 123
'toilers', 26
'tolerance, benign' (official, of NGOs), 146
Tol'ko mama, 125
Tolstaya, Tat'yana, 102
Tolstoi, Lev, 101
Tolstoyans, 115
Tomsk, 170, 173
Tomsk Popular Movement, 173
totalitarianism, 5–6
trade unions, 26, 42, 68, 71, 151, 154
TransEXPO, 164
'transmission belt' organizations, 42, 45, 68–9, 72, 81, 86–99, 121, 178
transplant surgery, 119
transport, public, 74, 120
Trans-Siberian Railway, 72
'trial by charity', 145, 151
trudyashchiesya, 26
Tsentr lechebnoi pedagogiki, 118–19
Tyutchev, Fedor, 2
Tula city/*oblast*, 91, 101, 156, 229n.18
Tver *oblast*, 122
twins, 174
typology of official atittudes to NGOs, 146–56

Ufa, 69, 72
Ufa Disaster Victims' Society, 72, 174
Ukrainian Red Cross, 87
Ulan-Ude, 91
umbrella organizations, 119, 127, 144, 174–5, 189, 190
unemployment, 74, 188

see also disability
Union for Revolutionary Perestroika, 170
Union of United Cooperatives, 110
United Way, 84, 190
Urals, 59, 156, 190
Urals Association of Refugees, 190
Urban, Michael, 103, 146
USA, 71, 84–5, 100, 123
USSR Ministries
  Coal Mining, 101
  Defence, 72, 173
  Finance, 68
  Foreign Affairs, 123
USSR/Russian Ministries/local departments
  Education, 24, 79, 109, 149, 162
  Health, 24, 27, 82, 92, 95, 110, 112, 130, 149, 161, 162

van der Voort, Feodor, 63
Vasil'ev, G, 172
Verbitsky, Andrei, 105
Vestnik (Iskra), 57
veterans, 29, 68, 87, 105, 121–2, 129, 130, 154, 170, 177, 190
  see also Afghan veterans, Organization of Veterans
Victims of Illegal Repression, Associations of, 152–3
victims of miscarriages of justice, 159
'victims of repression', see Stalin
Vietnam War syndrome/veterans, 137, 174, 236n.109
Vinogradova, Irina, 53–4
Vishnyakova, Nina, 49, 53, 217n.8, 220n.45
Vladikavkaz, 73, 162, 173
Vladimir city/*oblast*, 59, 94, 123, 190, 229n.18
VOG (Russian Society of Deaf People), 14, 45, 62, 68, 81, 126, 135–6, 151, 157, 183
VOI (Society of Disabled People), 13, 14, 16, 62, 80, 126–34, 142, 148, 154, 155, 160–1, 163–4, 165, 168–9, 171–2, 173, 177, 180, 183–4, 186

origins, 44–62, 126–9, 183
and other NGOs, 122, 125–6
see also LGOI, MGOI
  (Leningrad, Moscow branches)
VOIN, 56
Voinovich, Vladimir, 102
Volgograd city/*oblast*, 14, 123
voluntary organizations, official, see
  CPSU-supportive NGOs
voluntary organizations, post-1985
  business activities, 89, 94, 96,
    97–8, 108, 126, 132, 163
  charters, 142, 157, 161
  cohesiveness, 74, 134, 161–4
  conferences, 80, 175
  emergence in 1989: 118, 147
  emergence in 1990: 147–8
  leaders, 16, 82, 105, 162, 163
  membership, 15–17, 105, 168
  networks, 106, 127, 173–6, 189,
    190–1
  number, 12–13, 188
  politicization, 159–61
  professionalization, 107, 189
  size, 13, 105, 107, 113, 118, 119,
    121, 125, 126, 130, 132, 135,
    136, 137, 150, 155
  typology, 14, 118
  Western, 84, 190
  see also civil society, registration
'voluntary' work pre-1985: 42–4,
  182
volunteering, culture of, revival
  post-1985: 67, 76–7, 184, 189
volunteers
  age/generational issues, 16, 93,
    104–5, 106, 119–20, 162, 180
  enthusiasm, 107, 112, 145, 162
  FMZ, 93
  party affiliation, 101, 161, 168
  sex, 16
  social class, 16
  training, 189
Voronezh, 12, 91, 95, 110, 151,
  152, 155, 188
  disabled activists, 56–7, 59
  Miloserdie 103, 106, 145, 150,
    151, 152
VOS (Russian Society of Blind
  People), 14, 45, 62, 68, 81, 95,
    126, 133, 171, 174
voting, see elections, electoral
Vozrozhdenie, Leningrad, 114, 149
Vserossiiskoe obshchestvo glukhikh, see
  VOG
Vserossiskoe obshchestvo invalidov, see
  VOI
Vserossiskoe obshchestvo slepykh, see
  VOS
VTEK, 36, 37,167
Vtoraya zhizn', 119
Vysotsky, Vladimir, 8

'war of laws and parliaments', 131
  see also decentralizing trends
war veterans, see veterans
Weigle, Marcia, 146, 150
welfare state, chs. 2, 4
  see also *Minsobes*, USSR Ministry
    of Health
Western charities, 84
wheelchairs, 26, 79–80, 90–1
women
  blame for public morals, 78, 96
  conferences, 175
  councils, 5, 91, 125
  disabled activists, 55, 57–8, 60
  employment/self-help, 74, 189,
    191
  prisoners in Stalin's camps, 102,
    177
  pensioners, 16, 110–11
  'spinsters', 188
  staff of NGOs, 16
  status of women's organizations,
    5
  see also mothers
workers, 17, 30, 86, 101, 132, 172
work ethic, 26, 29, 37–9, 45, 54,
  56
World and Man/Person, 108
World Family Association, 115
World without Violence, 101, 156

Yakovlev, Aleksandr, 89, 148
Yaroslavl, 93, 190
Yekaterinburg/Sverdlovsk, 49, 60,
  77, 128, 135

Yeltsin, Boris, 82, 99, 102, 129, 147, 186
YMCA, 166
Young Disabled People's Organizations, USSR Association of, 134
young people and students, 7–8, 16, 27, 43–4, 60, 104, 106, 111, 123, 134–7
Youth Service, 77
Yunost', 103

Zabota ('Care') campaign, 69

Zagvozdina, Tamara, 51, 54–6, 57–8
Zaslavskaya, Tat'yana, 41, 222n.2
Zaslavsky, Il'ya, 38, 131, 148, 170–1
Zavertaeva, Tat'yana, 225n.107
Zdorov'e, 54
zhensovety, 91, 125
Zhiteli blokadnogo Leningrada, 121
Znanie Society, 93
Zorza, Victor, 84
Zvezda, 51